W9-CGT-108

Date Due

83491

```
971      MacDonald, E.
.103       The rainbow
0924     chasers.
MacDo
                    1695
```

83491

```
971     MacDonald, Ervin Austin, 1893-
.103      The rainbow chasers / Ervin Austin MacDonald.
0924    Vancouver : Douglas & McIntyre, c1982.
MacDo     272 p. : maps.


        1. MacDonald, Ervin Austin, 1893-
        2. Pioneers - British Columbia - Biography.
        3. Pioneers - Alberta - Biography.
                (Continued on next card)
0888943695                          1702009 NLC
```

hewed off the quarter round, from the wide end of the log to the top. A good broadaxe man could do this job without leaving a single axe mark. The second, third and fourth quarter round was hewed off in the same way to leave a square timber ready for export. An average pine prepared in this way was twenty inches across each face, though some were as broad as three feet. Octagonal timbers were made in the same manner, though the square ones were more common. Hewn timbers were far easier than round logs to raft down the rivers to the seaports and permitted great savings of space aboard the ships bound for Europe.

When freeze-up came each winter, the men in the lumber camps poured water on the snow leading down to the river bank to make an icy chute so they could slide the logs onto the river ice. Then they made the logs into rafts, and when the ice broke up in the spring, the rafts would start moving downstream. When they hit deep water, they were made into "cribs," that is, twenty squared timbers bordered by unpeeled logs and bound together with crosswise logs. The unpeeled logs took the damage from pegs or nails used to hold the crib together. Oak timbers were always cribbed with other lighter wood since they were heavier than the water they displaced and would sink if cribbed alone.

Whenever the crib approached a waterfall, the oak logs had to be hauled by land or they would be driven under the falls and lost. Downstream from the falls the crib was reassembled. On long stretches of calm water, as many as sixty of these cribs would be bound together to make huge rafts up to half a mile long. Sometimes sails were put up to speed the trip, for there were 700 miles of river to cover from the timber limits to the market. The men responsible for each raft set up camp on one or more of the cribs, making cabins of bark for shelter and building cooking fires on beds of sand.

The man in charge of the whole operation right from felling the trees to delivering the timber to dockside for shipment was called the "bull of the woods" or the "woods boss." This was the job my father earned when he was just twenty-one. He earned it because he knew the logging business better than any of the hundred or so men that he bossed, but he kept it because he was tougher than any of them.

It took a pretty strong-willed man to keep order and disci-

Most of his education was the result of my grandmother's tutoring during the long winter evenings. She taught all her children to read and write in both English and Gaelic, and to do arithmetic, because these were the skills they would need in their little community. When father was ten, a school was built four miles away. It was too far for his younger brothers and sisters to walk to, and the older ones were needed to run the farm, so my father was sent off alone. He was already big for his age, but since he had had no formal schooling he was put in the beginners' class. Every day he tramped the four miles to school to sit lonely and embarrassed among the little ones, then tramped the four miles home again. This went on for a month; finally he refused to go any more and returned to his mother's private lessons around the kitchen table.

Each winter after the hay and grain and winter vegetables were stored, the management of the farm was turned over to my grandmother, my aunts and the younger children, while grandfather and the older boys headed for their timber claims in the surrounding forests. Grandfather and Big John cut timber for ship spars and masts and for lumber, while the younger boys cut cordwood and hauled it to Bytown to sell for fuel. These were miserably cold trips for the boys, who sat on top of the load hunched against the wind and the driving snow, but travel was actually easier than in the spring or fall because the horses and sleighs could short-cut across the fields and streams: the snow was so deep that all the fences were buried, and the ice crust was firm enough to hold both horses and sleighs.

When he was fifteen, my father graduated from hauling cordwood to a place in the family logging business. In those days, logging was a craft: everything had to be done by hand. First the trees were carefully selected, then felled with a crosscut saw. In the forests along the Ottawa River and its tributaries, the timber was pine, oak, maple, basswood, butternut, hickory and cedar, and most of it was used in shipbuilding. Once felled, each tree that was considered suitable for ship's timbers was stripped of its limbs and bark with axes. Then one man walked the length of the log marking a chalk line down one side, and returned marking a matching line down the other side. Next the loggers took up their twelve- or fourteen-inch-bladed broadaxes and from the wool. I can still remember a dark grey homespun suit that my father wore when I was a boy. He had owned it for more than thirty years by that time and it showed little sign of wear.

In the traditional Scottish way, my grandfather MacDonald was the patriarch of his family. This meant that he gave orders which everyone obeyed. Even my grandmother accepted this although she had come from the prominent MacDonnell clan, had been raised in the castle of the chief, and had an exceptional education for a woman of her times. It had been grandmother who organized much of the journey to Canada, and it was her influential cousin, the Bishop of Upper Canada, who had helped with arrangements on this side of the Atlantic.

She had limited use of her right hand because of a childhood accident, but still she had been considered very marriageable and had only escaped wedding a wealthy older man by eloping with my grandfather, a man from the Isle of Skye with little education and even less wealth. Although grandfather deferred to her where her education was required, in all other things his word was law.

All the MacDonald children were healthy, well built, strong and tall. The boys all grew to six feet and more. Big John was the tallest at six feet four inches but Little John was only an inch shorter. Several of the girls were five feet eleven inches.

Archie, my father, grew to be six feet one inch, square shouldered and quick in his movements. His features were sharp and rugged, his skin fair, his eyes blue and his hair black and wavy. As soon as he reached manhood, he grew a long black beard of which he was extremely proud. When it became almost waist length, he wrapped it in a piece of thin, soft buckskin and tucked it inside his shirt. Though he led a very rough life, he could be gentle and tenderhearted. He was stubborn, even bullheaded at times. He was deeply religious and every night of his life he got down on his knees and repeated his prayers in Gaelic, because while other Catholics may talk to God in Latin, the MacDonalds knew He spoke Gaelic. Father was a clean-living man; he never drank more than an occasional glass of port, he never gambled and never used tobacco in any form. And he never forgot the lessons his parents had taught him of thrift, hard work and moderation in all things.

4

I

Lumberjack

M Y FATHER WAS born on 16 July 1839 and was christened Archibald Rory MacDonald, the sixth child in a family of seven sons and six daughters. His parents, Angus and Catherine Ann MacDonald, had arrived in Bytown, Ontario, in the spring of 1837 with a group of families of the MacDonald clan, who had left Glengarry, Scotland, in order to escape the restrictions that the government imposed on Roman Catholics.

After a few years in the new country, my grandfather Mac-Donald settled his family on a thousand-acre tract of timbered land twelve miles from Bytown near a village called Eastman Springs (later renamed Carlsbad Springs). During the first winter, with the help of his young sons, he began clearing land close to the unnamed stream that ran across the property. This was to be pastureland for the family cows. One day while cutting down a large hollow oak, grandfather and his eldest son Big John disturbed a large bear that had settled there to hibernate, and from that day on the stream beside it has been known as Bear Brook.

The growing MacDonald family was soon producing most of their own food on the farm; in fact, even their sugar supply came from their own sugar maple trees. They raised sheep, and my grandmother and her daughters knit sweaters and wove cloth

3

began with the California gold rush and slowly faded after the Klondike gold rush, thousands of men took up prospecting, chasing the rainbow throughout the west, unable to quit because there was always a chance that the pot of gold was just over the next hill. Father used to joke about it, telling the story of Old Sourdough Pete who died and got turned back at the Pearly Gates because there wasn't any more room in Heaven, Prospectors' Division.

"Can I just go in and have a little visit with some of my old friends?" he asked St. Peter.

"All right," said St. Peter. "I'll let you have an hour with them."

So Sourdough Pete went through the Pearly Gates and was welcomed by his old buddies.

"Any new strikes?" they asked.

Now Pete really had not heard of any new strikes in quite a while but he did not want to disappoint them, so he said, "Well, there's been a big gold strike at the head of Wild Goat Creek, and they tell me it's running an ounce and a half to the pan!"

Pretty soon Pete noticed that his audience was drifting away, and then he was all by himself. All his old buddies were heading for the Gates with packs on their backs. Since his hour was up he followed along, but St. Peter stopped him and asked where he was going.

"My hour is up so I'm leaving."

"Well, that won't be necessary now. So many of the boys have left that we've got plenty of room for you to stay."

Pete stood there scratching his head and looking apologetic. "Thanks, St. Peter, that's nice of you, but I think I'd better check this story out myself. It could be my last chance to make a really big strike!"

Prologue

I MUST HAVE BEEN no more than three years old when I first saw a rainbow. It was in the spring of 1896. There was a shower that afternoon, and when the sun came out again, I remember sitting with my mother on our verandah steps.

"Look, Ervin!" she said. "Look at the pretty rainbow!" I strained to see what she was pointing at. Though I was not much more than a baby, I didn't have any trouble finding that bright band of colours. Then with my mother's arms around me, I watched until it faded from the sky.

My father saw rainbows, too, but they were the kind no one else could see. Ephemeral bands of colour hung in the morning skies just beyond the misty mountains on the horizon, anchored there by a pot of gold nuggets. All his long life, my father chased his rainbows, sometimes almost touching one in Mexico or Montana or the Yukon, but he never quite got his hands on a really big one. So he was always travelling on: one man mounted on a saddle horse leading a couple of pack horses along some mountain trail, looking for a strike. Looking for gold.

First and last, my father was a prospector. Whenever he did make a strike, he worked it only until he got an offer from some development company. He had no interest in mining. For him the thrill was in the search. He was not alone in this. In a period that

1

Contents

To my wife Ann, my daughter Ruth Roberts,
my niece Vivian McGarrigle and my friend Flo Ivison,
without whose constant support and encouragement
I could not have written this book

Douglas & McIntyre Ltd.
1615 Venables Street
Vancouver, British Columbia

Published with assistance from the British Columbia Heritage Trust

Canadian Cataloguing in Publication Data

MacDonald, Ervin Austin, 1893–
    The rainbow chasers

    ISBN 0–88894–369–5

    1. MacDonald, Ervin Austin, 1893–
2. Pioneers—British Columbia—Biography.
3. Pioneers—Alberta—Biography.   4.
Frontier and pioneer life—British Columbia.
5. Frontier and pioneer life—Alberta.   6.
Overland journeys to the Pacific.   I. Title.
FC3824.1.M32A33   971.1′03′0924
F1088.M32A33   c82–091316–2

Jacket design by Richard Staehling
Jacket illustration by Ken Mimura
Typesetting, design and maps by The Typeworks
Printed and bound in Canada by D. W. Friesen & Sons Ltd.

The Rainbow Chasers

Ervin Austin MacDonald

Douglas & McIntyre
Vancouver/Toronto

pline in the camp and subdue the men who challenged his authority. And it took extraordinary courage to be able to step without hesitation into the middle of the fights that broke out between the lumberjacks. With a mixture of half a dozen or more nationalities in each forest camp and each man proud of his origin, any slur or insult, real or imagined, to any man's ancestry turned the camp into a battleground.

For six months of each year the men led a lonely and primitive life away from their families. Thirty or forty of them slept in a log "shanty" and were fed meals of salt pork, pea soup, dried peas or beans, coarse bread or hard biscuits, a little dried fruit and lots of boiled tea. To help pass the long winter evenings, they held contests, betting their wages on the outcome. Kicking contests were the favourite. Some of the champs could kick the stovepipe where it went through the ceiling, a height of some nine feet. They had three ways of doing this: a straight running high-kick, a hitch-kick from a standing start, and a double hitch where they kicked first with one leg and then the other. My father was one of the all-time champs at this sport.

But the favourite pastime of the men was fighting, especially using their boots with their three-quarter-inch-long sharp steel calks. They would kick out viciously for the stomach, the head or neck, or the groin, and if their opponent went down, they would stomp on him with both feet.

When they weren't fighting their fellow shantymen they were fighting the rival logging outfits, especially the French Canadians—"muskrats" or "logrollers" as they were called because they specialized in saw logs that they floated downriver in booms to be made into lumber at the sawmills. The logrollers used the same waterways, and often the square-timber men would find booms of saw logs strung right across their path. As soon as the square-timber men tried to make a passage through the boom for their own rafts, all hell would break loose. It was no-holds-barred fighting with axe handles, cant hooks, clubs, fists, boots and anything else that was handy. The fight ended only when one of the square-timber men succeeded in opening the boom and the current of the river carried the raft and its share of the combatants downriver.

Of course, if the rival groups met later in some saloon, the battle was on again. It was dangerous for any lumberjack, but most especially for a noted fighter, to go out alone because his rivals could gang up on him. The best friend of my uncle Big John MacDonald was badly hurt in this way by a gang of French Canadians. When Big John heard about it he vowed to teach the leader of the gang a lesson he wouldn't forget. He had to canoe nearly two hundred miles to find the man but he left him crippled for life; then he paddled back to tell his pal he had been avenged, only to find the poor fellow had died of his injuries.

Although my father was a robust man, he relied heavily on his agility whenever he was forced to fight. Then his fists would come out of nowhere and he would land a couple of punches that would lift his opponent right off his feet. But he hated all the fighting that went on in the camps; logging was dangerous enough as it was. Every step of the process took its toll in maimings and deaths, but the most dangerous part of all was rafting the logs through rough water on their way to market. Sometimes the timber, hurtling over a waterfall, would wedge between the rocks and then all the other logs would lodge behind them, held in place by the force of the water. Pretty soon a pile of logs thirty or forty feet high choked off the river, causing it to flood its banks.

Only the most agile and knowledgeable lumberjacks could break this kind of logjam, because the key log had to be found and either cut or pried out of the pile to free the rest. This was one of my father's skills. He would fasten a long rope to his waist and hand the other end to the men who waited on shore. Then barefoot and shirtless, with his single-bladed axe in hand, he would work his way over the jammed logs looking for the key one. When he found it, he had to be sure that he had correctly calculated his distance from the shore and gauged the force of the water behind the jam, so that when the logs started to move, he could save himself. Finally, he would start to chop, listening carefully after each axe blow for the first sound of moving timber. At any moment the tower of jammed logs above him might crash, grinding him to pieces or tossing him under the logs to drown. At the first crack, he threw his axe toward shore and began leaping from log to log for safety while behind him the jam broke with a roar and the logs rushed downstream.

Occasionally, the key log could not be pried or chopped loose and then father would have to blast the pile, but this was a last resort because valuable timber would be damaged. It was generally considered better to lose a man than lose good timber and as a result, probably one out of every three jambreakers did not make it back to shore when the jam broke. Those who did not make it to shore on their own two feet were pulled from the water by their "safety" lines and buried on the river bank before the lumberjacks hurried off to follow the logs downstream. On the other hand, the jambreakers who lived through the ordeal became famous throughout the Ottawa Valley.

The dangers were not over once the men left the rivers. Often when crossing Lake Ontario they were caught in storms that caused worse havoc than the rapids and falls. On one occasion, my father's raft began to break up in a violent storm, so he had the tender boat moved to the safest side of the raft and told the ten-man crew to abandon the raft. With cant hooks, two of the strongest men kept the boat from smashing against the raft while the crew transferred. Two of the men slipped and fell into the freezing water, but they were pulled into the boat and survived the mishap. As soon as my father was on board, they rowed for the safety of a nearby island. The raft broke up and nearly all the logs were lost, a huge financial loss. Other rafters were not so lucky. There were only two survivors from one crew whose boat was smashed against their disintegrating raft by the huge waves. The two who were saved had tied themselves to drifting timbers.

To the whole of the lumbering industry, my father proved himself to be a first-rate woods boss. In fact, one old-time lumberjack told me that father had been the best logging boss he ever worked for. Unfortunately, my grandfather was not equally impressed with his capabilities, and when the time came for the old man to choose one of his sons to succeed him as head of the family lumbering business, he chose his second son, Rory. The rest of the family fell into line behind Rory but not my father. He had become a very independent man even within that close-knit family, and he refused to knuckle under to his brother. He disagreed with his policies and fought all his decisions. He demanded more money for the dangerous and responsible job he held, and he accused Rory of pocketing too much of the family profits.

In 1864, rebelling at Rory's continuing attempts to make him toe the line, he announced his intention of joining the American

Federal Army so that he could collect the bonus offered to enlisting Canadians. The family persuaded him not to go, believing that he and Rory would resolve their differences in time. But the disagreements went on and father now began to talk about going west. He had heard stories of the fortunes to be made in the gold and silver mines of the west, and he knew of men from the Ottawa Valley who had left the dangerous life of the lumberjack to go prospecting. But the family ties were so strong that he found it hard to just pack up and take the same trail, so instead he decided to branch out in the lumbering business on his own. Therefore, in the spring of 1868, when he was twenty-nine years old, he left his younger brother Dan in his place as woods boss and went off to bid on some timber leases. However, Rory had learned of his plans and underbid him for the timber; when my father confronted him, a violent quarrel broke out.

In the midst of their fight, word came that Dan had been killed trying to break up a logjam in the river. My father was stricken with remorse. He felt responsible, because if he had been on the job, he would have been the one to venture out onto that logjam; since he was far more experienced than Dan, he would probably have survived. And though nobody actually accused him, he knew the family held him responsible for Dan's death.

He knew he had to go away. After the memorial service when the whole family gathered at a relative's house, father hurried home and packed a few belongings. Just as he was about to leave, he was stopped by his ten-year-old brother Angus who had stayed home from the funeral to look after the livestock.

"Where are you going, Archie?" he asked.

"To find a rainbow," said my father. Then as he was leaving he added, "I'll come home when I've got the pot of gold in my pack."

He never went back. He never even wrote a letter to say where he was. And he never spoke of Dan's death or Rory's double-cross. When I asked him in later years why he came west and why he didn't write to his family, he said, "I set out to make a million dollars. I couldn't swallow my pride and go back without it, could I?"

It was only in 1972 when Angus's youngest son Percy came west that I learned the true story.

2

Prospector
and Cowboy

IN THE SUMMER OF 1868, my father arrived in the city of St. Louis, Missouri. He had travelled this far by train and boat to the jumping-off point for prospectors. Here they outfitted themselves for the long journey west. He bought himself a good saddle horse, two pack horses, a small tent, a tarpaulin, wool blankets, cooking utensils and grub, a pick, a shovel, a gold pan and a miner's candle holder. This last item was nearly a foot long with a seven-inch point that could be stuck into wood or dirt, or shoved into a rock crevice or between the logs of a cabin. It also had a hook near the candle end so that it could be hung over the branch of a tree or from a shelf. I still have it today.

When he had loaded his prospecting outfit on the pack animals, he started west to find the pot of gold at the foot of the rainbow. Sometimes he travelled alone, sometimes he joined up with others on the trail. Along the way he stopped to prospect, taking side trips into areas like the Black Hills of Dakota. He learned his new calling by asking questions, by hiring himself out to other prospectors and miners, and by simple trial and error.

It took him a year to reach Denver, where he stayed several weeks to learn about that country before heading southwest to Leadville. Along the way, he kept meeting up with miners whose paths he had crossed before. None of them was exactly a friend because he was such an independent man and decidedly different from them. He did not drink, smoke or gamble and he never joined in their other pleasures either. He was friendly, of course, and helpful, but he always had a certain reserve. Since the other men could not decide what ailed him, they resented him and referred to him scornfully as "The Canadian," a name that stayed with him for years.

Leadville, Colorado, was the wildest mining town in the west in those days. Every gambler, claim jumper, grafter and thief seemed to have congregated there, and since unfortunately it was the only supply centre for a very large mining area, every miner had to show up there eventually and run the risk of getting fleeced. It was here that father replenished his grub supply before heading off into the mountains again. In the summer of 1870, he made his first strike, a rich outcropping of galena ore containing lead and silver in Buckskin Joe Gulch. He staked a claim and began an exploration tunnel. The rock was fairly soft and he made good progress, so as soon as he realized that he had the makings of a profitable investment, he took a few days off to build himself a log cabin and a blacksmith shop for sharpening his steel drills and repairing his equipment.

Then one day, after returning from Leadville with a load of supplies, as father approached the mouth of his tunnel he heard voices inside. He crept closer.

"This is too good for that damn Canadian!" said one voice.

"We can fix that," said another.

Father knew how claim jumpers worked and he got fighting mad. He ran back to his cabin, loaded his rifle and slipped back up the hill to hide behind a huge rock near the tunnel mouth. In a little while two men emerged, talking in low voices and peering cautiously around.

"I wonder where he is," one whispered.

"Right behind you," said father, stepping out from behind the rock.

The men whirled, reaching for their guns, but changed their minds when they saw father's rifle.

"You damn sons-of-guns can't be trusted with guns so you

can just undo your belts and drop 'em. One at a time." He motioned to one of them. "You first. Carefully now. Just let 'em lie at your feet." When the gunbelts were on the ground he said, "Now let's see how fast you can make it out of this gulch. And don't come back or I'll put a bullet in you!"

The two men started down the hillside at a dead run, but just to see if they could go any faster, father fired a few shots at their heels as they fled. Accidentally he shot the heel off one of the men's boots and that certainly did speed them on their way. When everything was quiet again, he collected their guns. They were six-shooters and such accurate shooting pieces that he kept them for many, many years.

In Leadville, the story spread quickly, and suddenly the scorned "Canadian" became the much-admired "Buckskin Archie." He was accepted as "one of the boys" at last, but it did not change the fact that he was still prey to claim jumpers. Playing a lone hand in the mining business was risky, because all a claim jumper had to do to steal his mine was establish possession when father was away getting supplies. He decided that he had to have a partner.

He had been hearing rumours that there was another Canadian in the Leadville area and he sounded as if he might make a good prospecting mate, but no one seemed to know where to find him. Then one night father dropped into a saloon. There he had his usual glass of port while the crowd at his table enjoyed the round of drinks he bought. Across the room was a prospector who reminded him of a lumberjack he had known in his Ottawa Valley days, so he asked someone who the man was.

"That fellow with all the hair? That's Big Jim Thompson."

So father pulled up a chair opposite Big Jim and by the time they left the saloon that night they had agreed to become partners.

Big Jim was so hairy that it was hard to see his face. He had long black hair, great bushy eyebrows, huge moustaches and an enormous wavy black beard. The only features discernible through all this were a prominent nose and piercing blue eyes. He was a couple of inches taller than my father but like him, he was long, lean, muscular and hard-working. Like father, he was

13

devoted to prospecting and had no intention of settling down. Unlike father, he was a heavy drinker. Once he got into a saloon, he was pretty hard to drag away.

Father and Big Jim worked the claim in Buckskin Joe Gulch for another ten months before they decided to sell out. They knew they would have to sink a shaft to follow the vein of ore and they had neither the capital nor the equipment to do it. So when a mining company came up with a substantial offer, they took it.

With money in their pockets and fresh supplies loaded on their pack horses, they headed for Mexico where big silver strikes had been making news. After nearly a year of combing the hills of Sonora State, they discovered a promising outcropping of silver-bearing ore. They staked and registered two claims and set up a permanent camp. Over the next few months they uncovered the main vein of ore, and when it assayed extremely high, they were pretty confident that they had found the rainbow's end.

Mexico seemed like a wonderful country: the climate was ideal, fruit and vegetables were plentiful, and there was lots of game for the shooting. Only a couple of things were wrong with the place. One was the people. They were so hotheaded that even peaceful, easygoing men like my father and Big Jim had to be always on their guard to avoid creating an excuse for a fight. Another problem was the government, which was very unstable and had little control over conditions outside the capital, and it was not long before they found out just how little control it had in Sonora. They had gone out hunting for a fresh meat supply and returned to camp in the late afternoon to find a band of gun-toting Mexicans settled comfortably in their camp.

"What's going on here?" father demanded angrily.

The leader looked him over calmly and then said, "This is our mine now. If you're smart you'll get on your horses and go back where you come from." He waved his pistol in a northerly direction. "We don't need you here!"

Father and Big Jim were looking into the barrels of nearly thirty guns. There was no point in arguing. They mounted their horses again and rode out of the camp. They had lost their mine and all their equipment but at least they were still alive. As they rode north, their spirits gradually began to lift. Maybe it had not been such a great mine anyhow. Maybe that vein would have petered out, and besides, how could they stay in a country full of wild men? Maybe the strike of a lifetime was waiting just over the next ridge.

They worked their way north through California without any luck at all. In the fall of 1873 they struck out across Nevada by way of Virginia City and stopped to see the Comstock Mine, at that time one of the richest in the world, though the prospectors who discovered it had sold it for eleven thousand dollars. They wintered near Carson City, then set out for Montana early in '74. They moved slowly from place to place with no particular destination in mind but prospecting every foot of the way. There was little difficulty finding base metals like lead and zinc and copper if you were any kind of prospector at all, but these were too hard to mine and too expensive to ship. Their ideal strike was gold or silver that would quickly attract a development company.

It took about three years for them to work their way from Helena to Bannock, Idaho, to Kellogg, with side trips to Coeur d'Alene and into the sparsely inhabited region at the northern end of Kootenay Lake in Canada. But around 1877 they returned to the Butte, Montana, area and stayed there for four years prospecting and hiring themselves out as miners whenever they needed money for a new stake.

In 1881, they packed up and moved north to the Flathead Lake area, and it was here that they became acquainted with the Flathead Indians and their head chief, Grey Eagle. The chief was an impressive figure with piercing black eyes flecked with grey like the eyes of the eagle. He was a stern man, dealing severely with those who broke the tribal laws or imposed on his hospitality. He was friendly to a certain point but did not allow anyone to take liberties that he had not offered, and he was extremely sensitive to real or imagined slights and insults. Big Jim and father, therefore, were always extremely careful not to offend him, because their safety in the Flathead country depended on his goodwill. But the chief liked the two big, black-bearded men, and always called my father "Canada" as a mark of his esteem.

Grey Eagle and his people raised big dapple-grey part-Arabian horses, the descendants of horses brought into Mexico by the Spaniards in the sixteenth century. They were trained to a running walk and some of them could reach a speed of nine or ten miles an hour and maintain it for hours. My father was an admirer of fine horseflesh and he started hankering after one of the Flatheads' horses from the moment he saw them. He knew that if Grey Eagle knew how badly he wanted one his chances would be spoiled, so he sat around the campfire talking to the old man several times before he brought up the subject of buying a horse.

"No, Canada," said the chief, "you can't buy my horse. But I tell you what. If you can ride that big horse over there I will give him to you." And he smiled as all the Indians listening laughed out loud. The chief felt perfectly safe in making his offer because this four-year-old stallion had already thrown everyone who tried to ride him.

"That's a deal, Grey Eagle," said my father quietly, "but I'm using my own saddle."

As the news spread through the camp, everyone crowded around to watch the fun, cheer and taunt. Four or five men corralled the horse, roped him, and with considerable difficulty got a hackamore and blindfold on him. Then father brought his saddle and it was cinched around the horse's belly. When this was done to father's satisfaction, two husky fellows eared the horse down until father had mounted. Then the blindfold was whipped off, the ropes dropped and the animal was turned loose.

That horse put up a terrific fight. He went straight up and he came straight down, he bucked and he twisted — but he could not get rid of the man on his back. Father had a number of advantages over the Indians who had tried to ride the horse earlier. He was taller and heavier and his long legs could get a better grip on the horse's belly. His sense of balance had become highly developed during years of riding logs down chutes and through rapids. And he had a better saddle. In fact, most of the Indians rode bareback or with just a strap around the horse's body to hang on to.

Finally, unable to buck my father off, the horse changed his tactics. He plunged into the side of the corral in an attempt to smash him into the poles. Instead the poor beast broke his own neck. The contest was over.

The Indians got a great laugh out of father's unexpected success; the loss of the horse seemed to be of little consequence.

16

"Well, Canada, this horse has gone *mimaloos!*" said Grey Eagle.

Father waited, wondering whether the chief was going to demand that he pay for the dead animal.

Grey Eagle appeared to be deep in thought. At last he said, "I'll give you his three-year-old full brother instead."

And that is how my father became the owner of the fine big horse he named Frank. He was a one-man horse, a very independent animal, and sometimes he even bucked when father got on him. I can recall an occasion when I was about four when Frank bucked father off, right onto a picket fence. He was quite a while recovering from those injuries.

In the summer of 1881, about two months after father had earned his new horse, he and Big Jim established their main camp on the shore of Flathead Lake. From this vantage point, they took light packs and worked their way up the streams that led back into the hills where they prospected and did a little placer mining. It was an ideal campsite: fish and game were plentiful and there was good grass and water for their horses.

Often while they prospected they met small bands of Indians out on hunting and fishing expeditions. My father had a great respect for the Indians but he had found in his many years of prospecting that a hungry Indian was a dangerous Indian and when well fed was inclined to sleep and take life easy. So whenever he and Big Jim met a bunch of Indians, they would cook up a kettle of rice and raisins, a pot of tea and plenty of meat, and everyone would sit happily eating around a campfire.

A couple of weeks after setting up camp, they returned from the hills to find that Grey Eagle and about thirty-five of his warriors had made camp a short distance away along the shore. Father had actually been hoping to meet them again because he had left a beautiful buffalo hide with one of the women to make into a coat for him. He particularly prized that hide because it was a glossy black instead of the usual brown. The woman had finished sewing the coat and had done an excellent job. It fitted him perfectly and he wore it every winter for the rest of his life.

Grey Eagle's people settled down in their new camp for a couple of weeks of hunting and fishing, and nearly every evening the two white men were invited to join their campfire to talk of the game and the country around them. About ten days after the Indians' arrival, father and Big Jim decided there was enough colour and fine gold in one of the creeks they had been following to build a sluice box on it. Before building, they staked two claims and made plans to head for civilization the following day to register them. But as they neared their camp that afternoon, Grey Eagle rode out to meet them with an invitation to join him and his two sub-chiefs in a ceremonial feast the next day. There went their plans to register their claims since they did not dare to offend the chief by not accepting. They insisted, however, that they be allowed to supply the coffee and a kettle of boiled rice and dried apples.

The next afternoon, father and Big Jim approached Grey Eagle's tepee with curiosity and a little apprehension. Inside, the three chiefs and the two white men sat in a circle. The feast was served by the chiefs' squaws. First the men were brought the peace pipe which was passed around the circle after Grey Eagle had taken the first puff. When this ritual was over, chunks of roast beaver on wooden skewers were served to each man. Now, my father had been eating moose meat and venison and buffalo meat ever since he started prospecting, but he drew the line after these three wild meats. He considered all the others to be totally inedible, and beaver meat was prominent on his list of inedibles. Yet he ate every bit that was offered to him: he could not offend the chief.

The next dish was the highlight of the feast—boiled white dog, a dish served only on state occasions. The dog had been killed ceremonially by striking it on the head, then skinned and eviscerated and hung from a scaffold opposite the powwow tent. After a week, it was ready to be boiled over the campfire.

The pot of boiled dog meat was placed in the centre of the circle and each man reached his hand into the pot and fished out a hunk of meat. For my father and Big Jim this was an entirely new experience, but it only took them a moment to realize that they were expected to show their enjoyment by smacking their lips and sucking the juice from their fingers. And above all, a smile like the moon coming from behind a cloud must light up their faces. Both men were almost sick to their stomachs but they smiled like idiots and plunged their hands into the pot. Finally, the rice and apples and coffee were served and the feast was finished.

When the women and children had finished their meal, the chiefs and their guests moved outside. Here the main campfire was piled high with dry wood and the Indians began to dance and chant. Grey Eagle disappeared into his tepee. When he reappeared he was wearing a very fine headdress of eagle feathers and he was leading a pretty young woman by the hand. This was his favourite daughter.

Slowly, the two walked into the clearing near the fire. Grey Eagle stood before them looking proud and serious; his daughter's eyes were downcast. The people gathered around. Grey Eagle beckoned my father to stand before him. Big Jim edged closer to see what was going on; neither he nor my father had any idea what was coming next. Grey Eagle held up his hand for silence.

"Canada, in your country, you would be great chief. Here, you are friend to my people. To show you my friendship, I make you one of my tribe, and I give you my daughter for your squaw."

My father was horrified.

"Tomorrow," continued the chief, "I will send braves to hunt and fish. I will send braves to tell all the people to come. After seven sleeps we will have a big feast. Then my daughter will be your woman."

My father had no intention of getting married, even to please the chief. He had been single for forty-two years and he could see no reason to change his status at this late date. Besides, there was still the small matter of that pot of gold waiting somewhere for him. On the other hand, Grey Eagle would be a dangerous enemy if he were offended. Father decided to stall for time.

"Oh, great Chief Grey Eagle," he said humbly, "I am deeply honoured to be chosen as a member of your family and your tribe. I am pleased to accept your daughter as my woman. Please allow me to bring rice, dried fruit and tea to the feast seven sleeps from now."

The chief nodded, pleased with my father's reply, and gave the signal for the dancing and chanting to resume. In their dances the Indians went through all the manoeuvres of hunting, stalking and then shooting the game with imaginary bows and arrows. While this was going on, father made his way slowly back to where Big Jim stood. Neither man spoke but after a while both of them began to drift out of the circle and back toward their own camp.

"What are we going to do, Archie?" asked Big Jim, as usual looking to father for direction.

"We're getting out of here," muttered father. "And we're going to do it pretty quietly because I'd feel awfully naked without my hair."

"You're not going to marry her?"

Big Jim was relieved to realize that he was not going to lose his partner to matrimony, though they could both lose their lives if Grey Eagle got hold of them.

In their tent, the two men talked in low voices, deciding at length that they might have a chance of escaping if they could get a good head start on the Indians. They would have to make it look as though they had gone off prospecting in the morning as usual. This would mean leaving behind their tent, pack horses and most of their supplies and equipment. They would only be able to take light packs tied behind their saddles. But one thing my father refused to give up was the beautiful buffalo coat, so even though it was midsummer he wore it. In preparation, they put light picket ropes on their saddle horses and tied them to their wrists so they would be able to find the animals in the dark. As final insurance, they cut up a saddle blanket and wrapped the pieces around their horses' hoofs to deaden the sound.

Then they sat down to wait. The Indians danced on and on into the night. It seemed they would never tire. At last the fire was reduced to glowing coals and the last braves wandered off to their tepees. There was silence except for the sound of the waves lapping the shore and the wind rustling the trees. After another hour had gone by, father and Big Jim rose, felt along their picket ropes and began leading their horses toward the lakeshore. For half an hour they walked ahead of their horses, glancing back from time to time. Their greatest fear was that the two young Indian boys who regularly practised their stalking techniques on them as they prospected up the creeks would pounce on them out of the shadows. But no one intercepted them, and after half an hour they mounted and turned south in the direction of Missoula, Montana. For the rest of the night they rode on, keeping to low ground and avoiding the skyline in case they were being followed.

When daylight came, they were travelling on a rocky ridge where they did not have to worry about leaving tracks, but since it was unsafe to travel in daylight, they began looking for a place to hide. Off to their right a bushy ravine offered cover and they made their way down, being careful to leave no sign of their passage. As they expected, there was a creek at the bottom of the ravine and they picketed their horses beside it. After they had eaten, they took turns sleeping and watching the trail.

About noon, Big Jim woke father gently and pointed to the ridge above them. Several of Grey Eagle's braves were coming in their direction along the ridge. Had their absence been discovered already? Were they being tracked? Silently they rolled up their packs, then held their horses' noses so that they could make no noise. Overhead the Indians approached in single file—and rode silently on, not showing the slightest interest in the ravine or in any tracks that might have been left by the two men. Father and Big Jim sighed with relief, realizing that these were just hunters going out for game for the wedding feast.

The day passed without anyone else coming near their hiding place, and when night came they continued on their way. By the third day they felt it was safe to travel during daylight. Eventually they reached Missoula where they purchased new camping and prospecting outfits and three new pack horses.

They knew they would have to stay clear of the Flathead district for a long time, but they were still interested in the mountains of western Montana and the panhandle of Idaho. During the next two years they worked their way to Butte, then westward through the Nez Perce Pass into Idaho and on to the Clearwater Mountains. Finding nothing worthwhile, they rode on to Coeur d'Alene and finally back to Libby, Montana.

They set up camp at Libby intending to stay awhile. They were deeply discouraged. In the two years since they had fled from Grey Eagle, they had not seen a glimmer of gold or silver.

The expense of buying a new outfit had taken all their cash reserves and they were having to hire themselves out more and more often just to pay for their grub supply.

The winter of 1883 was disappointing, but in the spring of the following year the talk around Libby gave father and Big Jim new hope. It was said that the contractors building the Canadian Pacific Railway were paying top money for beef cattle to feed their crews, and the biggest camp was just over two hundred miles to the north at Revelstoke in British Columbia. Neither father nor Big Jim had ever handled beef cattle but they decided to investigate the business of buying and selling cattle and cattle drives. They were agreed that nothing could pay worse than prospecting had in the last couple of years.

The first thing they learned was that they would need more hands for a cattle drive. They found one good wrangler in a man called Simmons who had spent most of his life herding cattle. Their other man was Hood Formwalt, a long lean Texan of about fifty years. He was a first-rate cowboy and an excellent cook. On cattle drives he proved to be absolutely reliable, but he had a few odd ways which made father and Big Jim suspect that he had had trouble with the law. He never started a conversation himself, and when anyone did get him talking he was exceedingly reluctant to give out personal information. But he was very easy to get along with.

With their crew hired, father and Big Jim began buying up range cattle in Montana where, because of a minor depression caused by a big drop in silver prices, cows were going cheap. There were few problems on the drive. Most of the trails north were clearly marked and the cattle (mainly Herefords and shorthorns) followed them instinctively. When they came to rivers, the cattle and horses simply swam them. Everything worked out well and when they reached Revelstoke they were paid handsomely for their beef.

Having succeeded with one cattle drive, they went back for another herd, and then another. Then there was just time for one last trip before winter. As usual, the cattle followed the trail easily and swam the rivers until they were just a few miles south of Revelstoke. There while crossing the Columbia, one steer refused to swim, so the drovers decided to lead him behind a rowboat they had rented. Hood lassoed the animal, settling the rope around his horns, then led him down to the river. He put the other end of the rope in a coil in the bottom of the boat. Off they went with father rowing and Hood on horseback forcing the steer into the water. This system worked perfectly until the animal reached shallow water just below a large sandbar in midstream. As soon as his feet touched bottom he started to run, tangling the rope around father's feet so that he was yanked out of the boat. He was plunged into the cold water feet first and dragged up onto the sandbar on his face, over rocks and snags and into a patch of brushwood.

It all happened so quickly that vital moments were lost before any of the others reacted. It was Big Jim who shot the animal, and all three men scrambled over the rocks and driftwood to find father. He was unconscious. Gently, they examined him. Both legs were broken in several places, his ribs were broken, and he had cuts from head to foot. But even more serious were his abdominal injuries where his guts were showing through holes gouged in his flesh.

Carefully, they carried him to a deserted shack on the river bank and did what little they could for him. They made a makeshift bed on the floor with blankets from their camping gear. They covered him up well and built a rip-roaring fire in the rusty old stove that stood in one corner of the room.

They decided to leave him there by himself while they drove the cattle into Revelstoke. The foreman at the construction camp was in quick agreement that they should get father to a doctor as fast as possible.

"But there's no doctor up this way," he said. "You've got to go back over the border to Fort Colville to find a doctor!"

Fort Colville had originally been a Hudson's Bay Company trading post, but when the border was established and the Bay men had withdrawn, it became an outpost for the United States Army. Because of its importance as an administrative centre for Indian affairs, it was well equipped and had a hospital and a doctor.

"But that's more than two hundred miles!" said Big Jim. "We can't put him on a horse! Besides, he's not even conscious."

"Build a raft," suggested the foreman. "You can follow the

Arrow Lakes down into the Columbia and you'll be just about there. You can take what you need to build it from the camp and I'll lend you a couple of men to help."

The foreman gave them some disinfectant and bandages, and Big Jim bought a bottle of rum from the camp stores to ease father's pain. Inevitably he also decided that it would be a good idea for all of them to ease their pain somewhat, and four hours later the three men were still sitting around with the construction crew drinking.

In their absence, my father drifted in and out of his pain-filled world. Once when he became partially conscious he thought he smelled smoke, but he slipped into unconsciousness again before he could be sure. Then suddenly he was fully awake.

It *was* smoke. The shack was on fire! The overheated tin stovepipe had set the roof on fire. Still in a daze, he struggled to sit but fell back in agony. Obviously he was not going to be able to get up and run out of there. But he was not a man to panic. He was too tough an old bird and had been through too much to give up without a fight. He felt his arms. There was nothing wrong with them. "Good!" he thought grimly and started pulling himself toward the door on the other side of the room.

Hot coals and pieces of burning wood fell on him as he struggled, his wounds gaping open with each movement. At the door he stretched upward for the latch, and from the pains in his chest he realized for the first time that his ribs were broken; he slid down against the door. Then in spite of the hurt, he stretched once more and jiggled the latch up. There it stuck, and he threw his weight against the door as hard as he could and fell out into the fresh air. Then painfully he dragged himself to the river's edge and slid into the shallow water to put out the fire that was smouldering in his clothes. He could feel burns on his face and smelled the singed hair of his beard. Unconsciousness again overtook him.

When the three men finally came back along the river and saw the blazing shack, their hearts hit their boots. They came running but they could not get near the shack. They knew that nobody could still be alive inside that inferno. Then Hood spotted father lying motionless in the water.

24

Big Jim was cold sober as he kneeled in the river. "Archie, can you hear me?" Then he turned to the others. "I think he's alive! Here, give me a hand!"

Carefully they eased him from the water and carried him up the bank. They cut off the remains of his clothes, wrapped him in blankets and gave him a big shot of rum.

"Jim," said father as he regained consciousness, "what happened to that steer?"

"The one that got you? I shot him," said Jim.

"I want his heart," said father.

"His heart?"

Father nodded.

Big Jim was not one to turn down a dying man so off he went, found the carcass and cut out the heart.

"You want it cooked?" he asked father.

Father shook his head. Big Jim cut off a slice and handed it to him.

"There," he said as he bit into it. "That proves he's dead—and I'm alive."

Big Jim, Hood and Simmons went to work making a stretcher out of a couple of saplings and a canvas pack cover, and they left him at the first aid tent at the construction camp while they built a raft with the help of some of the camp carpenters. It was about eight feet wide and twenty feet long. In the middle, they erected a mast about ten feet high, and fastened sixteen-foot-long sweeps to posts at each end of the raft. They knew everything had to be very sturdy to withstand the rapids and swift water ahead of them on the long, dangerous journey down the Columbia River, into the long Arrow Lakes, then back into the Columbia as far as Kettle Falls, Washington.

When the raft was finished, Big Jim and Hood went back to the construction camp store for more medical supplies, food and a few bottles of 120 overproof rum. The liquor was intended as a painkiller, disinfectant and stimulant for my father as well as a nightcap for his conscience-stricken but unreformed companions. The stretcher was made as comfortable as possible before the patient was placed on it and well covered up. They strapped him down securely to prevent him from rolling with the movement of the raft, then erected a willow frame over the stretcher

25

area and covered it with a pack canvas to shield him from the weather. They were working as quickly as possible but it was early on the third day after the accident before everything was ready and they were able to cast off. Big Jim manned the front sweep and Hood the stern, while Simmons spelled them.

Their first overnight stop was at Arrowhead at the northern end of the Arrow Lakes. Although it was only twenty-five miles from Revelstoke, the men were exhausted from working the sweeps on the swift, rapid-filled river. They were all aware that their patient's pain had been made worse by the buffeting they took. On the river bank they put up their tent and carried father inside to tend his wounds and feed him.

At sunrise on the fourth day, they looked out over the calm expanse of Upper Arrow Lake. They anticipated a smooth ride though they knew the drifting current would slow their progress. Using the sweeps, they worked the raft well out from shore to take full advantage of the current: at first, they moved at a fair speed because the river was still pushing them along, but as the day passed the current weakened. On the sixth day, a wind came up and they rigged a canvas sail to carry them faster, but toward evening, when black clouds rolled in from the west, they took shelter at a small settlement. As they redressed father's wounds the people of the settlement looked on and shook their heads. They knew a dying man when they saw one. Before it grew dark, Big Jim and Hood shot game along the shore to replenish their food supply.

They could not set off the next day. Rain lashed at the water and the wind whipped up huge waves. The three men spent the day passing the bottle. From time to time one of them would peer out into the rain to check for some lightening of the sky.

That night the wind eased off and the rain stopped. At dawn the next day, the eighth since the accident, winter was in the air. Despite a stiff wind, the men felt they could not risk any more delay. They set the raft loose but stayed close to shore, ready to head for shelter if necessary. They made good time and it was nearly dark before they began looking for a campsite.

By morning the wind had died, and all that day they drifted, their sail hanging slackly. Hood and Simmons fished from the stern and that night when they tied up the raft to some overhanging "sweepers," they dined on fresh trout. Father, drifting in and out of consciousness, sang Gaelic songs.

At midmorning of the tenth day, they reached the foot of the lake and began to negotiate the stretch of river separating it from Lower Arrow Lake. They stopped at a small homestead for the night and were able to buy fresh eggs and milk. There was a good wind to fill the sail the next morning and they made better progress. The following afternoon a storm developed and they were forced off the lake. The next day, the thirteenth since the accident, they sat in their tent and listened to the wind and the rain. Father's condition did not seem to be any worse and some of his wounds were healing nicely, but because he had little appetite he was growing steadily weaker. Big Jim, who had been father's only family for nearly fifteen years, could not bear to think of losing him, and finally shuffled off into the rain with his gun to shoot grouse. Action was the only way he could express his emotions.

On the fourteenth day, they set off in a stiff wind, but late in the afternoon it died and they settled down to their usual drifting pace. There was no wind all the following day. Then about noon of the sixteenth day, they suddenly realized that the raft had picked up speed. The sail was slack; it had to be the current carrying them into the river once more. Down came the sail and they rushed to man the sweeps as they slipped past the small community that would one day be called Castlegar, and past the mouth of the Kootenay River, stopping finally for the night at the settlement of Trail Creek where the Dewdney Trail met the Columbia River. Patient and crew were all exhausted. The river, flowing between steep banks, had tossed them over one rapid after another. They had made ten miles an hour at times that day so they were much closer to Fort Colville by nighttime than they had expected to be.

Sympathetic people at Trail Creek warned them where to expect rapids ahead and how to avoid difficulty at the junction of the Columbia and the Big Pend Oreille, and encouraged them with the news that they should be in Kettle Falls the next day. Early on the eighteenth morning they pushed out into the current and began manoeuvring the raft through some of the worst rapids of the whole trip, but they were buoyed up by the knowledge that father was still alive and they were within a few hours of a hospital. In midafternoon they saw Kettle Falls ahead. Big Jim leaped from the raft, leaving the others to secure it, and soon came back with a rented team and wagon. Still strapped to his stretcher, father was taken over twelve miles of bumpy trail and carried into the Fort Colville hospital.

The doctor was flabbergasted when they told him the story of their journey. When he had examined father, he turned to Big Jim and shook his head. "The bones have already started to knit. Either I amputate your friend's legs or I break them again and re-set them. And let me tell you, resetting them is the most terrible and painful operation there is!"

Father was listening to this conversation and he called the doctor and Big Jim over to his bed.

"Jim," he said, "where's my revolver?"

"It's right here, Archie. Right here at the end of your bed." He waved the gun to show him.

"Fine. Now you hang on to that and you keep watch. And if anybody around here tries to give me chloroform with the intention of cutting my legs off, you shoot him. You understand? It's hard enough to go through life with two good legs, but it's damn near impossible to do it with no legs at all!"

The doctor got the point. My father's legs were broken and reset, then put in casts with heavy weights attached to pull the muscles into proper position. For nearly three months he lay flat on his back in constant pain while the wounds to his stomach and abdomen healed and the bones of his legs knit. The one bright spot in his life was the girl who nursed him, Mary Malinda Prouty, the daughter of the colonel in charge of the fort. She was only about five feet one and small boned with large dark blue eyes and long, wavy auburn hair. My father admired her very much, but so did most of the young cavalry officers of the fort.

At the end of four months, when he was nearly ready to leave the hospital, father was forced to accept the fact that he was a cripple. He would never again walk without crutches. He could never follow another rainbow to its end. So the next time Big Jim, Hood and Simmons came to see him, he told them he was turning his interest in their pack animals and their outfit (which they had gone back to Revelstoke to retrieve) over to them in gratitude for all they had done for him. The only thing he kept was the dapple-grey horse Frank that he had won from Grey Eagle.

His fifteen-year partnership with Big Jim was dissolved with a handshake, but both men felt the loss deeply. A few days later, Big Jim saddled up and with Simmons as his new partner headed off into the mountains. My father never heard from him again. Hood Formwalt went to work on a local ranch and remained my father's friend for years.

3

Family

RELEASED FROM THE hospital, father went to stay at a Fort Colville hotel. From there he set out on his crutches walking a little farther each day, stopping to talk with people and determined to lift himself out of the despair he felt. He had no idea how he could earn a living without use of his legs.

One day when he was out walking, he met a young man from Ontario who said that he and two partners had staked some claims on a high bunchgrass mountain four miles from Fort Colville. They had named the mountain and their mine "The Old Dominion" since they all came from Canada. They were now busy hauling the ore by wagon and mule team to Spokane, some ninety miles away. From there it was shipped by train to the nearest smelter which was at Butte, Montana. To the older, more experienced prospectors in the area, the Old Dominion Mine was a joke because they could not believe that a mine so accessible could be any good. A good mine had to be somewhere away off in the wilderness.

The three young men took a liking to my father and they respected his experience in prospecting and mining. Soon they developed the habit of coming to him for advice concerning their mining problems, and father realized that although they were shipping out a lot of ore, it was not making them rich. He advised them to hire an experienced man to sort the ore and ship only the high-grade stuff.

"Good idea," said their spokesman. "Will you take the job?"

Father's hospital and doctor bills had almost drained his bank account. "Yes," he said, "but it will have to be on my terms. First, you'll have to build a platform for me at the mouth of the tunnel. With a roof over it. And it'll have to be rigged so I can work sitting down. And I'll need a helper to move the sacks of ore for me."

The three young men nodded in agreement and then waited.

"My wages will be five dollars a day."

"Now, hold on a minute, Archie! That's a lot of money!" they yelped.

"Well, you're not making that mine pay the way you're working it, are you? And I'm darn sure it could pay, by what you've told me about it, if you have someone capable of sorting the good ore from the bad. So why not try me for two or three months? If I can't make your mine pay, we'll call the deal off."

The three men went off to talk the idea over, but pretty soon they came back to say they would hire him on his terms.

Although father could now mount and ride his horse Frank, it was still very painful for him and he decided to look for a place to board closer to the mine. When Mary Prouty heard of this, she took him to meet her family at their homestead close to the mine site. Col. Richard Austin Prouty had built a great log mansion to house his big family, and in the evenings the colonel delighted in entertaining family and friends by playing the violin. For this event, he stood in his dress uniform, complete with sword, just to the right of the huge stone fireplace and played tune after tune. To the left, his wife Esther Howe Prouty sat in her favourite rocking chair, smoking a delicate corncob pipe, a high point of pleasure for a southern lady in those days.

My father liked the Prouty family very much and when the colonel offered to take him in as a boarder, he gladly accepted. He would be able to get a ride to and from work with the Prouty boys who were working at the mine.

For the first few weeks of work, father was exhausted. He was almost too tired to eat at the end of the day, but his strength gradually came back. All day long he sat on the platform picking out the best ore and putting it in sacks for an assistant to haul away. When it reached the smelter it assayed out around a hundred dollars a ton and sometimes more. This was even better than father had expected, and the three young owners were very satisfied. At last they were making money.

It was not long before the monotony of the job began to eat at father. He longed for his old active life, but he was forced to stick with the job because he was a cripple, and cripples cannot chase rainbows. In the meantime, he was becoming more skillful with his crutches, and whenever he had time he went riding into the hills on Frank or hunting with the Prouty boys. Almost two years went by in this way, before father came to the conclusion that although his crutches were a nuisance, he was no longer a cripple. He had taught himself to do most of the things he used to do before the accident.

So one night at the Prouty supper table he announced, "I'm thinking of going to South Africa."

All the Proutys stopped eating and looked up.

"There've been some pretty rich gold strikes there. I'd like to get in on it."

Now the Proutys were not really all that surprised, because they knew he was a wanderer. But they had come to think of him as one of the family.

"Well, Archie," said the colonel, "I know you've been in Fort Colville quite a while and you're probably ready to move on, but this idea of going off to a foreign country ... have you given this careful thought?"

So father began to explain his decision, and all the Proutys joined in the discussion. Then suddenly Mary Malinda got up from the table and ran out of the room. Father stopped talking and turned to look after her, but the family paid no attention whatsoever and went right on talking and eating.

After dinner he looked for her and found her hiding behind the kitchen door, with tears rolling down her face.

"What's the matter?" he asked quietly.

His gentle voice started her crying even harder. "I don't want you to go away!"

He was bewildered. "But I can't stay here forever!"

"Then take me with you!"

Father was thunderstruck. He knew he loved Mary Malinda but so did half the young men at the fort, and here she was suggesting (unless he was badly mistaken) that she wanted to be with him. Unsure that she meant what she appeared to mean, he said, "Why Mary Malinda, I couldn't possibly do that! It wouldn't be right to take a young girl into a place like that! Besides, your father would never allow it."

There was a fresh flood of tears. "But I *want* to go with you!"

"Why?"

"Because I love you! And I just want to be with you always."

These were the most beautiful words that my father had ever heard but they were also the saddest. He was forty-seven years old, he would be on crutches for the rest of his days, he was a wanderer, and he had few prospects for the future. The girl before him was just eighteen, charming and beautiful and desired by all the handsome, wealthy young men in town.

"Mary Malinda," he said sadly, "I'm nearly thirty years older than you, and I'm a cripple. You should be marrying one of those cavalry officers who are always coming to court."

"I don't care if you're older. I don't care about your crutches. And I don't want to marry one of the little boys in the cavalry. I want to marry you because I love you."

For nearly twenty years father had been on his own with only Big Jim for a family, so he found it hard to believe that this wonderful girl really loved him and wanted to be his wife. But he was quite willing to be persuaded. He gave up his plans for South Africa and instead began building a small log house at the foot of the Old Dominion Mine. When it was finished, father and Mary Malinda Prouty were married in a quiet family ceremony.

Their first child, a daughter whom they named Lavena Anne, was born in August 1887, and shortly afterwards they moved to a homestead at the farthest end of a small valley, about eighteen miles from Fort Colville. Father had discovered the land earlier in the year when he was out hunting. There was a good creek running through the property which he promptly christened Bear Creek after the one on the MacDonald farm in Ontario. With the help of some hired hands he built a log house, big enough for a family. A large living room with a big stone fireplace was flanked by a bedroom on the north end of the house and a kitchen and

33

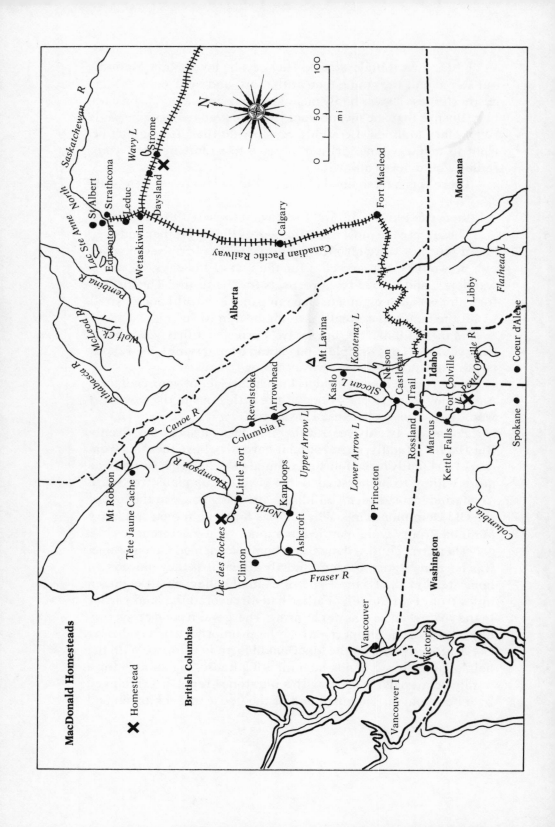

dining room on the south. A stairway led up to three more bedrooms. When it was complete, in spite of his crutches, father began clearing the land.

The job at the Old Dominion Mine lasted one more year after Lavena's birth. A sorter was no longer needed when the railway from Spokane to Colville was completed and it became just as cheap to ship all the ore as to sort it. But father had anticipated this day and had already contracted to act as field man for a couple of mining companies. He also began to stock his new homestead.

It was in the new ranch house on the new homestead beside Bear Creek that my mother gave birth to a boy, Angus, in 1889, and a second boy, Donald who was always called Dan, in 1891. And it was here in 1893 that I, Ervin Austin, finally joined this story. My youngest sister, Ruth, was born in 1895.

By the time I was born father had built up quite a good business buying and selling horses. He raised a strain called Cleveland Bays, heavy driving horses that weighed around fourteen hundred pounds at maturity. They were light bay in colour with silver manes and tails, very clean lined and high spirited. Any lover of fine horses could not help but be impressed by them; the Spokane fire department was one of father's best customers.

Buying and selling beef cattle was another of his farm enterprises even though it had been a steer that had almost killed him. One of his customers was a French Canadian, known simply as Antoine, who had won a contract to build freight barges to be used along the Columbia to Nelson before the railway was constructed. He hired a crew at Kettle Falls and built the barges there on the bank of the river. When he heard about father's excellent beef, he asked him to supply some for his crew.

They agreed on a price and also agreed that payment would be made after all the beef had been delivered. Once a week father butchered a fat steer and hauled the meat to Antoine's camp. Both men kept a tally of the amount that had been delivered.

One day after father had made his delivery, Antoine told him, "That's all the meat I'm going to need. The barges are almost finished. I will be pushing off in a couple of days."

"Well, Antoine," said father, "if that's the case, we'd better set-

35

tle up. According to my reckoning you owe me four hundred dollars."

"That's about right," said Antoine grinning, "and I've got the money right here in my pocket." He pulled a big roll of bills out of his back pocket and flashed it at my father. "Now you take a good look at it, Mac, because that's all you're going to see of it." And he stuffed the money back in his pocket.

Though father was thunderstruck, he said very calmly, "We made a fair deal, and you owe me that money. I kept my end of the bargain. Now it's up to you to keep yours or I shall have to take the money from you!"

Antoine laughed and laughed, and a crowd began to gather to see what was so funny. "You're a big man, Mac," he laughed, "but you're old and you're crippled! Go on home!"

Now father had a temper, and he began cursing that Frenchman out in Gaelic; Antoine goaded him, cursing him in French. Every so often there was enough English in the shouting match for the crowd to understand the issue yet no one made a move to try to make Antoine pay up. But the Frenchman had made two mistakes in taking on my father. First, he let my father know he had the money, and second, he believed that father would not fight for his rights. Unfortunately for Antoine, my father had never backed away from a fight in his life. When the Frenchman started taking mock jabs at him and laughing because father could not parry them, it was just too much for father's self-control. He dropped his crutches and stepped back out of Antoine's reach, then as Antoine lunged expecting to topple him off his feet, father socked Monsieur Antoine with a terrific left hook that knocked him out cold on the ground.

The crowd went wild. "Good going, Mac! He sure had that coming!"

Father bent over and pulled the roll of bills out of Antoine's pocket. He counted out four hundred dollars and asked the people who were standing around to witness the fact that he had taken exactly the amount the Frenchman had admitted owing him. He put the rest of the money back in the man's pocket, then walked back to his team and wagon and drove off. He had left the crutches lying on the ground beside Antoine.

When he got home, my mother watched him climb out of the

36

wagon and walk to the house. "Archie, what's happened? Where are your crutches?"

Only now did he realize that he had left them behind. He had depended on them for seven years and in a single moment of anger he had found out he could do without them. For the remainder of his life, he walked without crutches, only using a cane sometimes to favour his left leg a little when he was well into his eighties.

As time went by and his family grew in size, father went off on prospecting trips more and more often. He had not forgotten the prize waiting at the foot of the rainbow, but now he wanted it for his family. Since he was away so often we children were expected to do our share of the work around the ranch. I can remember weeding and thinning vegetables in the garden when I was no more than four years old. I did not mind being set to work in the carrots since I loved eating them raw.

One afternoon when all of us children were busy in the garden, we saw a tall, clean-shaven man dismount at the ranch gate and start toward the house. As fast as our little legs would carry us, we bolted for the house and dived under the beds. Who was this stranger? What was he coming here for? Here at the end of the road, outsiders were few and far between. We held our breath as we heard the man come into the house. Then suddenly we heard our father's voice and this gave us courage to come out of hiding, trying to look as if nothing unusual was going on.

"What were you kids doing under the beds?" the beardless stranger asked in father's voice. He had shaved off his waist-length wavy black beard while he was away buying cattle, and we had not recognized him even though he had kept his moustaches and was wearing familiar clothes.

"We didn't know who you were," we told him. "We thought you were coming to hurt us."

"Why did you cut your beard off?" Angus asked.

"It was a nuisance. It took too much time to groom," he said. He never let it grow again, though he still took great pride in his beautiful moustaches.

Our mother was not a robust woman and each of her pregnancies took its toll on her strength. It was impossible for her to cope with all the chores and all of us children when father was away, so father's solution was to hire help for her.

One time he hired a Dutch couple named Schmidt who had built a house about four miles away. They drove over every day by horse and buggy with their four children. The couple knew very little English and their children knew even less. Mr. Schmidt tended the garden and the stock and helped with the haying. His wife helped mother in the house, though her work was not up to mother's standards. Outdoors, we MacDonalds played and fought with their kids.

Sometimes when mother was sick my brother Dan and I were sent to spend a few days with the Schmidts. It made less work and noise for her with us out of the way. By our standards, the Schmidts had built a strange house. Set into a hillside overlooking Bear Creek, the house was supported in front on large cedar posts, while the back rested on the hillside, leaving a good space under the floor. They had levelled the ground and kept pigs under the overhang. The house itself had only one room. In one corner the stove had been set at an angle and above it small poles made a corner shelf so that the laying hens could have a cosy roost during the long winter nights. A team of horses, two cows and their calves shared a lean-to shed at the back of the house, entered by a door from the kitchen end of the room. The whole arrangement was snug, compact and labour-saving if you did not mind the smell and the noise.

Dan and I lay awake for hours our first night at the Schmidts. Mrs. Schmidt bedded us down on feather mattresses on the floor and covered us with a cosy feather comforter, and all the family settled down to sleep. But under the floor the pigs squealed and grunted, and in the shed the horses and cows chomped and stomped. Then just as I was dozing off, Mrs. Schmidt spoke.

"Androo! Androo, didja turn da scheekuns?"

"Yah, yah," said "Androo."

I fell asleep without finding out what this meant but I found out in the morning. After the "scheekuns" were settled on their roost for the night, someone had to turn each one with its head toward the cookstove so that its rear end would be in line with a board spread with sand behind the stove.

Though the Schmidts were goodhearted people, mother

could never become reconciled to the woman's standards of housekeeping, and she got tired of patching up our quarrels with the young Schmidts. Father agreed to tell them they would not be needed any more when he paid them off at the end of the week. The next time he had to go away, he hired a young Braid Indian and his wife from Coeur d'Alene in Idaho who had built a small cabin on Bear Creek just half a mile from our ranch.

Indian Joe was a very efficient worker and completely trustworthy; his wife Bedelia was an excellent housekeeper. They had both attended a mission school so there was no language problem to overcome, and since their own two children were well trained there were no kids' battles to annoy my mother. We spent most of our time following Joe about, and though he was strict with us he was always completely fair. He refused to allow us to swear. He knew we did not do it when our parents were around but we tried to outcuss each other when we were playing. He put a stop to that. And though Angus and Dan were only about seven and five at the time, he began to teach them a little about trapping and hunting.

There were few interruptions in our lives on the little ranch on Bear Creek, so that each new event stands out clearly in my memory. The biggest thrill of all was to go to Colville with my father when he had business there. We would be out of bed at four in the morning, have breakfast, harness a team and be on the road by five. Father would always take us to a restaurant for dinner and buy us some candy or an inexpensive toy. Then it was time to start home because the trip had to be made all in one day: we could never afford to stay overnight in a hotel.

We loved those toys that father bought us, but as a rule we made our own with mother's help. Once she made a little wooden wagon for Dan and me. The wheels were rounds cut off the end of a log about two inches across; the box was about two feet long, and mother fastened a tongue to the front axle. We could hardly stand the strain, hopping and dancing around her while she finished the last details. Then we raced off with it, taking turns riding in it. We used it to haul our share of the wood for the house and to carry buckets half full of water from the well. It seemed unimportant that half the water splashed out on the way.

Perhaps because she was still so young herself, our mother

took great pleasure in our games, often joining in and seeming to have as much fun as we did. But she worked very hard, too. Every springtime she gave the house a vigorous cleaning, and one year she decided she would paper all the walls and ceilings. She did not forewarn us, but at the last minute shared the secret with Lavena who was then nine, because Lavena was to be her assistant. She waited until father was away to start the job. She cut the paper to the right lengths and Lavena spread the paste. Between the two of them they lifted the sticky paper up to where they wanted it. It was a heavy and awkward job, especially doing the ceilings, but in a few days' time they had papered all the rooms of the house and it looked one hundred per cent better.

Father did not always take us with him when he went to Colville. In the late spring of 1896, when sudden warm weather had begun to thaw the snows much faster than usual, he went there alone over roads deep in mud. He finished his business quickly, anxious to be well on his way home before dark. When he reached the log bridge over Narcisse Creek, he found the water had risen to the floor of the bridge. He drove his team across very slowly and breathed with relief when he reached the other side.

By the time he got to the Little Pend Oreille River, it was quite dark, and he was still five miles from home. As he approached he could hear the river roaring. The bridge was still in place but the turbulent water was up to the floor. He had two choices: take a chance on the bridge or turn back to town, but if he turned back it would be days or even weeks before he could get home again. He cautiously eased his team and wagon onto the bridge, but as soon as their full weight hit, it broke away and began to float down the river. For a short distance it stayed intact and acted as a raft before the action of the current began to break it up. In that brief delay, father had time to walk up the wagon tongue, climb onto one of the horses, take out his pocket knife and cut the backstrap and the top hamestrap of the harness, releasing the horses. The floor of the bridge was almost gone by now with logs whittling off in every direction. The wagon and harness disappeared into the river as the two horses began swimming toward the opposite bank with father on the back of one. They were pulled downstream by the current but at last came up safely on the far side. Only then did father see that one of his horses had been struck by the logs of the bridge. Its front leg was badly crushed and father had to shoot it.

He rode the last five miles home, passing easily over the Bear Creek bridge. It was midnight when he unfastened the ranch gate. He had lost one horse, the wagon and harness, and all the supplies. It was a catastrophe. We had several other horses, but that had been our only wagon and double harness, and they would be costly to replace.

Every autumn a band of the Colville Indians would move into our valley. They would set up camp on the shore of the lake, turn their horses into our meadow and make themselves at home for three or four weeks of hunting. At that time of year there were always thousands of white-tailed deer along the timbered sidehills and farther back in the woods, and at the higher levels there were the big black-tailed and mule deer. Those Indians would set up a regular assembly-line slaughterhouse. The men killed the deer and the women went into the woods with pack horses and brought the carcasses into camp. They skinned them and prepared jerky and pemmican for their winter meat supply. For smoking, the meat was cut into long strips and hung on a rack over a smudge fire of green wood. They smoked fish in the same way. To make jerky, the meat was also cut in long strips but it was hung in the sun to dry. Pemmican was made from jerky or smoked meat pounded between two rocks until it looked like coarse flour or cornmeal; wild berries dried in the sun were mixed with the pounded meat and sometimes even melted deer or buffalo fat was added. All of this was stuffed into deer stomachs that had been thoroughly cleaned, and the end product was just like a big sausage or a haggis.

Father did not mind the Indians turning their horses into our meadow at that time of the year because the hay had already been cut and stacked for the winter. There was still plenty of grazing grass among the willows along the edge of the lake. Besides, he knew our valley had been a traditional hunting place for the Colville Indians. However, he worried about their visits, too, because they had become a pretty wild, foxy bunch of people since the white man had settled. They would hang around town waiting for a party of men to leave on a prospecting trip, then pack up and follow, looking for a chance to waylay and rob them.

If there was as many as five or six prospectors in the party, the Indians would wait until the men were out in the hills, then raid their base camp, stealing all their supplies, horses and equipment, and leave the prospectors stranded.

There were no incidents of bad behaviour among the Indians who came to our ranch each fall until one year when father was not on hand to see that they camped in the right place. We had two big stacks of hay about forty feet apart inside a corral. The Indians decided this was an ideal setup so they opened the corral gate and put up their tepees beside one of the stacks. Then they took corral rails for firewood and made a campfire between the stacks. They were as cosy as bugs in a rug.

Father had finished the year's haying but still had twenty-five acres of unripened oats, so the Indians turned their horses into that field. They were just like little children doing whatever came into their heads next.

Father arrived home when the women were busy preparing the evening meal. He rode straight into the barnyard, ran into the house, grabbed a bucket of water in one hand and his rifle in the other and headed for the haystacks. He threw the water on the fire, dropped the bucket and levelled his gun at the Indians standing there.

"You get the hell out of here!" he said. "Do you want to burn up my hay? And get your horses out of my oat field! You hear me? Move! You get back to your old campground on the other side of the lake and turn your horses into the meadow on the south side! And if you don't like that, you can get out of here altogether and never come back! Now get!"

Silently, they packed up; the braves rounded up their horses and drove them out of the oats. Then the whole band went off to their old campsite.

It took enormous confidence to walk into that camp full of Indians, douse their campfire and order them out. But few men have my father's kind of courage.

In the fall of 1896 the snow came early and the weather turned very cold. Father knew that the deer would starve that winter unless they were provided with feed, so occasionally he went out into the woods and cut moss off the tamaracks. There were lots of these trees around and some grew to be four feet at the stump and 100 to 150 feet tall. Since they were straight-grained hardwood we used them for fence posts. The moss that covered them from top to bottom was particularly relished by the deer.

Early in November, father began to find skinned deer carcasses in the woods. It was the work of two Scandinavians who lived in the little log cabin that was once Indian Joe's. They hunted on skis so it was easy for them to overtake the deer floundering along in the deep snow. The meat was of no use to them because the deer were too thin, but the hides brought a dollar apiece. Father was furious. After his efforts to save the deer, they were simply being butchered. He rode off to see the two men and announced that he was going to report them to the authorities. It was enough to scare them right out of the district.

Toward the end of that cold November, father was called away on urgent mining business. He was reluctant to go as mother was expecting another baby in January, but he finally left when my mother's sister and teen-age nephew agreed to come to stay. But before his business was finished, father had a terrible premonition that all was not well with mother and he started for home. It was a bad winter for travelling. He rode most of the way in a snowstorm and only reached Colville in the late afternoon of 3 December; there a friend told him that the doctor had just left for our place. Father hired a fresh horse at the livery stable since his own was done in and set out on the last eighteen miles through falling snow and a howling wind.

At midnight my Aunt Jenny met him at the door. Her sister Rachel was sitting by the stove rocking a tiny two-day-old baby who had been born prematurely. The doctor was with mother.

My mother's older sisters were competent midwives and had delivered many babies, including me; however, mother had developed milk fever after the baby's birth, and though the women had tried various herbs and old-time remedies, she got steadily worse.

The doctor had heard father arrive and beckoned him into the bedroom to see mother. Later he explained that although her condition was grave and she should be hospitalized, it would be impossible to take her there because of the storm. He stayed with her all night, then left in the morning after giving my aunts more medication and instructions.

Later that day we children were sent to stay with the Schmidts, but each afternoon father came for us and took us home to see mother and the new baby for a few minutes. Each day she grew weaker, and on the evening of 7 December 1896, at the age of twenty-eight, our mother died. When father brought us home the next day, it was to see her in her coffin supported between two beds in the big bedroom.

I was not yet four years old but I still remember going in the sleigh down the road to the cemetery in Colville. The air was clear and very cold. Snow was piled high on either side of the road and it hung in clumps on the branches of the evergreen trees. On the road it was packed so hard that it was like riding on glass, and I was sure that we were standing still and the trees were sliding past us.

It was very cold standing by her grave.

One week later the sad process was repeated when her grave was reopened to receive the body of our new little brother whom my father had named Joseph.

Aunt Jenny stayed on with us until father made up his mind what he should do about his children. He was almost beside himself with grief. When a man who has been a bachelor for so many years finds love at last, it is far stronger than any young man's love. Father's Mary Malinda had been a greater prize to him than any pot of gold at the rainbow's end. He could not believe she was gone.

Mother's married sisters looked over the situation calmly. They saw a man of fifty-seven with no great wealth and five children aged two to nine years. Gently but firmly they urged him to split the children up between them. They had, in fact, even decided who was to take whom when father put his foot down.

"No," he said. "As long as I draw breath my children will be brought up as one family. They are not going to grow up strangers to one another. I appreciate your generosity and kindness. I'm not sure what I'm going to do but something will turn up."

He knew he could not be home all the time to care for us because he had to earn money to feed and clothe us. Even if a housekeeper had been available, she would never have come to our remote little ranch. And there was no question of father marrying again.

One of the shareholders of the Spokane mining company for whom he acted as field man was a doctor named Burns, and he and my father had become close friends. Father took his problem to him. It happened that the doctor was the medical supervisor of St. Joseph's Catholic Orphanage in Spokane, and he suggested that father put us there. He thought it over for a while and decided it was the only answer to his problem. The arrangements were made. Lavena, Angus, Dan and I would go to the orphanage. Our little sister Ruth, who was only two, would go to live with our Aunt Annie and Uncle Dick Queener. When she was four she too would come to the orphanage so that we could all be together.

4

Orphanage

IT WAS SPRING when we went to Spokane. I can remember standing on the Colville station platform waiting for the train to come in. I had never seen a train before, and the ringing of the bell and the noise of the escaping steam nearly scared me out of my boots. If father had not been there to hold me tight, I would have taken off for the tall timber.

When we arrived at St. Joseph's Orphanage, father was ushered into the office of the Mother Superior to pay for our board. Then he said good-bye to us: his face was serious but he never broke down even when we wailed and clung to him, for he firmly believed it was a sign of weakness to show his feelings. I stood at the window watching him drive away in the rig that had brought us from the station. The world had come to an end. I was in a strange town among strange people. I had never before seen more than ten boys together in one place and here I was surrounded by at least a hundred of them.

I thought of the little wagon that mother had made us and the other special playthings around the farm, and I wondered whether they would still be there when we got home again. To add to my loneliness, the boys were separated from the girls in the orphanage, so while I could see Angus and Dan, I did not often see Lavena. Only because we were so homesick, the nuns gave special permission for us to visit together in the common room on rare occasions. Then the four of us would talk out our troubles and Lavena would soothe her unhappy, miserable brothers. And sometimes when no one was around, we talked over the fence that separated the boys' and girls' playgrounds.

The first question the orphanage boys asked a newcomer was "What's your name?" The second was "Can you fight?" Then, "You got any money?" And last, "Where d'ya come from?" When these were answered to their satisfaction, one boy about the same size as the new arrival would pick up a chip of wood and place it on his shoulder, daring the new boy to knock it off. It was immaterial whether the newcomer won the fight or not. If he put up a good fight he was considered to be okay. But if he refused to even try, he was reckoned to be a sissy and had to take an awful ribbing from the rest of the kids. It was therefore better to fight regardless of the outcome. If you happened to be a good fighter and won, you became a great hero and every boy wanted to be your friend. Oh, the glory of being handy with your fists! We Mac-Donalds were soon heroes because we could fight. Almost from the time we could walk, father had taught us the proper techniques so that we would be able to take care of ourselves. We had displayed all our black eyes, bumps and bruises to him proudly.

Angus would fight at the drop of a hat and ask questions later, so his second day at the orphanage he got into a fight when he thought one of the other boys was making fun of Lavena's nickname, "Veeny." Frank Dalston, a boy about Angus's age who was choosing sides for a game, came up to him saying, "Eeny, meeny, miney, mo..." Angus had never heard this jingle before and when the other boy pointed at him and said, "Meeny," Angus swung and hit him on the nose, hard. When blood spurted, Angus had firmly established his status as a fighter. Later he and Frank became the best of friends.

St. Joseph's was a three-storey wooden structure, the biggest building we had ever been in, and I could not believe I would ever be able to find my way around in it. There was no central heating system, just large sheet-iron Queen heaters in all the rooms. I soon got to know one of these stoves quite well. I had been there no more than a year when I fell heir to the job of looking after nine or ten boys my own age and younger. Every morning, after

47

our six o'clock breakfast, I would lead my gang outdoors to play when the weather was fine; when it was cold, we went to a ground floor playroom which was dominated by one of these Queen stoves. I was responsible for building a fire in the heater and keeping it burning until nine o'clock when we went off to the kindergarten classroom. Why the teachers chose me to be the leader I do not know, though it may have been that they considered me too ornery to be bossed around by any other kid.

When I was seven years old I lost this job and became a full-fledged schoolboy. From then on, besides being in the classroom from nine in the morning till four in the afternoon with an hour out for lunch, I had chores to do. Both boys and girls had to scrub floors, make beds, wash dishes, set tables, wash windows, dust, clean the school desks, and do any other jobs the nuns could think up. This is how I got an early start in learning to be a housekeeper, and it certainly came in handy in later years.

The boys also had to cut all the wood for the stoves. All summer long, cordwood was delivered to the orphanage in big wagons drawn by four-horse teams and unloaded onto stacks 150 feet long and eight feet high. Then the cutting began. Two boys would put a stick of this four-foot-long cordwood onto the sawbuck and hold it steady, then four boys, two on each end of a six-foot crosscut saw, would cut it up into sixteen-inch lengths. Meanwhile, another team would be busy piling the cut wood in the woodshed, and a couple of boys would be getting the cordwood down from the pile and placing it near the sawbuck. There would be three or four such crews at work at the same time, and the job went on day after day except on Sundays and religious holidays. Every boy from seven years of age had to take his turn, and though our father paid the Sisters well for our room, board and schooling, we still had to work like any of the other slaves. The Sisters never hired any hands.

The Sisters worked hard too, of course, though one or two of them seemed to remember what it was like to be young. Sister Oswald was a jolly young Dutch woman who spoke with quite a heavy accent. She was in charge of the stables, the milk cows, the two driving horses and the garden. She also supervised the boys' woodcutting and all their outside chores. She had her hands full even though she did not actually do any of the work. Because she was a good sport and very fair in all her dealings with us, if she happened to catch two boys fighting—which happened pretty frequently—she would stand back to referee. If they fought fair and square, she never interfered until the fight was over; then she would give them a mild scolding, tell them not to fight again and make them shake hands. But if the fighters started to run away when they saw her coming, she would call them back and box their ears good and hard.

"You sneaks," she would scold, shaking them so their heads rocked. "You rogues! If there's anything I don't like, it's a sneak!"

Sister Oswald dearly loved to play marbles with the boys in the springtime. She was very good at it, too, but she was not above fudging a little just to make the game more interesting. And when baseball season rolled around, she would tuck up her long skirts and be the first one out on the playground. And she could play with the best!

Sometimes one of the teachers would drive the democrat into the country to get vegetables, taking one or two of us kids along to help. Occasionally the excursion took them into the main part of Spokane to buy groceries and other basic supplies. When Sister Oswald made the trip to town, quite often she had me go with her. For these occasions I was given a decent pair of trousers to wear since our regular pants had holes and patches. Whenever Sister went into a store, I would stand outside smartly in my knee pants and long black stockings, holding the horses' reins. After the shopping she would take me to a restaurant for lunch, and even though I was not permitted to choose the menu, it was a big event. That Sister was very good to me, but, of course, she had found a useful way to keep track of me and any mischief I was up to.

Food at the orphanage was plain and unvaried: mush with brown sugar but no milk, a lot of stews and beans, and once in a while a plate of boiled beef. For a special treat at Sunday breakfast we had bread and crude molasses which we called "stay," because we associated it with The Lord's Prayer: "Give us thistay our daily bread," we would chant each Sunday morning, and that is how molasses became "stay." For Sunday supper there was cinnamon cake, and we looked forward to it all week!

During our first year at St. Joseph's father came to see us

quite often. He would begin each visit by talking to the Sisters about our school progress, health and behaviour. They seemed to have a high regard for him that went beyond the money he paid them, for he was a man who obviously cared about his family. Then we had a family visit in the common room. We always had lots to tell him, and each of us clamoured for his attention. It was wonderful to be together as a family again even though one of the Sisters always sat in the common room with us. But the highlight of his visits was when he took us to one of Spokane's nicest hotels for a meal. I guess oysters must have been our favourite food at that time because I can still remember the oyster stews he let us order. Afterwards, he would buy us all new clothes. We took real pleasure in them, though we soon learned that they would be taken from us as soon as we got back to the orphanage. They had to be kept for Sunday best, we were told, but we never saw them again. I think the nuns sold them.

Father spent his first year alone buying and selling beef, doing field work for the mining company, and prospecting a little east of Spokane. He wanted to be near his children so he could visit regularly. But in the fall of 1897, he quit the mining company and sold off all the stock on the Bear Creek Ranch. He was now fifty-eight, extremely depressed and broken in spirit. He had lost interest in the little ranch; there was no point in continuing there without his wife and children. He asked a neighbour to keep an eye on the place, then he packed his prospecting equipment, his bedroll and some grub and headed north alone. Rich strikes had been made in the Kootenays around Phoenix and Greenwood. Maybe he would find his pot of gold and be able to take his family out of the orphanage.

Father's visits had been the high point of our young lives. After he went north we were lonelier than we had ever been before, though in the coming years he always tried to be with us at Christmas and sometimes at Easter as well. In place of his regular visits we were now called on by his good friend Dr. Burns. Father had met Burns in his prospecting days, and as a company director, Burns had been responsible for getting father his job as field man for the mining company. They had a high regard for each other, and after father had been crippled, Dr. Burns had given him a blackthorn dress cane that had been in his family for two hundred years. Before he presented it, he had a silversmith put a silver cap on it engraved with father's name.

After that, whenever father was in Spokane with Dr. Burns and his swanky friends, he carried that cane and wore his swallow-tailed coat. Father could hold his own in society because as far as manners went, he was a lady's man.

Dr. Burns paid us frequent visits in the orphanage, but we liked it best when he took us to spend the day at his home. I can still see him filling the doorway of the common room, a huskily built man somewhat shorter than my father, with a full dark beard. He was always elegantly dressed. When he could not spare the time to come for us personally, he would send his driver and carriage. How excited we were when we saw those beautiful French coach horses and the gleaming carriage at the gate! We would scramble into our carriage seats ready for a holiday from dull routine. At the Burns house we would play for hours, then end the day with a decent home-cooked meal for a change.

When at the age of four our sister Ruth came to live in the girls' dormitory with Lavena, in a manner of speaking the family was all together again as father had wished. But she had come just in time to share the latest round of disease sweeping through the orphanage. This time it was diphtheria. Antitoxin for diphtheria had just been developed and it was used for the first time in Spokane on the children in St. Joseph's. Those who had been caught early enough survived with the help of the antitoxin, but many had already died. Dan, Ruth and I were all stricken, and I became delirious. I can still remember clearly snakes with vivid green spots and glossy black spots wriggling all over the dormitory walls. Poor little Ruth was sick for so long that when she got out of bed at last, she had to learn to walk all over again.

Diphtheria was just one of the many things that took me away from classes. Tonsillitis was my constant companion. I guess my tonsils should have been taken out, but no one did anything about them. I had toothache all the time and gumboils from infected teeth, but I was never taken to a dentist. I guess it was much the same for most of the children in that place. We all began our education at the age of seven but between the constant interruptions for sickness and for work, and because there were so many kids in each class, we really got scant learning.

After we had lived there for about three years, a new and

bigger orphanage was built nearby, all stone and brick with good central heating, eliminating a lot of the danger from fire. It had modern plumbing, too, a tremendous improvement over our old building. The boys were now housed in the dormitory in the west wing, the teachers lived in the centre, and the girls were in the east wing.

The new school had another advantage that the Sisters never knew about. Just beyond the back wall of the woodshed out behind, there was a railroad track and beside it a deep ditch. Now since the woodshed had been sided with one-by-twelve vertical planks, it was a simple matter for a number of us boys to take one of the boards off the back wall and fasten it back in place with a single nail at the top so that it could be pushed easily aside or swung neatly back into place. Unseen, we would drop down into the ditch below and creep along it until we were out of sight of the school.

Once in the town, we foraged along the back alleys looking for old rubber boots, copper wire, bits of zinc or lead, and anything else we could turn into cash. Nickels and dimes were few and far between inside St. Joseph's, so there was nothing we would turn down that might bring a little pocket money. A pair of old rubbers, for example, brought five or ten cents since they could be melted down to make new ones. When we had gathered up everything we could find in the time we could risk being away, we sold it and took our ill-gotten gain to the Golden Rule Confectionery on Boone Avenue to exchange for jawbreakers and licorice whips and pocket knives and marbles. Back at the orphanage we were everyone's friends until the candy ran out.

Not many of the boys had the nerve to pull this stunt because the Sisters truly knew how to hand out punishment. I was never caught but I came close to it. One afternoon while slipping out of one alley toward the next, we suddenly spotted the orphanage buggy coming at us down the street. We hid underneath a farmer's buggy, none of us daring to breathe, and watched the wheels pass us by.

Father's trip to the Kootenays in the fall of '97 took him to the settlement of Nelson on the east bank of Kootenay Lake, where he met a young Scot by the name of Norman "Red"

McLeod. Red had gone in for a bit of horse stealing when he was a little drunk over in Creston and had escaped the law by packing over the Purcell Range. He went prospecting in the Lardeau and in the nearly uninhabited area north of Kootenay Lake. Eventually he had to come out to civilization for supplies, which was when he and father met. I don't know whether father was ever aware of Red's horse-stealing habits, but if he was, it did not seem to alter his regard for the man. Not very long after they got to know one another, they realized that they both had their eye on the same outcropping, one that father and Big Jim had found years earlier but had abandoned since there was no transportation into the area. Now the Spokane Falls and Northern Railway ran all the way from Spokane to Nelson, and the Canadian Pacific was preparing to lay tracks through the Crowsnest Pass.

Father and Red went into partnership. They rented pasture for their horses and spent a week building a strong rowboat, adding a mast in case of favourable winds. They loaded it with grub and their camping and prospecting equipment and began rowing the seventy miles up the lake, keeping close to shore since the lake was famous for violent storms; nevertheless, they often found themselves rowing desperately in a rising storm below rugged cliffs with nowhere to beach their boat. And sometimes after they had found shelter, they had to delay two or three days for calm weather.

At the head of the lake was a beautiful spot where the settlement of Argenta would be established a few years later, and it was here that father and Red made their main camp. From this spot they travelled up a heavily timbered mountain, then up the bed of a stream (later named Hammill Creek) which emptied into the Lardeau River. Where the stream met the base of a steep rocky mountain, which they had sighted from the lake, they established a temporary camp, then began to climb again. Near the top they found a long ledge of rich lead and silver ore, so pure that it could be melted in a cast-iron frying pan. Father poured the ore into moulds that he made from clay and kept it for years as a souvenir. Since the mountain had no name, father christened it Mount Lavena for his first child.

After staking claims on the ore, the two men came down the mountain and rowed back to Nelson to register them. There they bought more groceries, then returned to camp. At the site of their temporary camp at the base of Mount Lavena they now built a good log cabin and a blacksmith shop, only to have them swept away in a snowslide. Neither man was hurt, so they set about rebuilding on a nearby ridge, where the remains of both buildings still stand today.

Until the snow put an end to activity for that year, they did exploratory work on their claims. One of their major difficulties was getting equipment up to the mine site. As well, they did not have enough capital to put the mine on a paying basis. The following spring they went back to work at the mine though they were still unable to begin development. Then one day when they were in Nelson to buy grub, an English syndicate's representative made them an attractive offer for their claims and they agreed to sell. Red took his share of the money back to Creston, hired a lawyer and got himself acquitted of the charges against him. In later years he returned and built a little cabin at Argenta and lived there for the rest of his life.

The English syndicate had paid a good price for the claims but it was no pot of gold. Father could not rescue his children from the orphanage yet, so in the late spring of 1898 he set out for the Yukon, riding old Frank and leading two pack horses. He could never pass up the possibility of being one of the lucky ones to strike it rich. He was gone for two years and returned without his beloved Frank. He never talked of his adventures up there, and this was strange because he loved to tell stories of the places he had been and the people he had known. My brothers and I concluded that the death of old Frank and all the other hardships and disappointments he had suffered had been so terrible that he could not bring himself to think about them once he was safely home again.

He returned in 1900 with a few thousand dollars, but that was just peanuts compared to what he had dreamed of finding. For the next two years he prospected in the Lardeau and Slocan districts, and around Rossland, Greenwood, Grand Forks and the other Boundary points. He staked several claims in the Red Mountain area near Rossland, and when one of them assayed a little better than the rest, he contracted with two Cornishmen, or

"Cousin Jacks" as they were called, to sink a shaft a hundred or so feet to see how the ore would assay at the lower depth. Once they were started he returned to his prospecting, but every now and again he went to see how the work was coming along. One day he arrived at the claim just in time to see one of the men pick up a piece of timber eight feet long and about six inches through and drop it down the shaft, which by that time was at least thirty feet deep. When the timber hit bottom there was a roar from below and some of the fanciest cuss words imaginable drifted to the surface.

Father rushed to the head of the shaft to see what the trouble was. The "Cousin Jack" who had dropped the timber turned to father grinning and shook his head.

"Listen to that damn growler down there! He just growls all day long!"

His partner at the bottom of the hole was in a killing rage. He had to jump out of the way every time a timber came down but he had nowhere to go in that narrow shaft.

"Why aren't you using a winch?" asked father. "Cousin Jack" smiled and shrugged. Father stayed at Rossland on that visit long enough to make sure they were using safer methods. In the end the ore proved to be quite rich and he accepted a tip-top cash offer for the claim by a mining company from Spokane.

Early in 1902 father returned to the Bear Creek Ranch. In his pocket was the money from the sale of the claim. It was not much to show for five years of prospecting.

At the ranch he found that most of the equipment and furnishings we had left behind had been stolen. The buildings were run-down, the fences sagging. For a week he stayed there alone, trying to make plans for the future. He was lonesome for his children, but they had become strangers to him. He knew they were adequately cared for at St. Joseph's but it was not like being a family. If he brought them home to the ranch, they could be really together, but could the ranch support them all? At last he decided he must give it a try.

When the orphanage classrooms were closed for the summer holidays, he came for us. This time the train held no fears for me. I was nine years old and we were going home. Almost the first thing I did when I got there was look for the little wagon but it was gone. I was too old to play with it now anyway but somehow it was awfully important to me.

Father had already planted a garden and fixed up the house a bit so that it had begun to look as it did when mother was alive. He had bought a team of horses and democrat, as well as a wagon, tools and equipment to run the ranch. A creamery had been built in Colville since we had been gone, so now father bought fourteen dairy cows instead of the beef animals that we used to raise.

Father was a particular man and liked everything to be ship-shape. "Take your time, boys," he would say, "do a good job—but for heaven's sake, hurry up!" He had so much energy he could not stand anyone else being poky. He allotted certain chores to each of us: Angus had the horses to care for; Dan and I brought the cows in from the pasture and milked them with Angus's occasional help; Lavena, our "Little Mother," did the cooking and housework; Ruth, who was only seven, helped her. Ruth had one other self-appointed task: she was always trying to make everyone happy.

Nearly every Saturday evening father would say, "Well, boys, tomorrow is Sunday and we won't do very much work." It was true that he did let us sleep a bit later, but I think we worked almost as hard on Sundays as on the other days. There were fences and machinery to be repaired, barns to be thoroughly cleaned, horses to be shod, and all the other chores that there was no time to do during the week.

Then early Monday we would be awakened by father saying, "Come on, boys, time to get up! Here it is four o'clock, tomorrow is Tuesday, the next day is Wednesday, half the week's gone and nothing's done!"

Whenever father had to go to Colville it was an all-day trip from four o'clock in the morning till after dark, so he assigned us plenty of work to keep us out of mischief. There was always weeding the carrots and cultivating the corn, and hoeing the potatoes and so forth. Only when the chores were all done were we allowed to go fishing. Now all of us, especially father, enjoyed a dinner of fresh brook trout, and though father found fishing too dull and slow a task, we kids dearly loved to head for one of the three creeks that ran nearby for a day's outing. We were the only ones who fished there so we had no difficulty coming home with a fine mess of trout.

In order to have more time to fish while father was away, Angus invented a primitive cultivator as well as a rig to hill the potatoes and corn. Dan and I pulled these contraptions while Angus guided them. Up and down the rows of vegetables we went on the run, doing a much better and faster job than we could do with a hoe. The result was that we could be done with the garden by ten o'clock in the morning, pack a lunch and head for the creeks for the rest of the day.

When father inspected our garden work the next morning, he would congratulate us on a job well done. We never told him about Angus's inventions because he was of the school that believes the only way is the slow, hard way. If he ever suspected how we had done so much and still had time to go fishing, he never said a thing.

In those days it was the fashion for farmers to take the occasional Sunday off from pressing chores and drive around visiting relatives and neighbours. Everyone dressed up in their best clothes for the event and sat in each other's parlours as though they were all city people. We MacDonald kids, however, had just got used to working every day of the week when one Sunday afternoon, father said, "I think we'll visit the Bryan family today."

The five of us all whooped and hollered. We scrubbed ourselves clean, dressed up in the best clothes we had and climbed into our new democrat. The Bryans had a nice farm on Narcisse Creek, not far from our place. They had built their house on the top of a little knoll near a fair-sized pond.

The Bryans had three boys, and we had great fun playing together, raiding their springhouse every so often for something cold to eat or drink. Most of the afternoon was spent beside the pond, throwing rocks. Late in the afternoon more visitors arrived and down to the pond came a boy of about eight, all dressed up in a sailor suit with a big white collar. His hair was long, blond and curly, and he was just too good to be true. Angus, Dan and the Bryan boys grabbed him and threw him into the pond while I danced around clapping my hands in glee. Then up the hill I rushed and into the Bryans' parlour where all the grownups sat balancing cups of tea on their knees.

In the midst of this sedate company I roared happily, "They threw Percy in the pond!"

You never saw a room empty so fast as they all rushed off to rescue poor Percy. Unfortunately, father did not share our pleasure in Percy's dunking, and we boys found it more comfortable to stand for the five-mile ride home.

That September, Dan, Ruth and I went back to St. Joseph's for one more term. Angus and Lavena were needed at home. How we hated going back after those three months of freedom, but in spite of our protests, father insisted we return. We settled down to the old routine until the end of May 1903, when classes were over again for the year. The following day father came for us and this time he took all our belongings home, too. It was a happy day for us. We said good-bye to the orphanage that we hated so much, knowing that we would never have to go back.

Father had high hopes of making a living at dairy farming alone, but he soon realized that this was impossible, so occasionally he returned to his old practice of buying beef cattle in the Colville Valley and driving them to Northport, Washington, on the Columbia River and on to Rossland or one of the other mining centres in the Kootenays where he could sell them to meat dealers and butchers. He made a fair profit this way, but best of all he got the ready cash he needed to support his family.

On one of these trips in 1904 a man who had a small dairy in Rossland asked whether father could supply him with thirty-five or forty head of good milk cows. He had realized that the big mining camps could use a regular milk supply. Father knew there were plenty of milk cows to be had in the rich farming district around Colville, so an agreement was drawn up, and father returned home very happy.

In Colville, he left word with various merchants, the bank, and Graham and Walsh's Livery Stable that he wanted to buy a few good milk cows. For cash. It was not long before everyone in the area had heard that Archie MacDonald was paying cash for good milk cows—not trade or barter, but real gold pieces. Now, cows were plentiful in that district but hard cash was pretty scarce, and though the farmers could always trade milk or butter or eggs for groceries, they needed money for things like taxes and new farm machinery. Within a week, father had enough high-quality milk cows to fill the dairyman's order and ensure himself a good profit.

When the herd was ready for the drive to Rossland, he told Angus, now fifteen, that he would be making the trip with him. The third member of the crew would be father's old buddy, Hood Formwalt. Since the cows could not be hurried, it was going to be a four- or five-day trip. Twice a day all the cows would have to be milked, quite a chore even for three men. Along the way they were sometimes close enough to a settler or small-scale farmer to give the milk to, but most of the time it had to be spilled onto the ground.

Angus was very happy to be included with the men and he started off proudly on Buck, a big buckskin horse with a clay back—a narrow, dark brown strip along the back from withers to tail. He was a well-trained cow horse but he had a mind of his own. Whenever one of the cows made a break for the brush, Buck went after her and all Angus could do was go along for the ride. Off they would dash through the thick thorn brush along the banks of the Columbia River, with those needle-sharp thorns ripping through Angus's clothes and into his hide, but Buck would always return proudly with the rebellious cow.

At Northport, Hood turned back. Father figured that he and Angus could manage the cows for the last few miles and he wanted Hood to keep an eye on the farm and us children while he was away. The remainder of the drive was without incident, and in Rossland they delivered the cows to their new owner and received the amount of money that had been agreed upon. Naturally, the arrival in town of such a large herd attracted a crowd of onlookers. Father noticed two men in particular who seemed to be taking a little too much interest in his business. They hung around longer than any of the others and asked questions. Where did he come from? How much money did he get for his cattle? Was he going to stay in town tonight? Or was he starting back that afternoon?

Father tried to put them off by saying he was not sure when

he would leave since he had other business to look after and friends to see. And before he did anything else, he and his son were going to a hotel for a darn good dinner.

They took their horses to the livery stable and checked into the hotel, and all the time father was wishing he had not sent Hood back home. That lean, tough old cowboy would have scared off guys like these. But since Hood was not there to help, father decided his best bet was to take his time. He sat down on the bed to think, and after a while it was obvious that he had come up with a plan. He told Angus they would try for a quick getaway that night. There would be no moon and they would stand a better chance in the dark.

They waited in their room till it was nearly dark, then went downstairs to eat. Although neither of them felt hungry any more, they dined in a leisurely fashion so that it was completely dark by the time they had finished. At a signal from father, Angus slipped out the back door of the hotel and went to the livery stable, saddled up the horses and took them out the back way to wait in the alley. Meanwhile, father paid the hotel bill saying they intended to leave so early that they would not have time to pay in the morning. He went up to the room, picked up their belongings and slipped down the back stairway to meet Angus. About twenty minutes had passed.

They rode slowly so as not to attract any undue attention until they reached the outskirts of town. Then they quickened their pace. At Northport they crossed the Columbia River, and had gone quite a way farther up the road when they heard the sound of horses coming up fast behind. Just to be on the safe side, they turned off into some thick brush where they dismounted and held their hands over the horses' noses.

In a few minutes, two horses passed them at a dead run. Father and Angus could not see the riders but as a precaution they stayed in their hiding place and waited. A half hour passed before they heard the horses coming back, this time slowly, and the riders were talking.

"You think that old son-of-a-gun and his kid got wise to us?"

Father and Angus could not hear the reply, but then the first one spoke again. They caught part of what he said. "Must have gone down the other side of the river." And the horses galloped off into the night.

Still they stayed in their hiding place. The night was absolutely quiet when the hoofbeats had died, but it was an hour before father decided that their pursuers had been thrown off the track and it was safe to continue.

Some time after midnight they came to a small roadside store; though it was closed, they stopped in the hope that they could buy something to eat since they had not really enjoyed their dinner. Father woke up the proprietor and then stayed outside to listen for their pursuers having told Angus to get a pound of cheese and a pound or two of crackers. Angus climbed back on his horse with a pretty big sack.

"What's in that?" asked father.

"You told me to get two pounds of crackers so I did." As they rode along, they ate cheese and crackers, but they ran out of cheese long before they ran out of crackers!

To reach Colville quicker they took a short cut through Echo Valley which father thought no stranger would know about. When they reached town, the first thing father did was deposit his roll of money in the bank, greatly relieved to have it in a safe place at last.

Windfalls like this certainly helped to augment our income from the Bear Creek Ranch, but even then there was not enough money coming in to support all the MacDonalds now that we were together again. And for father, the little valley held little charm now that mother was gone. He began to get that faraway look in his eye.

One day during the summer of 1904 he heard that the Canadian government was urging people to settle in Alberta and Saskatchewan, which were to become provinces the following year. He heard stories of cattle ranches of immense size, and waving fields of wheat, barley, oats, flax and rye as far as the eye could see. He tried to picture it, but he had never seen anything remotely like it, yet the more he thought about it the more he wanted to see the Canadian prairie. Then one day he announced he was going there to see what the prospects were for making a home.

He went alone that fall, leaving us boys and our two sisters to look after the ranch and get things ready for winter. We listened to his instructions carefully, knowing that when he told us to do something it had better be done. We dug the potatoes, turnips, onions and parsnips and stored them in the root cellar. Then there were eight pigs to butcher and the meat to cure. We began by making lard, which meant cutting all the fat from the carcasses into small strips and placing it in the oven with the fire burning low until most of it was melted. The fat from around the kidneys was rendered down separately because it made the best pastry. All the lard was poured into containers where it cooled and hardened for storage. The cracklings — the residue left when the fat was poured off — were mixed with lye and simmered for hours. When cooled, the solid brown mass that rose to the top was soap, which was cut into squares and used for all our general cleaning.

When it came time to smoke the meat, we found we had half a dozen hams and shoulders for which there was no more room in the smokehouse. In the hot weather of early fall they would not keep long, so we had a problem on our hands. It was typical that Angus was the one to solve it. He was a bit of a genius in figuring out how to get a job done with a lot less work, usually by inventing some simple tool or gadget.

He told Dan and me to get the stump burner, a large sheet-iron stove just like the old Queen heaters but with no bottom. It was about seven feet across and seven feet high. Whenever we had to burn out a stump, we dug around the roots to a depth of about eighteen inches, then lifted the burner up and over the stump. We started a fire inside and when the stump was burning, we banked dirt around the stove to make it airtight. After a while it would be vibrating like a steam engine, and in about a week's time a four-foot-wide stump would be burned out well below ground level.

This time Angus had us set the burner on gently sloping ground in a shallow ditch, and we dug a ditch about three feet long down the slope from the lower side of the burner. An eight-inch stovepipe laid in the ditch led from under the stump burner to an old stove set in a three-foot hole. Everything was well banked with earth. We fired up the old stove with a mixture of

62

dry and green alder, and hung the meat on a green wood rack inside the stump burner. It made an excellent flyproof smokehouse, and the hams smoked in it were delicious. There was only one problem: we had misjudged the heat of our fancy smokehouse and the meat was not only smoked but cooked as well. But none of it went to waste because it made perfect sandwiches and quick snacks.

Father was gone nearly three weeks and he seemed pleased with what we had accomplished, though he never made a fuss over us. He was happy, too, with what he had seen in Alberta. He brought back coloured folders showing miles of golden fields with ripening grain and an even more golden sun coming up over the giant grain elevators. He told us it looked like a really prosperous country, and that we would probably like living there.

To us children, raised on the bunchgrass and timber hills of eastern Washington where clearing an acre of land meant months of digging and burning stumps, this country with its miles of clear prairie looked like paradise. We were ready to go right that minute. But with winter coming on, it was a poor time to put our farm up for sale.

"We'll go next year," said father, "if we can find a buyer for the farm."

One hot afternoon towards the end of July 1905, when we were all out stacking hay, two men drove into the field where we were working. We recognized one as the real estate dealer from Colville; the other man appeared to be a cowboy and was introduced as "Mr. Hill from Wyoming."

"He's looking for a ranch where he can raise horses," said the agent.

Well, if Bear Creek Ranch was suited for any kind of ranching it was about perfect for raising horses. We had miles of adjoining rangeland with no other stock running on it. There was not much hayland, so the number of cattle we could raise had been limited, but horses could always rustle out most of the winter because they could paw away at the snow to get at the grass underneath.

Hill looked the ranch over and told father he would like to buy it. They agreed on a price and terms and the next day father went into Colville to sign the necessary papers. When Hill had gone back to Wyoming to settle his affairs there, we got on with our haying, then found buyers for all our cattle. The horses and farm machinery had been sold to Hill with the land.

One afternoon in late August he drove into our yard with a four-horse team and a big covered wagon loaded down with his things, followed by twenty head of mares and ten or twelve colts. Behind them came a great big grey horse and a collie dog. The horse was saddled and bridled with the reins wrapped around the saddle horn but there was nobody riding it. Hill had trained it so well that horse and dog had driven that band of horses behind the wagon all the way from Wyoming!

Hill drove the mares and colts up the trail behind the house to the bunchgrass hill. Once they got used to that nice grass they would stay put, but for the first day or two he would have to keep an eye on them or they would take off for Wyoming again.

Hill joined us for supper but turned down our offer of a bed. "Thank you, but I'll be fine in my wagon," he said. "I've got to listen for my horses."

About two in the morning his horses decided to head for Wyoming. Hill heard the leader's bell coming down the hill from the range, and scrambled out of the wagon pulling on his pants. Within minutes he was mounted on his saddle horse, heading those pesky mares back up the trail. He was pretty worn out by all this work and he slept late in the morning.

The MacDonalds, however, were up bright and early because this was the day we were to leave the peaceful little valley where all of us except Lavena had been born and where our mother had died. Father had seen a different rainbow this time, arching over miles of waving wheat with a golden sun overhead, and we were all going to share in this new pot of gold.

On this last morning, Dan and I traipsed back and forth between the house and the wagon we were loading. Suddenly we began finding five- and ten-dollar gold coins scattered on the ground. There were nine or ten of them! Where had they come from? The mystery was cleared up when Hill woke up and told how the horses had decided to leave in the middle of the night. He had been in such a rush getting out of his wagon that he had held his pants upside down, dumping the coins out of his pockets. So it was not raining gold coins from heaven after all as Dan and I had wanted to believe, and we would be leaving our old home just as poor as the day we were born into it, twelve and fourteen years before.

We loaded the last of our belongings into the wagon and drove out through the ranch gate and down the road.

In Colville, Lavena went to Grandmother Prouty's house where she would stay until she married Jim Case in the spring of the following year. Ruth went back to live with Aunt Annie and Uncle Dick Queener at Bosberg, a small town on the Columbia River about twenty miles from Colville. Father had decided to take Angus with him to Alberta to find land, but Dan and I were to stay behind until the spring; father had found a boarding school for us. A Catholic mission school intended primarily for Indian boys, it was situated just eight miles from Colville in a little village called Marcus. The Fathers at the mission assured our father that they would take good care of us; father paid our board in advance and said good-bye.

Dan and I took an instant dislike to the place. We got into a fight with the Indian boys the first time we set foot in the school-yard, and we kept fighting all the time we were there. When the battles got too hot for us, we would grab baseball bats or sticks and stand back to back to beat our attackers off. Only if it looked as though one of us was likely to be murdered did the head of the school or one of his assistants step in to break it up and take us into the washroom to patch up the black eyes and bloody noses. Afterwards we were given a lecture, but the next day we would be back at it, Dan and I against the rest of the school.

In the mornings we all attended classes. The afternoons were spent in cutting cordwood or fishing in the Colville River to supplement our bill-of-fare. As far as Dan and I were concerned, the fishing was the only good thing about the school, especially since it improved on the mission food which certainly was not up to Lavena's cooking standards.

Whenever we went fishing, one of the priests would go along to keep order, for the mission even had rules and regulations about fishing. The most important rule was that we could not go more than two hundred yards up or downstream from the bridge: our supervisor would stand on the bridge as command-ing officer to make sure we obeyed, with the result that this stretch of the river was badly overfished.

By the time we had been at the school five days we had

already been fishing twice and not caught a thing. So on the Saturday when it was announced that we were going fishing, Dan and I decided to hell with the rules! We slipped away from the main group and went upstream by ourselves. In a few hours we had caught about thirty-five lovely trout which we cleaned just as father had taught us. Unfortunately, we lost track of time and were late getting back to the bridge. Our supervisor, looking very cross, was standing in the middle of the group of boys. Just as we expected, he gave us a good scolding for going so far and coming back late, and then he said, looking very self-righteous, "And as punishment you will not have any of those fish for supper!"

All those lovely trout were going to be fed to our enemies instead!

Now, Dan and I had both inherited a good bit of father's highland "scotch" and we could feel it pumping hotly in our veins. We ran to the river bank.

"To hell with you and your Indians! You're not going to eat these fish!" And we chucked them into the water. Every last one. It certainly wiped the smiles off the boys' faces!

Our punishment was to be sent to bed without supper— considering the food, not a terrible punishment. Locked in our room, we contemplated our situation. Each day is getting worse, we told each other. By the time father comes back for us there won't be anything left of us to take to Alberta. There was only one solution. By hook or by crook, we would have to get out of that place. We had to make up a story to tell the head priest in order to make good our escape, and when we settled on one at last, we rehearsed it in every detail.

On Monday morning we went to the head priest and told him that father had instructed us that if he did not come to see us on Sunday morning at the school, we were to meet him in Colville on Monday morning before he and Angus left for Alberta so that he could buy us our winter clothes while we tried them on for size. The poor man did not know whether to believe us or not, but because of the way we had been carrying on, he must have thought we were too dumb to have dreamed up such a story.

"Are you positive, boys?" he asked. "Are you sure that's what your father told you to do?"

"Oh, yes," we lied glibly, "that's what he said. And if we don't get a ride back in the afternoon, we're to walk back, he said." We knew this would sound plausible because eight miles was not too far for two healthy boys to walk.

We started out right after breakfast, leaving behind our clothes and everything we owned even though we planned never to go back. But father had always said that you must travel light if you want to stay free, which had certainly been true when he escaped from Grey Eagle.

Unfortunately, we did not get a hitch to town, so it was after ten o'clock when we arrived there. Because we had had little supper the night before, we were anxious to find some place to eat, but we were even more anxious not to run into father. We had no idea what day he and Angus planned to leave town since he had a lot of business to attend to, but we knew they had been staying at the Colville Hotel and would spend part of their time around Graham and Walsh's Livery Stable. We slipped around to the stable to see if they were there. Not seeing them, we got up our courage to ask one of the men if he had seen father around.

"No, boys," he said, "your father and Angus left for Alberta on Saturday morning."

It was a tremendous relief. Dan and I would rather have faced a grizzly bear than father when he got his "scotch" up. Now everything looked rosy. We went into a small restaurant where we had eaten many times with father and put out twenty-five cents each for a full-course meal. After six days at the mission school, we were starved.

Our grandmother Prouty's house was four miles from town away up the Monson Hill Road. We started walking in the hot sun, but we had not gone far when a generous man driving a team and wagon offered us a ride.

Grandmother, Aunt Annie, Lavena and Ruth could not believe their ears when we told them we had run away from the mission school.

"There's no use sending us back," I said, "because we won't stay there." Then we told them about the fish and all the regulations and about the fighting, and showed them our bruises and Dan's split lip. We could see the mounting sympathy.

While we gorged on cookies and apple pie and all the milk we could drink, our folks held a council of war.

"The boys can stay with us," said Uncle Dick, and Aunt Annie agreed. This suited us just fine as we liked both of them very much, and Ruth was already living with them. Uncle Dick was a veteran of the last Indian wars against the notorious Chief Joseph of the Nez Perce tribe and had been badly crippled by wounds received in those fierce battles. He made his living now with his team and wagon, hauling freight and express for the town and the district people.

The next day, Dan and I went to the annual Colville Fall Fair with all the family who were visiting at grandmother's, and just when we had completely forgotten that the mission school ever existed, we ran into a boy from the school. We were pretty sure he did not recognize us, so we asked him what he was doing at the fair.

"I came up with our teacher from Marcus," he said. "A couple of boys ran away and we've got to find them."

We hurried back to Uncle Dick's wagon and laid low for the rest of the day. The following day, Aunt Annie and Uncle Dick went to the school to get our clothes. They had quite an argument with the head priest but they came away with the trunk containing our belongings.

There was a lot to do on Uncle Dick's little farm at Bosberg before winter set in. The vegetables had to be dug and stored, firewood had to be cut and hauled from the woods. Father had given Aunt Annie a little Jersey cow when he sold the ranch and it was our job to milk her, as well as feed and take care of the horses, clean the barn and a hundred and one other chores that waited to be done, but they were all familiar to us.

After the first of October, we had school to attend, too. We had already received some schooling at the orphanage, and when we returned to the Bear Creek Ranch we went to school for two years, but it had been a tiny one-room place with only eleven pupils; our teacher, Jane MacEwan, was only seventeen years old and had not yet finished grade eight. Most of the time she studied along with us kids. Now at Bosberg we went to a real school for the first time and had a schoolmaster who could really teach.

During the winter months, Dan and I earned some pocket money by shovelling snow off roofs and cleaning pathways. We got twenty-five cents each for the steepest and most dangerous roofs and were pleased to put the money in our pockets.

68

5

Prairie

FATHER AND ANGUS set off for Alberta on the Great Northern Railway, transferred to the steamer *Kokanee* at Nelson, then caught the Canadian Pacific at Kootenay Landing. At Fort Macleod they had to change trains, putting up at a hotel overnight. In the morning, father laid a twenty-dollar gold piece on the counter to pay for their room.

"What's that?" asked the hotel manager.

Father told him.

The manager shook his head emphatically. "I don't take no funny money here! My customers pay with the real stuff!"

"There's no money more real than gold," said father.

But the manager was quite firm. He was not going to accept that funny coin. Father was equally firm. That coin was the only money he was going to pay with. Finally a friend of the manager came into the lobby and listened in on the argument. The manager turned to him for support.

"Walt," he said, "this guy's trying to pay his bill with this thing! Is it any good?"

"Sure is. It's worth twenty paper dollars anywhere. I'll change it for you if you like." And he brought out his billfold.

But at this point the hotel manager decided to accept the coin and gave father his change.

Later father had the same experience when he was buying a team of horses at a livery stable. As he had always valued gold so highly, he found it hard to believe that not everyone regarded it the same way, and he concluded that Albertans were just a little different from other folks.

The next train took them north to Wetaskiwin, from which the CPR was constructing a line east to Saskatoon. Since the railway had planned townsites every ten miles along the line, where grain elevators, blacksmith shops and stores would be established after farmers settled in the area, father decided here would be the best place to look for land. At the CPR land office in Wetaskiwin he was told that the company had an excellent salesman at the new town of Daysland about thirty miles east along the new line, so they hitched a ride east on a work train hauling supplies for the construction camps.

At Daysland, the salesman, whose name was John MacDonald, was most obliging and took them in his buggy to see the available pieces of land. Angus sat on the floor at the back with his feet hanging over the end, across his knees father's big Winchester rifle, an accurate shooting piece though somewhat heavy because of its octagonal-shaped barrel. As MacDonald drove across the prairie, occasionally the buggy disturbed nice fat prairie chickens which did not have the sense to take to the air since they were not afraid of teams and wagons. Angus could not resist the opportunity. Up went the gun and one prairie chicken was minus a head. MacDonald stopped the buggy while Angus retrieved the bird.

"Good shooting, my lad," said MacDonald, "good shooting! I'll bet your father taught you to shoot like that, didn't he?"

"Yes sir," said Angus.

They continued across the prairie. Suddenly MacDonald said, "Can you hit that one, lad?"

Angus raised the gun and another prairie chicken lost its head, neatly, without damaging the body at all.

"Good shooting, lad!" cried MacDonald. Father never said a word. Angus knew father was proud of his shooting just by the set of his jawline.

Three more chickens in a row met the same fate and each time MacDonald was loud in his praise. But the weight of the gun was beginning to take its toll, and when Angus raised it to shoot number six, his aim was off. He hit it in the body and blew it to pieces.

MacDonald frowned. "That's not very good, lad. You'll have to do better than that!"

Father glanced sideways at him but said nothing. Angus waited a while before he tried for number seven, then took careful aim and blew it all to pieces, too. He was disgusted with himself.

MacDonald reined in the horses. "There'll be no more shooting, lad. I must tell you that I'm a justice of the peace here, and since you're an alien and you don't have a hunting licence, it's against the law for you to shoot in this province!"

"Yes, sir," said Angus.

Father looked straight ahead.

At the end of the day, father had not seen any land that he liked, but MacDonald insisted that he and Angus come back to his home for dinner. What did his wife serve? Angus's prairie chickens with gravy and dumplings! And, said Angus when he told us the story later, that MacDonald fellow didn't have the least trouble swallowing the lion's share of those illegal birds.

After a night in the Daysland Hotel, father contacted a man named Brown, the agent for the Hudson's Bay Company which owned almost as much land in the district as the CPR did. Now, since news travels fast in a town that size, Brown had already heard about Angus's experience with the prairie chickens. Therefore, thinking he would get on the good side of father, he took down a shotgun from his office wall and handed it to Angus.

"Now, young man," he said, "I'm going to make a hunting licence for you, and as a present I'm going to give you this fine twelve-gauge shotgun and I want you to go out there and shoot as many prairie chickens as you want!"

"Thank you, sir," said Angus grinning.

"And when you're tired of shooting chickens, you can shoot ducks and geese because the property I'm going to show your father this morning is right beside the best duck and goose lake in the whole province." He turned to father. "Mr. MacDonald, you're going to like this piece of land!"

He drove them to the new townsite of Strome, ten miles east

71

of Daysland, and showed them a piece of land right between the proposed townsite and Wavy Lake—three-quarters of a section. He said that this 480 acres belonged to the Hudson's Bay and the remaining 160 acres in the section was government land open for homesteading. It was the best land they had seen so far, so father agreed to buy the Hudson's Bay land at $6.50 an acre.

The next day, father and Angus went back to Wetaskiwin to buy a camping outfit, a wagon, and team of Percherons, among other equipment, and while they were outfitting themselves, met two young Englishmen just recently arrived in the country. They were also buying their outfit to go to their new homestead, not far from our new land. Someone had sold them a team of oxen and a wagon, and though they were obviously well educated, they knew absolutely nothing about farming and even less about handling oxen. On top of that, these were not even good oxen, actually just a couple of old range bulls.

In 1905 ox teams were in great demand on the prairies, because they were cheaper than horses and extremely strong. For those who knew how to handle them, they were very dependable for farm labour. However, the good heavy steers that were normally broken as draft animals were pretty scarce, so some of the feed and sales stables were buying old bulls and breaking them instead. The oxen that these young Englishmen got were not the most co-operative beasts in the world.

That evening, after they had bought all the supplies they needed, the two Englishmen with the help of father and Angus removed their wagon box from the running gear and loaded about two thousand feet of lumber between the uprights of the bolsters. Then they perched the wagon box on top of the lumber, filled it with their camp outfit, grub and other gear, and covered the whole thing with a tarpaulin.

Next day the two outfits made good time on the level prairie road, but when dark clouds gathered ahead they made camp early in the afternoon to give their teams a chance to rest and graze. Travelling and camping was an old experience for father and Angus but for the Englishmen it was something entirely new, though they were eager to learn. The stableman had sold them two pairs of hobbles and explained how to put them on the front feet of the oxen to keep them from straying too far at night, so with father's help they applied them when they stopped to camp. In the morning, the animals were easily caught and reharnessed.

On the second day, father allowed the ox team to go first so he could drive at a leisurely pace and give Angus a chance to hunt along the roadside with his new gun. He got a few prairie chickens and some ducks and even a couple of Canada geese in the sloughs and ponds.

Although most of the road led across flat prairie, there were occasional hills, some of them pretty steep. The worst one was Pipe Stone Hill near Camrose. Father was not too worried when he saw it because his wagon had brakes, but the Englishmen's cheaper rig had none. So there they were at the crest of the hill with this high, heavy load and nothing to stop them from landing in a heap at the bottom. Then suddenly one of them remembered the hobbles. Since they kept the oxen from straying too far the night before, surely they would stop the beasts from running down the hill out of control. So they got out the hobbles and fastened them to the animals' feet just as father had shown them, climbed back onto the wagon seat and started down the hill.

Within seconds, all hell broke loose. Without the full use of their front feet, the oxen lost their footing almost immediately, and the weight of the heavy wagon threw them onto their sides. The whole business—oxen, wagon, lumber and all—went skidding helter-skelter down the road as the two men flung themselves into the roadside grasses. Luckily, about two-thirds of the way down the hill the wagon overturned, bringing the whole mess to a halt at last.

Meanwhile, father and Angus had come to the top of the hill and stopped to put a chain ruff-lock on the two back wheels to hold their wagon back. They were unaware of the disaster since the pile-up had taken place just around a bend in the road, and they set off down the hill. As soon as they rounded the curve they saw but could not stop.

In a few minutes, they returned on foot to find that the Englishmen were bruised and cut but otherwise all right. The four men unhooked the oxen from the wagon and got them to their feet. Those old range bulls were pretty tough. They were

73

badly scratched and bruised, and some of their skin and hair had been peeled right off their hides, but otherwise they were still capable of carrying on.

The whole wagon had to be unloaded and the box and lumber removed before the running gear could be put back on the wheels, taking the remainder of the afternoon, so that everyone camped right there for the night to give man and beast a little time to recover.

The morning was clear and uncomfortably hot by the time they got the wagons on the road. The oxen, still unhappy with what had happened to them the day before, were a lot unhappier with the heat, and the Englishmen had trouble getting them to move at all. Near noon they came to a big slough close to the side of the road, and those two old bulls headed straight for it and kept going until they were standing in three feet of water. They drank their fill and then refused to move. Coaxing, whipping, nothing worked. They had to be unhitched and led out of the slough one at a time, leaving the wagon in the water. Then father took our team into the water, hooked them up to the wagon and pulled it out. The oxen appeared happy with their show of independence and allowed themselves to be hitched to the wagon again without resistance. Eventually the Englishmen arrived at their homestead, but we never did learn what happened to the oxen.

Father and Angus reached their new property about the fifteenth of September and pitched their tent a couple of hundred yards from the camp of a big railway construction crew. After fixing dinner, they walked over to visit the camp and found, much to father's surprise, that it was owned by the MacArthur brothers from the Ottawa Valley. Father had grown up with them and was happy to meet them again after all those years and see how they had been transformed from backwoods lumberjacks to big-time railroad contractors.

The MacArthurs had 200 teams of big Missouri mules and 20 teams of Clydesdale and Percheron horses located at four or five camps along the right of way. The mules were used for pulling the wheel-scrapers (dirt plows or buckets on wheels) to build the railroad grade; the horses loosened the dirt to make it easier to load into the wheel-scrapers.

The MacArthurs' camps were located at the townsites so

they could have one crew building a siding and two more crews grading the roadway for a distance of about five miles both east and west from the camp. As soon as that section was completed and the steel laid, the camp was moved on to the next townsite. This siding at Strome, however, was taking a little longer than usual because the CPR planned to make it their main marshalling yard for empty boxcars. Duncan, who was head of the MacArthur Brothers Company, was worried.

"I don't think we'll get this one finished before freeze-up, Archie. And that means money lost because we'll have to bring the crews back here in the spring before we can get along to the next site. I'd bring in more equipment but we've none to spare."

They went on to talk of father's reason for being at Strome.

"I've just bought that land where I've pitched my tent. My son and I are going to start building there."

"Well, since you're so close," said Duncan, "come and have your meals here in camp as long as we're here!"

When father started to protest, Duncan just laughed. "When you're feeding over two hundred men, two more won't make a bit of difference!"

So father and Angus wasted none of their precious time cooking as long as the camp was there, giving them more time every day to get the necessary work done on the land. Their first job was to build some sort of shelter for the horses. They cut small poplar trees growing along the shore of Wavy Lake to make a frame for a barn, then put a layer of diamond willows from the lakeside over the frame to support a roof. They bought hay from three brothers who lived two miles away. Jim, Bob and Will Lindsay were Lowland Scots who owned two sections of land. One was cultivated to grow grain; the other was still raw prairie and it provided them with the kind of hay known as prairie wool or bunchgrass. Since they did not have enough stock to feed it to, each year they acquired a few more haystacks, and they were quite happy to get rid of some of their two-year-old hay to father at two dollars a measured ton. Father then induced them to lend him a wagon and hayrack to cart it away.

He and Angus piled the hay over the frame of the barn until it looked like a huge hollowed-out haystack. It proved to be a dandy snug place for the horses.

Next on their list of priorities was a corral and pasture for the horses. For this they went twenty miles to the banks of the Battle River to cut diamond willows for fence posts and cotton-wood poles to brace the corners. After unloading them near their tent site, they sharpened one end of each post with an axe to make it easier to drive them into that hard-packed ground.

They were finishing the pasture fence when freeze-up came and they had to quit. Next door at the construction camp, the men began packing up their equipment and driving their horses and mules toward Wetaskiwin. The siding had not been finished in time and would have to wait until spring.

When father and Angus had stapled several strands of barbed wire to their fence posts, it was the beginning of November. About this time a young neighbour, Stuart McCullough, dropped by to invite them to dine with himself and his sister Marcella. They were glad to accept the offer of a home-cooked meal, and during the course of the evening they discovered that Stuart and father were distant cousins. The visit passed quickly in talk about families and farming, and it was very dark when they said their good-nights. But father and Angus had not walked far when they realized that it was starting to snow. Before they got back to camp it was a raging blizzard. They could not see their hands in front of their faces and the cold pierced right through their clothes.

They lost all sense of direction and stumbled around on that wide open prairie, hanging on to one another so they would not get separated. They knew if they did not find their tent soon, they had no chance of survival. After what seemed like hours, Angus's feet stumbled over something in the snow.

"Just a minute, father," he shouted above the storm. He got down on his knees to feel around in the snow and his hands touched the chopping block and the pile of chips from the fence posts. "I've found the chopping block! The tent must be here somewhere!"

"Stay there," called father. "Don't move! Just holler every few seconds. I'm going to circle round your voice!"

A few minutes later, he tripped over the guy rope of the tent, which was still standing, and was able to direct Angus to join him. They were soon inside with a roaring fire going in the cast-iron cookstove.

After that blizzard, the weather grew colder and colder, and they knew they would never survive the winter in the tent. There was also the constant danger of the wind carrying it away. One day they harnessed the team to the wagon and set off for Daysland to buy lumber for a cabin. Unfortunately, the only kind that could be bought at that time of the year was green shiplap, which had already frozen into a solid block so that each board had to be pried from the pile. But they hauled it home and set to work building a cabin fourteen feet by twenty feet with a boxcar roof, the quickest and easiest kind to make. It was built on skids so it would be easy to haul later to a permanent location to use for grain storage. The walls and roof were a single layer of shiplap with a layer of tarpaper on the outside held in place by laths. They placed their cookstove at one end of the room near the door and at the other end they set up a big cast-iron heater that they had bought in Daysland.

For the first week after they moved from the tent into the cabin, they kept telling each other how nice it was to be warm again. But soon they were finding it difficult to keep ice from forming on the inside walls even with both fires going full blast: the shiplap was drying out from the heat of the stoves and in a short while there were cracks half an inch wide between the boards. And to make matters worse, the wind whipped the tarpaper right off the outside walls letting the snow drift in through the cracks.

For father and Angus, it was the longest, most severe winter they had ever put in, though the old-timers told them it was milder than usual.

Once the cabin was finished, father bought eight more draft horses and hired three teamsters. With five teams, he now got himself a contract for hauling freight to the small towns along the railway right of way; it would be another year before the trains arrived.

It was the first of February when Mr. Brown, the real estate agent from the Hudson's Bay Company, arrived at the cabin.

"Mr. MacDonald, I've come with bad news," he said looking nervously at father's stern face.

Father waited. He hated people who beat about the bush.

"It's this property, sir. I made a mistake. You see, you can't

77

have it."

"What do you mean, I can't have it? I've got it. I bought it and paid for it and I've got the papers to prove it."

"But I made a mistake in selling it, Mr. MacDonald. It didn't belong to the Hudson's Bay Company. It belongs to the CPR."

"There's no problem then," said my father. "You just give my money to the CPR."

"But they won't take it. It's against the CPR's policy to sell waterfront land or land adjoining a townsite, and this piece of land does both. I'm very sorry, Mr. MacDonald, but you'll have to leave."

"You can be as sorry as you like, Mr. Brown, but this is my land. I've built a cabin and made fences. I'm settled here. I don't see how you can do anything about it."

"Maybe I can't, sir, but the CPR can. Look, I can give you a piece of land every bit as good as this just six miles south of here in the next township. It's section twenty-six just like this one. It belongs to the CPR but they're willing to sell it . . . well, that is, exchange it for this land. I'm really sorry about all this—"

"No!" said my father. "This is my land and I'll take the matter to court before I give it up."

"You won't win. It will cost you a fortune in legal fees but the CPR will still win. Please, Mr. MacDonald, this little piece of land is not worth throwing away your hand-earned money."

Father turned away.

"Look," said Brown, "why don't you come and see this other parcel? I know you'll like it. And there's another six hundred and forty acres right next to it that you can buy at the same price."

Father finally agreed to look at the other piece and the two of them rode off in Brown's buggy. Father had to agree that there was nothing wrong with the land, but he refused to give Brown a firm answer.

"I'll let you know in a few days," he said.

In Wetaskiwin he talked to a lawyer whose opinion was as gloomy as Brown's had been.

"The CPR will stall you in the courts for years. You'll keep paying lawyers just to keep your hand in the game, and when you run out of cash or have a couple of bad crop-years, they'll run you off the land. Then you'll have nothing. You might as well take the other land now and save yourself all those years of grief. But make sure they pay for the improvements that you've made!"

So father agreed to take the parcel of land six miles to the south with the understanding that he could stay where he was until spring, that he would get compensation for his improvements, and that he could move his cabin to the new property.

On 20 February 1906 when father came back, by himself, to get Dan and me, it was already spring in the Colville Valley. We had mixed feelings about his return because we knew that Aunt Annie had written to him about our running away from the mission school; we were mighty worried about what he would say. He could be pretty tough when we did not follow his orders.

We need not have worried. All he said was, "I'm proud to have two boys who had guts enough to look after themselves when people tried to mistreat them!"

With that off our minds we began asking questions about Alberta. Father told us as much as he could about our new home but it was hard for us to picture it. One thing we were sure of: it was nothing at all like the Bear Creek Ranch.

Lavena had married while father was in Alberta and settled with her husband on a bit of land near Bear Creek. Ruth would continue to live with Aunt Annie and Uncle Dick since father considered her too young for the rugged life on the prairies. We were going to miss our sisters and all the Prouty relatives who had been so good to us. Father was usually able to leave family and friends behind quite easily when he set out on one of his journeys, but he seemed to understand that Dan and I were feeling the wrench of parting very deeply, so he took us on a round of visits to our relatives to say good-bye.

He even took time to pay a visit to the teacher at the Bosberg school. We liked Mr. Anderson very much and were always anxious to please him and do our school work just as well as we possibly could. He seemed greatly surprised that father was taking us out of school.

"What chance is there for further schooling for your boys where you'll be living?"

"There's no school there at all," said father, "and none within riding distance."

"What a pity," said Mr. Anderson shaking his head in disapproval. "Your boys seem to be intelligent, too."

He was silent for a moment or two and father stood up to leave. Mr. Anderson stopped him.

"Mr. MacDonald, as you probably know, my wife and I have no children. Would you consider leaving your youngest son Ervin with us? We would be very glad to have him and we would see that he got a good education. He's only been here about four months but I feel sure he has the ability to go quite a way if he gets the opportunity."

Father did not even think over his offer. "I thank you very kindly for praising my boy's capabilities and for your kind offer to see that he gets more schooling, but I can't accept. I've been without my sons for too long."

So at the advanced age of almost thirteen years I said farewell to school and to the one and only teacher whom I had ever learned anything from.

On 26 February, Dan and I were finally Alberta-bound with father. On the first leg we travelled on the Spokane Falls and Northern Railroad which was a daily train with three passenger coaches and a baggage and mail car. From Bosberg to Nelson was only a few hours' run, but since the train did not leave until evening, it was quite late when we arrived. Father took us to the Queen's Hotel on Baker Street where he had stayed on a number of occasions. Since it was the first time that Dan and I had ever stayed in a hotel, we were thrilled as well as somewhat bewildered.

It is a wonder that either of us slept at all that night, but suddenly there was father calling us to get up so we could be on our way. At breakfast in the hotel dining room, the tables were decorated with centrepieces of pretty glass bowls filled with bright red apples. As soon as we sat down I reached out for one but the waitress whisked the bowl off the table and onto the sideboard.

"Would you like porridge?" she asked me.

Porridge? I had never heard of it before but I decided it was worth a try. And what did she bring? Plain old oatmeal mush that I had eaten every day of my life! What a letdown.

At the dock we caught the steamer *Kokanee* for the trip up

Kootenay Lake. It was a slow journey: the *Kokanee* would swing in toward the shore every so often and put down her anchor while some farmer rowed out with a couple of sacks of apples, potatoes or other farm produce to be delivered to a logging camp or sawmill along the CPR line.

At Kootenay Landing, the end of the boat run, we transferred to a mixed passenger and freight train, which ran through beautiful country with thick forests of fir, larch, cedar and birch trees growing right up to the edge of the right of way, giving the impression that we were travelling through one long tunnel. Now and again we passed through a small clearing with a saw-mill and a cluster of buildings where a few lonely souls made a living from the forest. Occasionally the train would stop to load or unload freight or mail, and once a passenger climbed down and vanished among the trees. All afternoon the train crept on through forest, then near evening we reached the mountains and the Crowsnest Pass. After that the dark forest and the grandeur of the Rocky Mountains slipped into the night.

It was one o'clock in the morning when we arrived at Fort Macleod, and since the connecting train was not due to leave until the next morning, father decided we would go to a hotel. The railway station was about a mile from the town, so father hustled off to find a hack. Dan and I grabbed our bags and followed him but we were not prepared for the weather outside. When we left Bosberg the wild buttercups had been in bloom; here it was twenty below! We had never experienced anything remotely like it in our lives and we were sure we would freeze to death before we got to the hotel.

Father never bothered to tell us that this was considered to be a mild winter in those parts: I think he had his own misgivings. But he kept them to himself.

From the train the next morning we got our first look at the prairie. We were overwhelmed by the vast expanse of level land. There was not a tree or bush in sight, just a monotonous flat white country as far as we could see.

"Look out this way," said father. "You can see the Rocky Mountains! See the snow on them?"

But they were so far away that they seemed absolutely unreal; our eyes wandered back to the prairie sliding past the other window. Where were those golden wheat fields and the golden sun that we had seen in father's folders?

After a long stop at Calgary, the scenery changed very little, but sometime around midafternoon Dan poked me in the ribs to point out some bushes, clusters of them here and there in little gullies. But around them the old prairie rolled on.

We came to Wetaskiwin in the late afternoon and stayed overnight. In the morning father got his team and light sleigh from the livery stable and we headed east, Dan and I huddled down as low as we could under the rugs to escape the cold. On the evening of the following day, 1 March 1906 — my thirteenth birthday — we finally arrived at our new home on the wide open prairie.

Anxious to escape the cold, we rushed into the cabin where Angus was cooking dinner for father's three teamsters. It was not much warmer inside. The wind had taken every bit of tarpaper for a tour of the western prairie and snow drifted through the cracks and across the floor. That night we followed Angus's and father's example and loaded ourselves down with blankets so that only our noses were exposed, but in the morning we found that our breath had put an edging of frost on the blankets next to our faces. Before we could prepare breakfast, we had to thaw out the food we were going to eat.

This was our initiation into life on the bald prairie.

In spite of the cold and the depressingly flat land, we Mac-Donalds were happy. Father and his three boys were together again, and there was work to be done. We waited for father to assign our chores.

Before he had come to fetch us from Colville, he had bought 3,000 bushels of oats and 2,000 bushels of wheat from an elderly Scotsman, Mr. Struthers, who had a well-established grain farm about eighteen miles away. Aware that the railway had bypassed Struthers's farm leaving him with little market, father drove a hard bargain and got the wheat at thirty-five cents a bushel and the oats at twenty-five cents, on the understanding that Mr. Struthers would put up the teamsters and teams when they came to haul it away.

Father had also bought a fanning mill to remove the weed seeds and wild oats from the grain, but since there were no gas engines in those days to power the thing, it had to be operated by hand. This was where Dan and I came in. Together we manned the handle that turned the big wheel which made the screens in the mill vibrate back and forth and which made the fan blow the chaff from the heavier oats and wheat, leaving only clean grain. The cleaned grain dropped into a hopper at the bottom of the mill, where elevator buckets picked it up and lifted it into grain sacks. Whenever a sack filled up, one of us had to drag it aside and sew up the top with a big sack needle and binder twine; the other one had to keep the handle turning. We cranked that thing all through March and April and well into May, till at last the mill was darn near worn out and Dan and I had man-sized biceps.

All that dirty, dusty, monotonous work produced 2,000 bushels of cleaned wheat and nearly 200 bushels of cleaned oats for seed. The rest was used for feeding the livestock.

As soon as the frost came out of the ground, work on the railway right of way could begin again, but the MacArthurs decided not to bring in a big crew to finish the Strome siding. Instead, they came to father to see if he would put his teams to work on the job.

"But I've had no experience of that kind," he said.

"We'll lend you some of our wheel-scrapers, and three of our best men," said Duncan MacArthur.

"I've a lot of work to do to get ready for planting—" said father.

"You've more than a month of cool weather before you can seed, Archie, and this little job will take less time than that."

So father agreed to do the job, and for a month that spring the MacDonalds became railway builders. We were able to begin about mid-April. Father used his five teams, and his crew consisted of himself, Angus, our three teamsters and the three men from MacArthur's crew. The siding was just across the section line from our place so the men did not have far to go to work. Dan and I alternated now between cooking meals for the crew and operating the fanning mill. Just as Duncan MacArthur had predicted, the little job on the railway was finished to the MacArthurs' satisfaction before it was time to seed.

During the winter, our neighbour Stuart McCullough had asked father if he would like to lease their farm for one crop season since he was too busy operating his livery and sales stable in Strome. Father agreed with a few stipulations. He wanted the property fenced: he would furnish the diamond willow posts and put up the fence; Stuart was to supply the barbed wire which he had already bought for the job. The posts that father intended to use were the ones he and Angus had cut during the winter to fence the land at Strome, no longer needed now that we had to give up that property and move south. We would also use our cabin as a granary on his place. Once the deal had been made with Stuart, father turned around and gave two young homesteaders a contract to do the fencing, for we would all be busy with other work.

On our own land we had already fenced 320 acres for livestock pasture, and in one corner we fenced in four acres for the house, barn and other outbuildings. Now father gave the two young men a contract to fence the land reserved for hay fields.

He bought a seeder to plant the wheat, then put one of the teamsters and a four-horse team onto the job. Angus and Dan harrowed the ground ahead of the seeder; father and Angus treated the wheat seed for smut and hauled it to the field where it would be handy to load into the seed hopper. Since seeding time was so short, it was vitally important to keep the seeder operating, but it was such hard work that a four-horse team would be played out by noon and have to be replaced by a fresh team.

It took eight days to seed the land leased from Stuart McCullough, and then came the task of moving the cabin onto his place. This turned out to be much easier than we anticipated as we simply hitched two four-horse teams to one end and hauled it across the prairie on its skids. With the cabin in place, it now became a granary, and we moved all our belongings to our own new property, put up our tent, and beside it erected another tent borrowed from the McCulloughs.

We now began seeding our own property. Father put four-horse teams on the gang plows and on the disc harrow, and in this way the men were able to get six or seven acres of ground ready for seeding in one day. About once a week, father would put the discing team onto the seeder to plant the prepared ground.

In all we planted about eighty acres to wheat and about forty in oats. By this time father figured it was too late to plant any more grain so we seeded about the same number of acres to flax and sold off all the leftover seed grain. Since good cleaned seed was at a premium, we got a dollar a bushel for the wheat and seventy-five cents for the oats. A nice profit from Dan's and my hard labour.

While Angus and the hired men had been doing the plowing and seeding, the rest of us, with the help of a carpenter, began building our new house. It was a frame structure, twenty-four by twenty-six feet, a storey and a half high. It did not have a basement, only cedar-block pilings. On the outside, we covered the walls with tarpaper and siding; the roof was cedar shingles. The inside walls were shiplap covered with grey building paper but the ceilings were V-joint lumber. When it was completed inside and out, we boarded up the crawl-space under the house and banked it well with earth. There was no insulation in those days, no luxuries such as indoor plumbing and electric wiring to install, and no building inspectors to satisfy, so it did not take long to build a house.

Inside, there were a living room, kitchen and dining room combined, plus a pantry, on the main floor. Upstairs were three bedrooms, and every room had plenty of windows. It was quite warm once we moved in the stoves from the cabin. Beyond them we owned very little furniture, but we felt as though we were living in a palace after the cabin and tents.

For Dan and me, building the house was certainly a welcome change from cranking the mill, and it certainly beat plowing and discing. We learned a lot about carpentry from father and most of the time managed to satisfy his standards of workmanship. He taught us how to shingle and turned the roofing job over to us, only coming around now and then to supervise. Though he never told us that we had done well, we knew by the way he nodded when he looked the job over. We never expected more.

At the beginning of June, Lavena and her husband Jim Case came to visit, bringing our eleven-year-old sister Ruth with them. Dan and I had been doing the cooking but now Lavena and Ruth took over all the cooking and housework, leaving us more time to work outside. I am sure that father and my brothers were even happier to see them than I was. At last they would get some relief from Ervin's sourdough and baking-powder biscuits. If a person was really determined, he could eat one of these things when they were fresh out of the oven (if they were not burned too badly) but, in some mysterious way, as soon as they cooled off they got as hard as the lumps of coal they usually resembled. I have often wondered if people still find them scattered around the prairie and think they have stumbled on the makings of a coal mine.

Angus and his brother-in-law broke up more land with gang plows and six-horse teams, and by the middle of July they had prepared 160 acres. Then it was time to start cutting hay for winter. The prairie wool was about fifteen inches high and as thick as a carpet. Because of Alberta's dry climate it did not require much curing so we were able to stack it soon after it was cut. Using first-rate teams of horses and with all of us working from daylight to dark, we made excellent time. Angus and Dan drove the teams on the bucking pole that pushed the hay into the stack. Father pitched it up, and I was given the honour of building the stack sixteen feet wide, ninety feet long and twelve feet high. This is the hardest of all the jobs in haying, but I had the rare pleasure of hearing my father say, "Well done!" when I climbed down from the second seventy-ton stack. The haying was all done.

When Lavena, Ruth and Jim departed to Colville, I had to return to my cooking duties as well as work in the field. Now it was time to cut the grain. We soon discovered that cutting and stacking hay was child's play compared to harvesting grain. Angus and father drove the three-horse teams on our binders, while Dan and I came along behind and stooked the grain. We would grab a sheaf in each hand — each sheaf weighing thirty-five to forty pounds — and pull and tug them to the spot we had picked for the stook. There we would jam the butt end hard on the ground and angle the sheaves so they would brace each other. Ten or twelve sheaves went into a stook. Later on we loaded them onto wagons and hauled them into the stack yard to make round stacks. We were spared the job of threshing the grain since we had no threshing equipment of our own. Father let this job out on contract.

After the threshing was finished in early October, Angus, Dan and I hoped for a little respite, but that was not to be. The land had to be disced to get it in shape for next year's crops. The barn and the chicken house had to be finished. The garden vegetables had to be dug and stored, and a good quantity of groceries had to be hauled from Strome and Daysland. And then there was coal to be hauled home for winter fuel. Fortunately, fifteen miles away on the banks of the Battle River was a beautiful seam of coal which the owners sold at a dollar a wagonload. We got enough to last us for a couple of months, and planned to get the rest during the winter.

By 15 October, we were well into our preparations for next spring. Dan was discing with a four-horse team; father, Angus and I were at work on the sod barn and the chicken house. About two o'clock in the afternoon, Angus stopped nailing rafters on the chicken house and waved his hammer toward the southwest.

"Look at that!"

A great cloud of smoke rolled up into the sky, perhaps five miles away. We had been told enough about prairie fires to know we were looking at one. We were worried, but figured our own place was safe since we had dusty roads on all four sides to form fireguards. However, several families lived right in the path of the fire, so father and Angus rode off on our two light workhorses in the direction of the smoke, while Dan and I went back to our work.

But soon after they left, the fire veered in our direction. The land just south of our place was virgin prairie covered with thick dry grass. As soon as the fire touched the edge, it came roaring toward our farm with a strong wind behind. Dan brought his team in from the field and we stood watching that raging fire coming closer and closer.

"It'll stop at the road," Dan said. I nodded. No fire could cross the sixteen-foot-wide dirt road that separated the burning wild-hay field from our own field.

But we had no real idea what a prairie fire can do, and we were still standing there watching when it leaped the road as though no road had been there and came right on across our hay field. It slowed down because only stubble remained on this field but it showed no signs of burning itself out, and it was heading straight for our two haystacks. Unfortunately, neither Dan nor I had any idea how to fight it.

At that precise moment, into our yard rode a farmer who lived just east of us, someone who had lived on the prairie for several years and had seen many fires. He helped us hitch up the four-horse team to our big sixteen-inch breaking plow. We rushed out into the hay field with Dan driving the team and the neighbour handling the plow, while I went along behind to make sure the grass side of the sod was turned completely under so it would not catch fire. We plowed straight across the field toward the nearest haystack, but we were too late to save it. It was already burning in several places. We hurried to the other stack a quarter of a mile away and began plowing a fireguard around it. Our neighbour showed us how to start a backfire and we waited for the two fires to meet. It worked. In a little while we were able to head home across the field of charred stubble. The fire was out, at least on our land, and we had saved the second haystack.

The first stack blazed for three days. When it was finally out, only a pile of ash remained where seventy tons of hay had sat. Fortunately, our house and outbuildings had been in little danger because they stood behind the piece of freshly plowed ground that Dan had just been working.

When father and Angus came back from fighting the fire on our neighbours' land, father took one look at the burning stack and quickly harnessed a fresh horse to our light buggy and leaped into the seat.

"See to the chores till I get back!" he called, and was gone. He had worked building the barn all morning and fought the fire all afternoon but he had not even stopped to eat or rest. He was the fastest-thinking man I ever knew.

It was late the next day when he got back. While I put out his dinner, he explained.

"We lost seventy ton of hay in that fire, but there'll be others who've lost more. There'll be a shortage before spring so I went to buy some in Daysland."

"Who do you know that has hay, father?" we asked.

"One of the partners in the Daysland Hotel. He owns a couple of sections about six miles north of us near Wavy Lake. He has his hay put up each year on shares and I remembered him telling me when I was in Daysland about five or six weeks ago that he had more than three hundred ton of hay that he hadn't been able to sell."

Father had got to the man before news of the fire reached him and bought all his hay for $2.50 a ton. It was after midnight when he fell into bed in the Daysland Hotel with the bill of sale in his pocket.

The following spring the price of hay in southern Alberta went up to $40 and $50 a ton for those who were fortunate enough to be able to buy any at all.

With the fire over, we went back to our preparations for the winter. Then one evening a Mr. Peterson stopped at our house, driving three oxen hitched to a stoneboat and leading a Percheron mare. He had been working for the MacArthur brothers, using the oxen on the huge breaking plows to loosen up the ground ahead of the wheel-scrapers. The grading of the right of way had stopped for the winter and he was on his way back to his homestead.

"Could you put me up for the night?" he asked.

Father never turned anyone from our door so Mr. Peterson spent the night, and in the morning he hit father up for a trade. He wanted a mate for his mare and we had a nice grey Percheron mare, a dead ringer for his. They would make an excellent matched team. Father was always open for a trade, so he said, "I'll trade my mare for your three oxen, stoneboat, breaking plow and harness."

"Agreed," said Mr. Peterson. He was well pleased. He left with two fine matched Percheron mares, and left behind three of the most ornery oxen that God ever let live. We were now the proud owners of one big red shorthorn ox named Tom and two red-roans named Dick and Harry. They could kick the knots out of a two-inch plank at a distance of four feet.

"What are you going to do with them, father?" we asked, afraid we would end up behind them in the field when spring came around.

"God will provide, boys, something will turn up."

We were skeptical. Not even father had driven oxen before and I think even he had a healthy respect for those animals' feet. But God did provide in the form of a neighbouring homesteader

89

named Jack O'Toole who claimed to be an expert ox-team driver. Father therefore made a bargain with him to finish our fencing in exchange for those three fine healthy oxen. We furnished the materials for the fence and lent him our wagon to do the job. Thus we were rid of the oxen and a tough, tiresome piece of work at the same time.

Late in the fall father bought a couple of driving horses. One of them was a 1,200-pound blue-roan mare called Ruby which father used to lend out when necessary because she was a pretty wise animal and seemed capable of looking after herself. One day, Paul Lamoure, the stout French-Canadian blacksmith from Strome, came to hire a rig to drive to his homestead twelve miles south of us. We gave him Ruby.

Unfortunately, Paul made a mistake on his way back to our place: he decided Ruby was too slow. He got down from the buggy and headed for a small clump of willows by the roadside with the idea of cutting himself a nice long switch. Ruby watched him cut it, and started for home without him. She knew all about switches and buggy whips. When Lamoure ran to catch up with her, she ran, and when he got tired of running, she slowed down, just keeping her distance. The poor man walked all the way back to our farm.

Jim was the driving horse we boys liked the best. He was what was called a "French Canadian," a breed developed in eastern Canada. He weighed the same as Ruby but was quite blocky with a heavy coat of hair and a long wavy mane and tail. He was a beautiful example of the breed, coal black with one white spot on his forehead. Father had bought him from Stuart McCullough who had trained him for ice racing, a sport common at that time on the frozen rivers and streams of eastern Canada.

In those days Alberta had a Lord's Day Act that prevented anyone from doing labour for gain on Sunday. This meant that we could not work the teams plowing, discing, or hauling a load of grain or coal. There was even a ban on hunting and shooting game birds of any kind. The act was strictly enforced and anyone caught breaking it was liable to a heavy fine. The only activities permitted were driving a team to church or Sunday School and to visit neighbours. Father, being a deeply religious man, saw this as a good opportunity to send Angus, Dan and me to Sunday School.

We got there a few times, but most Sundays, especially if we had Jim harnessed to the buggy, the three of us would start off toward church and then detour out into the countryside. That Jim simply would not let another horse and buggy or sleigh pass him and he gave us many a wild, thrilling race across the prairie. It was great sport!

Father never learned of our escapades. We always returned home about the right time looking pious and meek, and when he asked us about the sermon or the Sunday School lesson, we gave him a good story. We had so little leisure from work, work, work that we felt little guilt about deceiving him.

On the first of November, Angus and father were putting the finishing touches on the barn. Dan was nearing the end of the discing that father wanted finished by winter, and I was busy scrubbing clothes. When I stepped out to call the others for the noon meal, I could see it was snowing. Just a few flakes drifting lazily down. Nothing to get excited about. But by the time they were ready to go back out to work, a full-scale blizzard was blowing. That night the temperature hit twenty below zero and it was only the beginning of our troubles. The record-breaking winter of 1906–7 had begun. It would prove to be the worst known in Alberta.

That first blizzard lasted for two days; snowdrifts piled up around the house and over the barn and chicken house. Everything froze solidly. The slough where we had been watering our cattle froze to the bottom, and it became my job to drive our two milk cows, fifty head of range cattle and twelve workhorses to a good spring in a draw about four miles away. It had never been known to freeze over even in weather fifty degrees below zero. The water bubbled up to within two feet of the surface, just close enough for me to be able to dip out a full bucket.

Driving all our horses and cattle to water early every cold, windy morning was no picnic. I would start them off on the trail, following behind on our little Indian cayuse. I rode bareback because we had no saddle for him. Once we got to the spring, I would tie his head down to his front foot since there was nothing

91

else to tie him to and I did not want the pleasure of walking home in that weather. Then I would dip my bucket into the spring and pour water into the wooden trough beside it. The horses always crowded in first, and when they had drunk their fill, they would start home at a dead run. They had been cold to start with and drinking that icy water made them even colder so they lost no time in getting back to their warm barn. The cows pushed in for their turn.

After each cow drank enough she left for home and by the time the last one had finished, there was a long string of cattle moving along the narrow trail. I made the cayuse wait till last to be sure of keeping him there, then climbed on his back and waited shivering while he drank. Dipping all that water took quite a while and it was bitterly cold out there. Many times that winter the temperature dropped to fifty below, though you would swear it was colder when the wind was blowing. It never got above ten below.

When that horse had drunk his fill, he would break into a dead run, dodging around the slow-moving cows, stumbling sometimes when his feet broke through the snow crust. It was like riding the tail of a hurricane.

Back home again there were chickens and pigs to feed, barns to clean and all the odds and ends of jobs that come up on a mixed farm. While I was busy with these chores, Dan and Angus hauled grain for shipping and brought hay from the stack that father had bought near Wavy Lake. Eventually he discovered that he had bought more than we needed, and was able to sell the surplus at an excellent profiit, but as far as Angus and Dan were concerned, the best thing about that sale was that the buyers came and hauled it away themselves.

Frequently the boys would arrive home after dark if they had had to shovel drifting snow off the haystacks or from the roads. Then as the winter wore on and the drifts built the roads up higher than the surrounding fields, the sleigh would keep sliding off and upsetting, and they would have to reload it. The same thing happened when they were hauling coal. To get the sleigh righted and back onto the road, they had to unload even more coal to make it light enough to lift. We all agreed it had been a mistake not to get enough coal before winter came, but we really had not expected the bad weather to arrive so early or be so severe.

Many times that winter, we felt we could not endure another blizzard or another snowdrift. Father suffered from pleurisy for almost the whole winter, and grumbled to us, "It's living indoors that does it to me, boys! I can't stand living in a house for long. Give me the fresh air and the mountains and I'll be right as rain!"

We knew this was true.

6

Overland

DURING THE LONG months that father had lain in bed with pleurisy, he had done a lot of thinking. When his body could not be busy, his mind was twice as active as usual. My brothers and I knew the signs and had learned to bide our time and wait for the outcome.

Then one morning in early March, he came downstairs to have breakfast, and we could tell that he was somehow different. I had no idea what it was but he had changed. We watched him limbering up. He was always a little stiff in the morning as a result of his old injuries.

"Good morning, boys!" he said. They were the same old words but they sounded different. He sat down to breakfast and started to eat. My brothers and I ate in silence, waiting.

"Boys," he said at last, "I had a dream last night and in it I saw the nicest layout for a ranch that you could ever hope to find. It was on a beautiful lake, with open fields sloping down to the shore. I have a hunch we should go and have a look for it!"

It certainly did not sound like any land we had seen in Alberta so far, but it sounded good to us.

"Where would we look, father?" asked Angus.

"The Cariboo in British Columbia!"

In those long winter months, father had come to the conclusion that he was not a wheat-growing man; he was a mountain man, and he belonged where he could see the mountains, not this flat never-ending prairie. He could never find his pot of gold here.

The Grand Trunk Pacific Railway was planning to continue its line right through the city of Edmonton, across the Rockies through the Yellowhead Pass, and along the Fraser River all the way down to Vancouver. It was the route the Overlanders had taken in 1862 when they were looking for gold, though some, of course, had followed the North Thompson instead of the Fraser since it was a much less dangerous river.

"I'm sure, boys," said father, "that somewhere along that railway line, somewhere west of the Yellowhead, that little ranch is waiting for us. What do you say we sell up here and go west? We'll pack in over the Yellowhead and find our ranch before the railway takes all the land."

For the first time in our lives, father was talking about a pot of gold that Angus, Dan and I could understand. And he was inviting us to go chasing one of his rainbows with him, one we could really see and share in.

Not one of us boys doubted the wisdom of setting off on this adventure. If father decided we were going to do it, then of course it could be done. He had never failed in anything he set out to do, so we knew he would get us there and we would find that beautiful ranch on the lake.

Father was, however, almost sixty-eight years old that spring of 1907, and he had suffered injuries twenty years earlier from which most men would not have recovered. His face was tanned and leathery from all his years in the open, and his hair was sandy grey, balding just a little on top. But he never wore glasses and could drop a deer on the run at three hundred yards. He had grown a third set of teeth when he was fifty and they sparkled when he smiled. He could ride a horse with the best of them, and was always the first one into the saddle when we were driving cattle, even in later years. In fact, few people ever realized his age because he could put men twenty years younger to shame when it came to energy.

I guess we boys really should have been worried about our own capabilities that spring. Father had taught us a lot about resourcefulness and taking responsibility, but we were actually not much more than kids. Angus was seventeen and a half, and he was the most independent and resourceful of us all. He could make anything using the simplest tools and materials, and invented equipment to make jobs easier. He was a cheerful, optimistic young fellow, always curious about things, always interested in people. Though none of us ever achieved father's six-foot-plus frame, we were all sturdily built, and Angus was the heaviest (though not in later years); but for all that he was strong and agile.

Dan, who was not yet sixteen, was the shortest and slightest, and he was also the gentlest. With his calm blue eyes and slow quiet speech, he could soothe any upset animal, but he was especially good with horses. It took a lot to get Dan angry, but if we teased him — and Angus was a terrible tease — he would finally explode and there would be fireworks going off in every direction.

I had just turned fourteen when father made his momentous announcement at the breakfast table. I was aware even then that I took after the MacDonald side of the family more than my brothers did, who were much more like the Proutys. I had father's stubbornness and his capacity for work; but I guess I had been taking orders from him for so long that I never really learned to deliver orders the way he could. Instead I became considerably more accommodating when dealing with people. This did not stop me from bossing my brothers around, however, if need be.

Alberta could not seem to shake off winter in 1907, and we all waited impatiently for spring when father would list our property with one of the real estate people in Daysland. Then on a morning around the middle of March when the weather was still bitterly cold and snow still covered most of our land, once more the answer rode into our yard. The stranger was from North Dakota.

"I'm looking for a piece of land for raising sheep," he said. "Have you given any thought to selling?"

Father shrugged, trying not to look too enthusiastic. "The thought has come to mind," he said.

Before the stranger left at noon, a deal had been made, and the MacDonalds began preparing to move.

There were a lot of things to dispose of before we could

leave, and the manager of the Daysland bank advised father that our best bet would be an auction.

"Everybody comes out for an auction," he said. "You won't have any trouble selling your gear."

Father contacted the local auctioneer, Mr. Hatfield, and set the date of the sale for a Saturday in April. In the meantime, we gave some of our possessions such as a set of dishes to the McCulloughs, who had been so kind to us, and stored a trunk with them containing clothes, breakables, important papers and pictures, a box of tools and father's precious buffalo coat. Once we were settled they would send it on to us. Of the animals, we decided to keep only three horses, two Clydesdale mares and one young stallion. These would be the nucleus of our new herd on the other side of the mountains. Angus would take them by train to Strathcona (which later became South Edmonton), the starting point of our journey.

The day before the sale, because the snow was still deep around the farm machines, Dan and father shovelled it clear to be sure that people got a good look at the inventory. In the house I was busy over the stove. I roasted beef and pork, and assembled pots for making coffee. Everything in the house had to be clean and the furniture ready for inspection. Early the next morning several of our neighbours came over bringing extra cups and they helped to make beef and pork sandwiches and lay out plates of crackers and cheese. We figured a lot of people would come just out of curiosity and a lot of the others would come for the free food since that was what had happened at all the auctions we had attended in Alberta.

They started driving into the yard around nine o'clock, and by ten you could not turn around in the house or the yard or the barn without getting somebody's elbow in your chest or trampling on some child. The table where we served the food was under heavy attack. Father and the bank manager took care of the money. Any sale under twenty-five dollars was cash. Sales over that amount required 25 per cent down and the balance secured by approved bank notes carrying 9 per cent interest.

Shortly after four o'clock everything had been sold. The place was stripped clean since almost all the buyers had taken their purchases away with them. The banker took the notes off to deposit in his bank and would collect on them when due. Unfortunately, that part did not work out too well because many of the buyers failed to make their payments, but on that April day we felt happy at the way the sale had gone.

This was the end of our brief life on the prairie. A few days later, father, Dan and I left the farm without a backward look and caught the train to Wetaskiwin where father bought four saddle horses and a pair of mules to use as pack animals. After a night in a hotel, we set off early on our new mounts, leading the mules and the fourth horse. By nightfall we were in the village of Leduc where we found a good livery stable and a hotel. By the next afternoon we had rejoined Angus in Strathcona.

He had made arrangments to board our animals at Colson's Livery Stable, at the south end of the future site of the high-level bridge. Before dark we bought ourselves a good camping outfit: one ten-by-twelve-foot wall tent, two tarpaulins, four galvanized kettles of different sizes with lids to fit, tin plates and cups, blankets, two water buckets, a dozen candles and a basic grub supply. Now equipped, we set up camp there on the bank of the North Saskatchewan River. But weather was bad, with rain and wet snow turning the ground to mud everywhere we went, and we were forced to stay put until the weather improved and the grass had grown enough to feed our horses along the trail.

Although father was eager to be off, my brothers and I really did not mind the waiting period. For once, there was almost no work to do and we had a chance to rest up. I was particularly happy about taking our main meal of the day at a small eating place nearby. The food was laid out on a long table and we helped ourselves to as much as we wanted. It was good food, too, and all it cost us was twenty cents each a day. Most important, I did not have to cook it.

Sometimes in the evenings we would sit on the river bank and listen to Scottish pipers playing their bagpipes as they walked back and forth in front of Cameron House hotel. We were enthralled by their splendid music, because in spite of our Scots heritage, we had never heard bagpipes before.

Directly across the river from our camp was the bustling young city of Edmonton, with several hotels, every kind of store, feed stables and blacksmith shops—all the establishments that one would expect to find in a thriving frontier city. But the streets were one hell of a mess. The frost was just coming out of the ground and streets which had been hard-packed and dusty last summer had become a sea of mud, in some places ankle-deep. The city fathers had hired teams to haul gravel from the river bank, but it was literally an uphill job. The gravel had to be loaded by hand shovel, then the teamster had to coax and beat his animals to get them up the long steep hill to the town. And it was all pretty fruitless because it was going to take thousands and thousands of yards of gravel to get those streets into condition so people could walk or drive a buggy down them.

When it was not actually pouring rain or snowing, we passed some time sitting on the river bank watching the teams struggle up that long hill on the other side. We seldom went to the city. By the time we walked down the long hill from Strathcona, crossed over the low-level bridge and climbed up the long hill on the other side, we had no more than a couple of hours to prowl around in the stores before setting out again for our camp. For the most part we were satisfied to sit on our side of the river and look across—it was a lot easier on the legs, and besides, we were not used to the bright lights.

In the long days while we waited in Strathcona, Angus came up with the idea of keeping a journal of the trip and he bought a little book to keep his notes in. After this, the book was always kept in his pants pocket and he took time to write in it every night. We also bought a small calendar to keep track of the passing days. The hours would have to take care of themselves, as father had packed his gold watch in the trunk we left behind.

Meanwhile, father searched for pack horses for sale, but he found that good ones were scarce because they had been bought up for the railway survey crews. He was assured that our mules would be of little use; their feet were not suited to the swamps and muskeg that lay along our route, so he traded them and our two Clydesdale mares, who were not very manageable on the road, to Mr. Colson for seven pack horses. We now had eleven horses and the young stallion from our farm.

The weather began to grow warmer and, eager to be on our way at last, we headed for the general store with our provi-

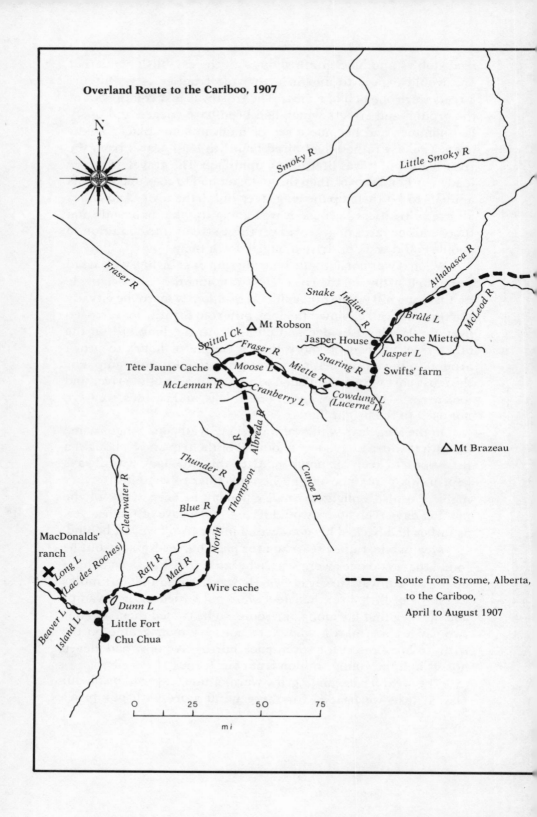

Overland Route to the Cariboo, 1907

N

Smoky R

Little Smoky R

Fraser R

Snake Indian R

Athabasca R

McLeod R

Brûlé L

Spittal Ck

Mt Robson

Jasper House

Roche Miette

Fraser R

Snaring R

Jasper L

Tête Jaune Cache

Moose L

Miette R

Swifts' farm

McLennan R

Cranberry L

Cowdung L
(Lucerne L)

Thunder R

Albreda R

Canoe R

Mt Brazeau

Clearwater R

Blue R

North Thompson R

MacDonalds'
ranch

Long L
(Lac des Roches)

Raft R

Mad R

Wire cache

Beaver L

Dunn L

Island L

Little Fort

Chu Chua

- - - Route from Strome, Alberta,
to the Cariboo,
April to August 1907

0   25   50   75

mi

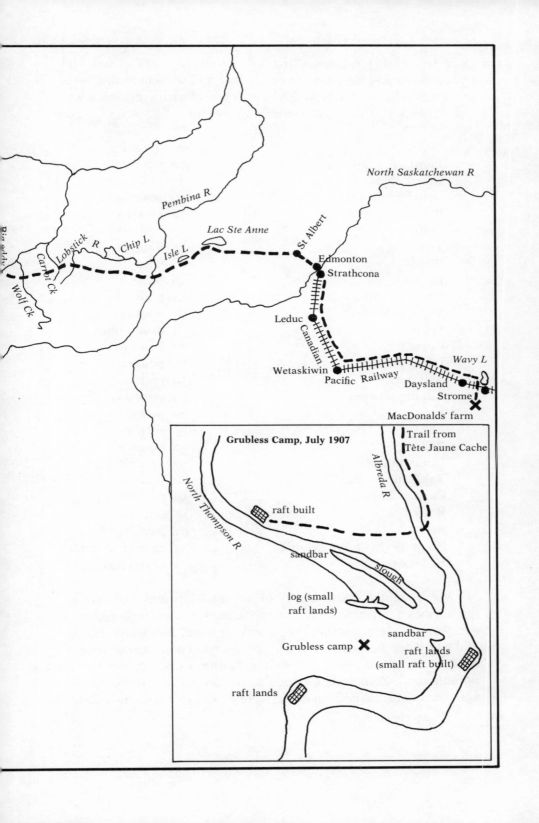

North Saskatchewan R

Pembina R

Lobstick R   Chip L   Isle L   Lac Ste Anne   St Albert

Carrot Ck

Big adder

Wolf Ck

Edmonton
Strathcona

Leduc

Canadian

Wetaskiwin
Pacific Railway

Wavy L

Daysland
Strome ✕
MacDonalds' farm

Grubless Camp, July 1907

Trail from
Tête Jaune Cache

Albreda R

North Thompson R

raft built

sandbar

slough

log (small
raft lands)

sandbar

Grubless camp ✕

raft lands
(small raft built)

raft lands

sions list. Father estimated that the trip would take us four or five months, and because we really had no idea where the next store might be, we knew we had better travel with everything we would need. Our list went something like this:

Sugar	200	pounds
Flour	300	pounds
Dried apples	25	pounds
Dried prunes	20	pounds
Raisins	10	pounds
Coffee	20	pounds
Tea	5	pounds
Beans	60	pounds
Bacon	150	pounds
Baking soda	4	pounds
Yeast cakes	1	package
Soap	1	dozen bars
Cornmeal	20	pounds
Dried potatoes	20	pounds
Salt pork	150	pounds
Baking powder	4	pounds
Lard	20	pounds
Salt	15	pounds
Pepper	2	pounds
Cinnamon	1	pound
Tapioca	10	pounds
Canned butter	50	pounds
Rolled oats	50	pounds
Rice	50	pounds
"Reindeer" condensed milk	1	case of 96 cans
Matches	2	dozen boxes

We bought a good supply of ammunition and two dozen horseshoes of assorted sizes. We took axes, wire pliers, augers, whetstones, five or six flat files, a pick, a shovel, handsaws, rasps and hammers. Father got a couple of new gold pans. In our medical kit we carried painkiller, iodine, Epsom salts, dry mustard, boracic acid, Zambuck, Carter's Little Liver Pills, some bandages, linament, carbolic acid, and a few things which I have long since forgotten. For extra clothes we packed bib overalls, heavy work shirts, socks, underwear, extra pairs of heavy work boots, denim jackets and wool mackinaws.

Then early on the morning of Saturday, 27 April, father had us scrambling out of our beds with: "Rise and shine, boys! The weather is fine, the sun is warm, there's not a cloud in the sky. So it's time for us to pack up and hit the trail for the Cariboo. We have a long way to go, and since we have no idea how long it'll take us, we better get going!"

We were on our way right after lunch and I have no doubt that we were the unlikeliest-looking pack train that ever left Strathcona. Father was a man who really appreciated good horses but he was plainly ashamed of half of these animals.

He led the way on a sandy-coloured mare appropriately called Sandy. She was a good all-round horse, though she was probably better as a packer than as a saddle horse. Behind him on a lead came our young stallion.

I came next driving my pack animals ahead and Dan followed with his; father was ready to give either of us a hand when we had trouble with an animal or a pack. Angus brought up the rear with his pack horses.

Jane came directly behind the young stallion in the pack line. She was a six-year-old bluish-roan Appaloosa of about 1,100 pounds who was terribly proud of her position as bell mare: she would kick any other horse that tried to get in front of her. She proved to be an excellent swimmer which made it easier for us when we had to make the horses swim a river along the trail. The next horse in the line was a French coach horse which had never been intended for anything but driving. He was completely nonplussed by a pack on his back and spent all his time trying to get rid of it. I followed him riding Lucy, a three-year-old Morgan and Arab cross mare who could run like a racehorse—a dark bay with brown shaded to black on her legs. Though she was a high-spirited horse, I still found her to be essentially gentle, and I rode her for many years after our great trip was over.

Behind me came Molly. Father had tried very hard not to buy any old horses but Molly must have been at least twelve years old when we set out from Strathcona. She had been an Indian cayuse and they had trained her to be a good pack horse, but she had become slow and poky with age. Jim was a sorrel gelding weighing about 900 pounds. I believe he was no more than six years old but he was a dependable animal. Both Jim and Molly were low-slung and barrel shaped.

Behind Jim came my brother Dan riding our hammer-headed, long-geared pinto which was never dignified by any name other than Pinto. That animal was so long in the body that he looked as if he needed another set of legs. He had a hump like a camel and crooked hind legs. It was father's decision that Dan should ride him since he was a real lightweight for his age, and Pinto turned out to be a good reliable mount, even if he did look strange.

Old Dan and Pete were Angus's first two pack animals, a pair of German coach horses bred to be drivers. Now, pack animals are supposed to be solid and chunky, but these two were tall and heavy, though they had little extra meat on them. They were so tall, in fact, that Angus darn near needed a ladder to put on their packs. Old Dan was about fourteen years old when father bought him, hardly in his prime. Pete, who was probably Old Dan's half-brother, was no more than eight or nine. Behind these two in the line came Big Billy, a dark brown gelding of about 1,100 pounds. At eight or nine years old, he was completely dependable and seemed to know exactly what was expected of him.

Angus brought up the rear riding Little Billy, a bay-coloured six-year-old Indian cayuse. He was no more than 850 pounds but he was stockily built and did his job well.

As we left Strathcona, father led the way as he did throughout our journey, but we nearly met with disaster before we even got out of town. A horseless carriage tried to crowd past and met a pair of horseshoes attached to the hind feet of our rangy French coach horse. It made quite a clatter and stirred up some excitement since the owner of the automobile was Mr. Alex Rutherford, Alberta's first premier, and he was riding in it at the time. When the commotion died down, we got our pack train moving again and made our way out of town.

Most of the horses were unused to packs so that first day we had the problem of their bucking their packs loose and scattering our provisions around the countryside. Each time this happened we would have to call a halt while we repacked, so it was almost dark before we reached St. Albert. We took our horses to the livery stable. Then since it was raining and there was no hotel and we were feeling fed up, we got the stable owner's permission to sleep in the hayloft. It was to be the last roof over our heads for the next sixteen weeks.

In the morning we woke up to the music of Sunday church bells from the nearby mission. While we prepared our packs, father held the livery stable owner in a long conversation about horses. The upshot was that the French coach stayed in St. Albert and we acquired one of the best saddle horses that we ever owned, a sorrel-coloured stock horse about six years old and so well trained that he was just a pleasure to ride. Father called him Frank, but I do not know to this day whether that was the name he came with or father rechristened him in honour of his first Frank. In any case, he was a fitting heir to the name.

We now set off on the road to Lac Ste. Anne about forty miles away. We took six days to cover this distance, camping out each night. We were in no hurry because father wanted to use this comparatively easy part of the journey to break the horses in to packing and teach them their correct positions in the line. This would save us a lot of crowding and confusion later on when we came to bad places on the trail.

One unexpected problem developed during these early days. Our young stallion Walter had to be watched constantly and kept away from the other horses. Though he was only a yearling he became possessive of the pack mares, and whenever one of the pack geldings came near a mare, Walter would attack kicking and, if we were not quick enough in separating them, biting the gelding in the neck, throwing him to the ground and then kneeling on him. We could not afford to lose any of our pack animals, so father realized regretfully that we could not take the stallion with us. We had had high hopes that he would sire our new herd on our far-off ranch but this could not be.

In 1907, Lac Ste. Anne was a bustling community consisting of one small hotel, a livery stable, an ice house, a post office, two stores, and a Mounted Police station with one lone constable. One of the stores belonged to the Hudson's Bay Company and was manned by factor Peter Gunn. These few establishments were the sum total of Lac Ste. Anne, but the size of the settlement had nothing to do with its importance.

For centuries it had been the spring fishing camp and meeting ground for the local Cree and Stoney Indians and for all the tribes of the adjoining prairies and the eastern slopes of the Rockies. When the Hudson's Bay Company sent its big dugout canoes up the Saskatchewan River to look for places to set up trading posts, this meeting place of the Indians seemed like a natural site. With the tremendous supply of whitefish and pike to be found in all the lakes and streams nearby, the Bay men knew they would never starve, and they knew they had the ideal location for capturing the fur trade. In time it became the focus of all social life in the area, because everyone going to or coming from the Yellowhead or the Athabasca passes went through Lac Ste. Anne. They came for supplies and to sell their furs and they came for news of the outside world.

In 1844, Father Thibault and Father Bourassa came searching for a site for a new mission and they chose a spot on the shore of the lake just east of the Hudson's Bay post. It was the fathers who named the lake after Ste. Anne de Beaupré, wiping out the old Indian name and the Hudson's Bay name, Devil's Lake. In 1852 the famous Father Lacombe arrived at the mission, and seven years later three sisters of the Grey Nun Order came to take up teaching and nursing duties.

When we arrived with our pack train on that May day in 1907, Father Lize had been the head of the mission for twenty years, and for eighteen of those years he had been leading a pilgrimage to the chapel of Ste. Anne de Beaupré on the Wednesday closest to 26 July, which is the saint's feast day. Indians, Métis and whites would travel 300 miles to take part in the pilgrimage and the giant feast that followed, and for days before and after there would be visiting back and forth between the camps along the lakeshore.

Although it was not Ste. Anne's feast day when we arrived, the community was a beehive of activity anyhow. We set up camp on the shore and made arrangements to pasture our horses in a field close by. After making up his mind to get rid of Walter, father had been worried that there might not be an opportunity to trade him, but now we could see this would not be a problem. Even as we pitched our tent, more and more people arrived, all of them mounted and leading pack animals. Someone here would want that stallion.

The next morning father found a Métis who was interested in our horse. He offered in trade a mare and her three-year-old colt, nice-looking horses, blocky and well built, so father agreed to trade. The mare became known by us as the Squaw Mare and we soon learned that she was a good pack horse but she would never make a saddle horse. Her colt, Jackie, a light tan-coloured horse of about 800 pounds, was a strong animal which we used for both riding and packing.

With two extra pack animals we needed two more pack saddles; then we could stock up on a few more supplies. The Métis told us about an old Indian who made them so we rode out to see him at his camp. Father knew a good saddle when he saw one; in the last forty years he had sat on more of them than chairs. He looked the old man's work over carefully.

"First rate," he said, and paid ten dollars for two of them without a word of complaint. That old Indian knew his craft.

We could hardly push our way into the Hudson's Bay store, it was so crowded with people. Up on the counter a good-looking young man stood tipsily, singing at the top of his voice. He was a fine tenor and knew all kinds of songs in French and Irish, German and English. He was putting on a great show and everyone was enjoying it thoroughly. Later, the factor Peter Gunn told us that the singer was one of three remittance men who had just arrived from England.

Of course, the crowd in the store had not come just to hear the young man sing. They were trappers recently arrived from the Rocky Mountains with their winter catch of furs, and prospectors heading in the opposite direction. Women and children had come to meet their menfolk who had been away all winter. Gunn was busy buying furs, and selling liquor, while the men settled their debts and gambled and made love and generally let their hair down.

In this atmosphere it was hard for us to get any business done, but we finally bought the things we had come there for and returned to our camp. The next day we made up packs for the two new horses and got everything ready for an early start. Life at Lac Ste. Anne at this time of year was a little too rich for the Mac-Donald blood. We were all glad to be off on the trail again, but I had no idea then that it was the last settlement I would see for four years.

With the addition of two new horses to our pack train, we had to juggle positions in the line. After father riding Frank, the dependable Big Billy and Jim were moved up behind the bell mare Jane. Dan now drove the cayuse Little Billy since Angus rode Sandy instead, as well as the new Squaw Mare. We put Jackie directly in front of Angus. From time to time we switched mounts to give the pack animals a rest because it is much easier for a horse to carry a 250-pound man than carry a pack of the same weight, which has no give. Sometimes we got down and walked beside our horses, especially when we had been travelling a long time without a few days' layover.

Lac Ste. Anne lay at the end of the wagon road. From now on we would follow Indian trails wherever they existed. Sometimes there would be no trail at all, or they were so poorly marked that we could not find them. In many, many places we would have to cruise out our own trail following streams and low-lying country as much as possible.

Indian trails are generally difficult to find because the Indians do not blaze trees as white men do. Instead, as they walk or ride along, every 300 or 400 yards and at every turning they break the end of a branch off, leaving it to hang down from the limb. I have ridden with Indians and watched them do this with one quick snap of the wrist. When they want to travel on that trail again they just look for these broken branches. Another challenge in following their trails was their infrequent use of an axe to cut a log or tree that had fallen across the trail. They took the time to find their way around such obstacles.

Although we were travelling the same route that the Overlanders had followed nearly fifty years earlier, we saw no sign of their passing. This was not really surprising because of the rapid growth of vegetation and the rough territory. Any trail markers that the Overlanders might have made had been blotted out by spring floods, winter storms and the rank growth of willows and birches.

As we left Lac Ste. Anne, Angus, Dan and I felt like real veterans of the trail. Most of our confidence, of course, we owed to father's instruction. There was not much he did not know about horses and life on the trail. He taught us that each horse must have its own outfit—blanket, saddle and pack: it was very important that the horse always keep the equipment it had become used to because it was less likely to get a sore back. Father had showed us just how to position the saddle blanket and pack saddle, how to put a cargo hitch onto the front and back forks of the saddle, how to balance the load and put on the canvas pack cover and, finally, how to place the all-important pack rope and to throw and tighten a diamond hitch to hold the pack in place. Some of the older pack animals had a few tricks that they would pull when we were saddling up. The horse would have taken and held a few big breaths so that we would think we were cinching tight, but as soon as we got out on the trail the pack would slide off. Father showed us how a good kick in the ribs as we cinched them up would let the air out. But then if you started cinching up too tight, you could get nipped in the elbow or the ribs. We had to learn to put that pack on just right.

On the trail, each of us boys tried to look after our own pack horses, but it was a comfort to know that father was always handy to help. So many things could go wrong, such as a horse bucking off its pack, or a pack coming loose, or a horse bogging down in a mud hole. Sometimes one of the pack animals, especially Pete or Old Dan because they were so tall, would get stuck between two trees growing close together—with the pack jammed in tight—unable to go forward or back. Then we would have to either cut down one tree or unpack the horse.

The pack horses established their seniority and their proper places in the line within a few days and after that the line was strictly maintained. They would take their places automatically. They could recognize a campsite, too, even if it hadn't been used for several years. When they approached one in midafternoon, all of them would break into a run, stop in the middle and wait to be unpacked. If we happened to think it was too early to camp, we had one heck of a job getting that bunch of knot-headed cayuses to hit the trail again. They seemed to think we were trying to get them to work overtime without extra pay.

They developed another little trick that wasted a lot of time. In the morning they would gather in a patch of thick bush or trees and stand absolutely still. Even Jane, our bell mare, would stand like a statue to keep her bell from ringing. There we would be, finished breakfast and all ready to ride out, but first we had to find that foxy bunch of broom-tails. We would look everywhere, stopping here and there to listen. Not a sound. We could ride within fifty yards of the grove where they were hiding and not see or hear them. Then finally old Jane would give them away when the flies and mosquitoes got too much for her and she had to shake her head. Just for mornings like this, father had us picket one of the horses near camp for the night so we would have it to ride while looking for the rest.

Although all of us were handy at cooking, it became my particular job when we were on the trail. I guess this was because I was the youngest and father thought cooking would be easier for me than taking care of the horses or setting up the tent. Besides, I had had plenty of experience in Alberta and my cooking had improved with practice. Cooking over a campfire, however, was an altogether different matter. Once again, it was father who instructed in the niceties of campfire cuisine. He showed me how to carry a sourdough jug on my saddle horse so that every evening I could make sourdough for the next day. Sourdough batter is a mixture of flour and water with a little bit of yeast added, though you can start the fermentation just as well using the water that rice or potatoes have been boiled in. (I have also used sour milk or buttermilk but these were not available on the trail.) Most of the time I used yeast as we had brought a good supply with us.

My sourdough jug was actually a four-quart kettle with a tight-fitting lid, and I kept it tied to my saddle horn to keep it warm and to make sure it didn't spill. At night, I stuffed it under my bedroll to keep its temperature just right and prevent the yeast from "dying," which gave me and my clothes a distinctly sour odour most of the time. To make biscuits or bread I mixed some of the batter with more flour to make a stiff dough, and for pancakes I thinned it with water. I had trouble keeping it from getting too sour, but I learned that a little baking soda would kill the excessively sour taste. One trick that father showed me was how to mix the dough right in the sack of flour by rolling back the top of the sack to make a ring, then making a deep hole in the flour, pouring in some of the batter from the jug, and stirring flour into it from around the hole. When the mixture reached the right texture, I put it into a galvanized kettle with a tight lid and placed it in a hole at the base of the campfire, right beside my kettle of beans and bacon or maybe beans and pork.

I put a green willow sapling through the wire bails, or handles, of the kettles to hold them upright, then supported the sapling on top of a couple of flat stones. I covered the kettles with hot sand and coals. As a rule, I did all this just before going to bed. In the morning we used a green willow hook to get hold of the handles and pull the kettles out of the ashes. When they were all cleaned off, we removed the lids and there was our breakfast of hot bread, beans and bacon or pork.

Dessicated or dried potatoes were a great help in making meals. They came looking like dried brownish shoestrings but they kept well for months. Just a handful of them put into a pan with bacon and water made a meal for the four of us. And we learned to love father's old standby of rice with dried fruit or raisins.

For washing dishes I used the gold pans that father had packed for so many years. In fact, when he got ready for a trip, those two pans and his prospector's pick were always the first things he put in his packsack. Father did not mind my using the pans for washing up or for mixing sourdough because we could carry only a minimum of cooking utensils with us, but I had to be careful to place them over a pile of hot coals after I had used them so that any grease or oil residue would burn off. When panning, small flakes of gold or gold colour will be floated away if there is even a trace of grease in the pan.

Very quickly, we developed routines for camping that were quite efficient and ensured that we got fed as quickly as possible. As soon as we stopped for the night, I would catch the horse that was carrying the kitchen equipment, unpack it, select a place for a campfire, get it burning and prepare supper. I needed a good bed of coals for cooking so I had to get that fire going fast. Next I set off to get water for cooking and cleaning up, then got the supper grub into the fire to cook, and mixed up some sourdough loaves. These loaves were the basis of our noon meal, too: each of us carried our own light lunch of sourdough bread sandwiches with filling of bacon or venison steaks or sometimes fried fish, jerky or smoked meat. The lunches were packed into cloth bags which we tied to our saddles. Once in a while we would stop to make coffee for lunch if we felt we could spare the time to make a fire, but as a rule we just had a few gulps of refreshing cold water.

Each night while I prepared dinner, Dan, Angus and father attended to the other chores, looking after the horses, putting up the tent and cutting and laying spruce boughs for our beds. These boughs were lapped one over another with the bowed side up. Properly done, this made a comfortable bed and kept us off the damp ground. Canvas was spread on top of the boughs and then blankets were rolled out ready for the occupant.

After supper was over, the dishes washed and the food put away so the bears couldn't get it, we would build up a big fire and sit around and relax. Then father would tell us of his prospecting adventures, about his escape from Grey Eagle, and his terrible journey down the Arrow Lakes. He would talk about his lumbering days and about all his brothers and sisters in the Ottawa Valley and about our grandmother who had lived in a castle. He would speak of our mother and how he came to marry her, and he would look fondly at Dan because of all of us boys only Dan resembled her with his gentle blue eyes. Though we had heard all the stories before, we listened intently. No one could tell a story like father could.

Two days out from Lac Ste. Anne, we found ourselves riding in a mixture of snow and rain, our hands blue from the cold as we gripped the reins. Hunched over in my saddle, I was thinking unhappily about building a fire and cooking dinner with the rain running down my neck, when the trail suddenly broke into a clearing. In the centre was a log shack and a small barn. This was the homestead of three young men, the Yates brothers, who were at work clearing land and making the improvements necessary to get a crown grant. They called their place Hobo Ranch.

The Yates were pleased to have company, for they led a very lonely life, and they gave us permission to pitch our tent in their yard. It was too early for grass but they sold us some hay for our horses. Meanwhile, I had been thinking of a way to avoid a wet campfire, and I told the Yates brothers that if they would let me use their stove, I would cook dinner for all of us. After all, if you are cooking for four, three more makes little difference. I still had some fresh potatoes and carrots bought in Lac Ste. Anne and our hosts provided fresh fish, so we had a good meal and a lively chat before it was time to turn in.

The Yates brothers told us a lot about the country just ahead of us, and when I asked where they had caught the delicious fish, they took us outside: it was just a little creek behind the house, no more than four feet wide but quite deep. In it were literally hundreds of fish, mostly jackfish or pike, about eighteen inches long, slender but solid. The brothers explained that they speared them with ordinary six-tined hayforks. When we tried our luck, in an hour we had all the fish we wanted. We cleaned them, sprinkled a little salt inside each one, then wrapped them in wet burlap sacking. When we packed our horses the next morning, we placed the fish on top of the pack covers to keep them out in the cool air, and in this way they stayed in good condition for a couple of days.

It was shortly after leaving Hobo Ranch that the first real mishap of the trip occurred. We were passing a small pond when Little Billy decided to lie down in the water: he was trying to roll his pack off. It was not the first time that one of the pack horses had pulled this stunt, but the tragedy this time was that Little Billy was carrying two 100-pound sacks of sugar! There was no more than two feet of water in the pond but it was enough to get his pack thoroughly wet before we could pull him to his feet. The sugar was well soaked. For days afterwards, the pack dripped syrup over the saddle, the saddle blankets, the ropes and Little Billy's flanks. Every evening we had to take a bucket of warm water and wash him and his whole outfit down.

On the first warm day, we camped over and tried to dry the sugar out without much success. Finally, it dried into a rock-solid mass, and after that whenever we needed sugar we had to chop a piece off with an axe and pound it in a canvas bag with a stick or a rock. This was wasteful and time-consuming but since it was all the sugar we had with us, we had no choice. Little Billy, of course, was not very popular with us, and we rechristened him

Sugar Billy, the sweetest little horse that ever went through the Yellowhead.

At two o'clock one afternoon we came to the Pembina River. The water was very high and swift from the melting snows, so we turned south and rode upstream from the regular crossing till a mile later we came to an old campsite. Just opposite it on the far side of the river was a ledge of coal that must have been at least forty feet high. Dan and Angus and I got excited and talked of staking it and making our fortunes.

Father shook his head. "Don't get your hopes up. That ledge must have been staked years and years ago."

We simmered down and began unpacking the horses and making camp. We would have to cross the river here but it was now too late in the day.

The Pembina was really not too deep for fording, but father, knowing we would have bigger and more dangerous rivers to cross farther on, decided this would be a good place to give us our first lesson in rafting a river. As usual, he was teaching us another valuable lesson. I never remember him being stumped for the answer to what to do next; he was an expert on just about everything.

To build the raft, he first scouted for dry spruce trees and instructed us to cut eight of them about twenty feet long. Then he got out the small horse collar and light single harness: we had been very puzzled about his reason for bringing it but now we found out why. Putting the harness on Sugar Billy, we hauled the logs to the river bank. We then cut two green spruce trees about eight inches in diameter and brought them to the river bank as well. The raft that father now had us assemble used no nails; it was the kind of raft unique to the Ottawa Valley logging camps.

He showed us how to lay the green spruce logs on the river bank ten or twelve feet apart with the small ends of both projecting out over the water, then place the dry spruce logs across them so they were parallel to the river. Finally we laced crosspieces to the logs with our pack ropes, making a good strong raft. Two poles about six feet long and two and a half to three inches in diameter were used as handspikes to pry the raft into the river.

While we loaded our supplies and pack saddles, the raft was

tied securely to trees along the bank. Next we saddled our horses and crossed the river. Father rode Frank and led my Lucy; the pack horses followed, and Dan and Angus brought up the rear. The horses had to swim for a short distance in the deepest part, but the crossing gave us no trouble.

When we reached the other side, Father and Angus rode back into the water to get the raft. Just before they untied it, they sent back their saddle horses, and then pushed off into the current. When they reached our side, Dan and I caught the raft, unloaded it and untied our valuable lashings. Once again we loaded the pack animals and set off on the trail.

The land on the west side of the river was quite level with just the occasional mud hole, so it was easy travelling. Just to the north of our trail was a fair-sized river called the Lobstick which we followed for several days, crossing a number of small streams which flowed into it. Eventually, the trail crossed the Lobstick itself, but by this time it was only a small stream and gave us no problems. We could tell that the place where we camped that evening had been a major Indian campground because we found the remains of dozens of old campfires and a lot of tepee poles leaning against the trees nearby. The people had come here to catch spring fish which came up the creeks as soon as the ice was gone. The Lobstick was already choked with fish and we caught as many as we could eat or salt to take with us.

A couple of days later when we crossed Carrot Creek, we found signs of another large Indian encampment. It had been used for so many years that all the trees near the creek had been used for firewood and we had to travel quite a distance to cut wood. After supper we stood watching the fish struggling up the stream to spawn.

"Well, the Indians didn't catch them all," I said.

"There's more than Indians come fishing here," said father. "Bears hang around spawning creeks, too. Remember, this is grizzly country."

We became more watchful after his reminder. It was now May and the weather was more pleasant, so father gave us all a break. The horses needed a few days' rest and grazing, for they were beginning to show the lack of good feed, and we needed time to mend our pack gear and wash clothes. Of course, we took time to fish as well, salting some of our catch to take with us. Sometimes we had the feeling that if we took off our undershirts we might find fish bones sticking out of our hides!

We hit the first muskeg a few days later. Time and again, the horses got stuck in the mud, and sometimes even had to be unpacked before we could get them out. We made only a half dozen miles a day.

After crossing Wolf Creek we camped for two days. We washed the muskeg off our clothes and off the horses and packs, then sat by the creek to haul out trout and jackfish. Father and Angus went off into the hills to hunt and came back with a two-year-old buck. Fresh meat certainly tasted great after the beans, bacon and fish we had been living on for so long. After supper, we cut some of the remaining meat into strips, salted it and left it in a pile overnight. In the morning we hung it on a rack and smoked it a little to help dry it. In this way we were able to pack it with us when we broke camp on the third morning. From then on, each night when we made camp we smoked it a little more until it was well cured. I used to cook up this venison, chopped into small pieces, with rice and bacon for a welcome change from bacon and beans.

After the crossing at Wolf Creek, the trail followed the creek north through low, swampy country with a lot of willows and other scrubby trees. Our pack train was strung out in its usual order with father in the lead looking out for the best trail, me next driving three pack horses, then Dan with his three, and finally Angus with his three. Toward midmorning, the trail worked its way up onto a ridge. On the right-hand side there was a steep drop-off to Wolf Creek about forty or fifty feet below; on the left was muskeg. Acres of it. This left only a strip of solid ground seven or eight feet wide for the trail. Father led the way slowly and cautiously. All we needed was one horse to stray a couple of feet from the centre of the trail or try to crowd past another one and we would lose a horse over the cliff or into that bottomless muskeg.

As we moved out along the ridge, Dan and Angus and their pack animals lagged a little behind so that father and I and my three pack horses were alone when we rounded a bend to find that the trail had narrowed to no more than four feet, then opened out ahead into a small clearing to the right of the trail. We moved cautiously onto the narrow section, and were almost across, when entering the clearing from the opposite side came a huge, shaggy grey animal. We were horrified. It had to be a grizzly, yet it was so huge and such a strange colour that we just stared.

In the second or two that father and I sat staring at the animal, our horses got whiff of him and all hell broke loose. They screamed and snorted, whirled around and headed back down the trail toward Edmonton, trying to buck their packs off as they went. The three horses I was driving, Jane, Big Billy and Jim, being closer to the grizzly got a stronger smell and a closer look. They went completely berserk. Unable to get past the horses behind us they whirled sharply right, plunged off the trail and instantly sank into the mud. Only their packs held them up. But even in the mud they still struggled to escape the bear and they worked themselves down deeper and deeper. The bear, meanwhile, had long since vanished over the cliff.

Father and I calmed our saddle horses and tied them to a tree. Dan's and Angus's horses were all safe, though their packs were scattered.

"Put the single harness on Sugar Billy and bring him up here," father shouted. "We'll need him!"

Father and I began the rescue. He told me to get the axe I always carried in a scabbard under Lucy's stirrup leather and cut and trim some small trees. We placed the trunks across the surface of the muskeg so that they lay around the horses, then laid the limbs across them just as if we were making a very lightweight raft. On this contraption we could crawl out to work around the horses and get their packs off without sinking into the mud ourselves. Once we had the packs off, father told us to leave the saddles on so that we would have something to fasten ropes to.

"Now we'll need pry poles," said father.

We cut four of them sixteen feet long and three inches in diameter. Then we fastened our lasso ropes to our trusty bell mare Jane who was closest to solid ground. We carried the ends of our lassoes to our three strongest saddle horses, Frank, Lucy and Sandy, and to Sugar Billy and spread the horses along the trail. Father stayed to lead Sugar Billy while we boys took one turn of our lassoes around our saddle horns then ran them back to Sugar Billy and hooked them to his singletree. Now we were ready. We mounted our horses.

"'Everybody ready...Pull!" yelled father.

It did not work.

There was not much room to work in so when we had to stop almost right away to take up the slack, poor old Jane sank back into the mud, more terrified than before.

"This time when you pull," father ordered, "keep your line taut until I tell you to take up your slack. We'll do it one at a time. Ready? Pull!"

It worked. Each of us took up the slack in his rope as father called out to us, while Jane held her new position closer to safety. Another pull and she moved to solid ground. One more pull and she was out.

One look at the other horses told us we had taken too long to save the packs and Jane. Big Billy and Jim had sunk so deep that only their necks and heads were above the mud. Father got his rifle and ended their suffering. It was a sad thing to have to do to horses that had been so reliable and faithful, but we could not leave them there to suffer.

My brother Dan found an easy place to get down the cliff and led poor Jane down to the creek to wash her off. There was no one like Dan for a way with animals and when we were ready to pack up again, Jane was almost her old self. Angus, father and I rounded up the other horses and then began searching the bushes for the stuff that had been bucked off. We were very nervous as we pushed through the brushwood knowing the grizzly might be prowling somewhere nearby. But our search had to go on because we were miles from civilization and we could not abandon sorely needed supplies in the bush. Although father had had a lot of experience with grizzlies when he wandered over the mountains looking for minerals, and though he had told us many stories about them, this was the first encounter for my brothers and me and it had been a shattering experience. Father tried to shore up our courage by saying that the bear must have been very old judging by his colour, and that he was most likely as frightened as we were and had headed for high country right after the encounter. We were not reassured.

At last we got everything gathered up, the horses repacked and ready to go on our way. Father rearranged the line-up, giving me Molly and Jackie to follow Jane, leaving my brothers with two horses each. The provisions in the packs of the two dead horses were divided among all the others. It was a very subdued and wary train that finally continued on its way.

About an hour later the trail left the ridge and returned to creek level again, and shortly after we found a good camping place beside the water. The next morning we were packed and on our way early, partly because we had lost so much time the day before and partly because we were still nervous in this area. At noon we stopped briefly for lunch and checked the packs.

The trail wound along the creek bank for another mile or two, then abruptly descended a very steep bank into a clearing that had been made by centuries of wood gathering by the Indians who had camped there. And right there beside the creek were two young grizzlies feeding on jackfish! They were not more than two years old but that was old enough for them to have that grizzly bear smell. Our horses stampeded. Fortunately, this time there was no muskeg for them to dive into and the steep bank we had just come down prevented them from getting very far. By the time we had them under control, the young bears had disappeared down the creek. We breathed a sigh of relief to see that our trail led west from the clearing, away from that grizzly creek.

The country we entered was lightly timbered, with rolling hills, long level stretches and very little mud. We could afford to relax a bit as we rode along, and for several days we made good time. Then one afternoon we realized that our easy riding had come to an end: from the brow of a hill we could see the mighty McLeod River in all its wild beauty — it was in spring flood by this time, gorged with the icy waters of the Rocky Mountain snow fields. We paused there on the crest of the hill and had a good long look at it.

I turned to look at my brothers. They were older than I was but they were just as scared. We had never seen anything in our lives before like that treacherous piece of water and we knew we had to cross it.

Father's face was unchanged. He had crossed worse rivers than this one, and I really believe that he liked nothing better than this kind of challenge. We took heart from his calm face and started down the hill.

We made camp on the river bank. Nearby were a lot of trees killed by forest fire some years earlier.

"They'll be just right for our raft," said father.

Since we had already built one raft, we were able to proceed with fewer instructions from father. Before dark we had cut the timbers, ten of them about ten inches in diameter and twenty-four feet long, and some others half as thick and eight feet long for crosspieces. Then we harnessed Sugar Billy and snaked them all to the river bank. The next morning, we laid out the logs as father had taught us and lashed the whole thing together. When it was ready, father made two sweeps about twelve feet long and fastened one at each end of the raft. In the middle of the raft we built a platform of small poles about ten inches above the deck to hold those things that had to be kept dry.

In midafternoon while we were still at work on the raft, three men on saddle horses leading four pack horses arrived at the river bank. They made camp nearby, then came over to intro-duce themselves. One of them was a huge man at least six feet five with massive shoulders, and the kind of face that makes you grab tight hold of your wallet. His name, he told us, was Bill Spittal. The other two were brothers by the name of Monahan, fine-looking Irishmen and obviously well educated. The younger one told us later, in fact, that he would be entering the priesthood when this trip was over. The three of them were on their way to inspect a placer mine that Spittal had discovered on a creek about ten miles west of Tête Jaune Cache. The Monahans had been sent out by the company that had grubstaked Spittal to make sure that the claim was as good as he said it was.

"What do you say we share your raft?" said Spittal.

Father didn't even look up from his work. "No," he said. "That's impossible. With all your saddles and supplies, plus the weight of the three of you, the raft would be completely over-loaded. Even if it didn't go under, it would still be too hard to handle."

Spittal's face looked dangerous but father still had not looked up.

He continued, "But I'll tell you what. If you cut your own logs, one of my boys will take Sugar Billy and haul them to the river bank for you."

Spittal agreed because he had no choice and the three of them set off to cut the necessary logs. Father instructed them just as he had instructed me and my brothers, while Dan snaked their logs down to a spot near our raft.

All this work had barely begun when another man on a saddle horse driving five pack horses appeared on the hill above us. Things were sure picking up on the bank of that wild river, and if it kept up we would soon have a full-fledged town.

The newcomer was Fred Stephens, but he was one man who was capable of looking after himself. He told us he was going first to the Smoky River and then to the Brazeau River country to trade with the Indians for furs. He had a fine outfit — good horses and equipment. An old hand at this kind of life, he asked for no help from anyone. He set up camp and went right to work getting logs for his own raft.

The following day when all three rafts were ready for the crossing, we herded the horses into the river and made them swim across. We watched their progress anxiously for they would give us an idea of the currents and the speed of the river. They were swept about a mile downriver, then we could see that Jane had touched bottom and she led the rest of them up the opposite bank. Being well trail-broken, they would graze there until their owners came for them.

Father was pleased with the horses' passage because it looked like a fairly simple crossing. Stephens was the first to push off and he landed quite close to the spot where the horses had come out of the river. Then Spittal and the two Monahans got ready to take off. They climbed aboard their raft, removed their boots and piled them on top of the load; then each took a long pull from the two-gallon keg of whiskey they had on board.

"Here we go to 'Frisco!" they hollered as they cast off.

From our vantage point on the bank we could see they were in for trouble. They had no idea how to angle the raft so that the current would take it across. As a result, it was heading downstream at a terrific pace, still on our side of the river. They had been caught in the current along the bank which was pushing them right into the "sweepers" or low-hanging branches dipping into the swollen river.

"Use your sweeps!" we shouted, but they were so busy dodging branches and snatching at articles being swept off the raft that they had no time to man the sweeps. It is sheer luck that none of them was knocked into the river, but before the raft disappeared around a bend, they had finally caught a current which took them out into midstream.

Before we turned our raft loose, father gave us a short lecture on the proper way to cross a river on a raft. He explained that when a large, swift river is in flood, it is higher in the middle than along the shore, so you must get your raft well out into the river as fast as possible. We all nodded to show we understood, but in reality the performance of Spittal and the Monahans had undermined our confidence.

"All right, let's go," father said quietly.

We turned the raft loose. Each of us taking a twelve-foot pole, we shoved hard on the river bottom. Father and Angus then manned the long sweeps, using them to keep the raft at the angle that would push it toward the far bank. Considering the size of the raft and the fact that most of the crew were green kids, we made a good crossing, landing close to Stephens's raft. There was no sign of the other three men.

Dan grabbed the halters from the raft and went to collect the horses on the sidehill. Then, while father and Angus unloaded the raft and dismantled it, Dan and I saddled up and began packing.

We searched through the willows for the trail and followed it upstream till we came to a sharp bend in the river where a huge eddy had formed. It was known to those who used this route as the "Big Eddy." There was a fine sandy beach which made a good campsite. Emptying into the upper end of the eddy was a big creek that had been christened Rock Creek, which we found an ideal place to catch Dolly Varden trout, a fine change from jackfish.

Nearby on the bank of the river in a little log cabin lived a tall slim man about forty-five years old who told us that he was there to take care of some groceries and supplies which were stacked on a long platform outside. It had been built a foot or so off the ground and covered with a tarpaulin. These provisions had been freighted in during the winter by teams and sleighs over the frozen lakes and rivers in readiness for the survey crews coming through for the new Grand Pacific Railway.

We set up camp a little distance from the cabin and Stephens set up his close by, but in a short while he came over to chat. This cordiality was something new on his part so we suspected there had been a change in his attitude toward us. Before the crossing he had obviously thought that father was a feeble old man and we boys were three babes-in-the-woods. I guess he was afraid we might become a liability to him if he had anything to do with us. Now, having seen the capable way father managed the crossing and the efficient way we young fellows had handled ourselves and the raft, and then quickly organized ourselves on landing, he had changed his mind.

"Mr. MacDonald," he said, "we'll be travelling in the same direction for some time to come."

Father nodded.

"Would you object if I joined your party?"

Father nodded again. "You might just as well move your stuff over here, Mr. Stephens. No use making two campfires."

After we moved his gear over to our camp, he and father set off to look for the three missing men. In the meantime, I got a fire going and started cooking supper; Angus and Dan set up the tent and cut the spruce boughs needed for our beds. Father had instructed us to set up a good camp since we were going to stay a few days. There was good grass here for the horses and it was important to our survival to keep them in shape.

Father and Stephens returned just as I had dinner prepared, for it had gotten too dark to look any farther in the thick bush. They would have to go out again in the morning. We rolled in early as we were all played out by the strenuous work and excitement of the day.

At daybreak, father and Stephens breakfasted, saddled their horses and started off on the search once more, en route rounding up the saddle horses belonging to the three men.

About midmorning they met the younger Monahan plunging

through the bush in search of their horses, but the poor man was so worked up over their experiences that he had forgotten to bring either ropes or halters.

"But you're all safe?" asked father in an effort to calm the man's babbling.

"Aye, all but my brother!" he said wildly.

"Your brother is lost?" asked Stephens.

"Nay," said the young Monahan. "'Tis his boots that are lost! They were knocked overboard!"

It seems that his brother's only pair of boots had been swept off the raft by a sweeper as they careened down the river. Monahan mounted his horse and the three continued on to the place where the castaways waited for him. There, Stephens took off his own boots and offered them to the older Monahan.

If they fit, you can wear them," he said. "I have some more boots and mocassins in my pack." He rode back to camp barefoot.

Our next prolonged stopover was at a place called Round Prairie. According to Stephens, it would probably be the last time the horses could get a good feed before crossing the Athabasca River. As usual, when we set up camp, father chose one horse to be picketed nearby in case we had to use it to wrangle the horses. This time he chose the colt Jackie; he threw a saddle on him and rode toward a bunch of willows to picket him. Suddenly a large sandhill crane, squalling and flapping its wings, rushed into their path, and it was more than a fat, saucy colt could stand. He put on a streak of bucking and pitching that would have brought them to their feet at the Calgary Stampede. But father's riding form would have won him first prize at any rodeo. At sixty-eight he could still ride with the best of them, and my brothers and I stood there open-mouthed with admiration. Stephens, who had started to run toward father and then realized he needed no help, was clearly amazed. That night around the campfire, we got father to retell the story of how he had earned a horse from old Grey Eagle. We thought Stephens would enjoy it.

The next day we rode among young trees in pleasantly rolling country; the sun was shining. Up ahead, I could hear father singing, and behind me Dan whistled a tune that more or less followed father's. Suddenly father reined in his horse and his song died. We drew up beside him, and Dan stopped whistling. We had come out onto a ridge above the wide Athabasca Valley; the thing that riveted our attention was the Athabasca River which we could see about a half mile away. It had already flooded its banks and even at this distance we could see uprooted trees being swept downriver. The roar of the flood waters was deafening.

We got the train moving again and rode along the ridge, never taking our eyes off the river. We knew we had to cross that terrible water, but we certainly could not cross it at this point. We left the ridge after a while and followed the trail down into the valley, but the closer we got to the river the more awesome and spectacular it appeared. For the next three days we rode beside it, judging its speed, watching the currents, looking for the right place to cross. At night we were all subdued as we camped. There was no whistling or singing. Even Angus forgot to whittle one of the bits of wood that he usually spent his evenings shaping. Father and Stephens would wander off to look at the river after supper, calculating our chances of rafting it safely.

On the third evening, just before dark, another man joined our campfire. His name was Donald MacDonald, the same as my brother Dan, but his nickname was "Mac." His father was a Hudson's Bay factor and his mother was a full breed Indian. A man of forty-five or fifty, he was at least six feet four and weighed about 250 pounds, all of it muscle. He was as active and agile as a kid in spite of his size, and as fast as lightning on his feet.

He told us he was on his way to Tête Jaune Cache and that he had three men and fifty head of pack horses following. They were carrying provisions for a man by the name of Finch who was planning to build a store there to be ready for business when the survey crews arrived later in the summer.

Mac knew the trail we were on very well, and told us he was going to block it off ahead of us at Disaster Point.

"There's a bad slide just beyond that point," he said. "It's too easy for a horse to lose its footing and slide right down into the Athabasca so I've cut a new trail to go around it. Since I'm going to be on my way before you, I'll mark where the new trail starts."

"How far is it from here?" father asked.

"Maybe three hours' ride."

Father thanked him for his kindness and told him we were not anxious to lose any more horses. Then we all chimed in to tell him about the loss of Big Billy and Jim.

"You were lucky you didn't lose the lot," Mac exclaimed. "I know one packer who lost forty mules in that same muskeg when they smelled a grizzly. You'd be wise to leave your horse bells on when you're in this country. Bears are shy animals and won't come around if you give them warning you're coming."

We thanked him for the advice and followed it religiously after that. We had no more trouble with bears.

Mac told us about some wonderful hot springs a little way back from the river. Angus, Dan and I wanted to go and see them but father and Stephens were anxious to move on the next day.

In the morning, Mac left several hours before us and, just as he had promised, marked the detour clearly. We followed his new trail until we came to Roche Miette, an enormous rock cliff towering a couple of thousand feet above the river. Mac was waiting there for us, for this was where the trail crossed the Athabasca River. We camped on a lovely grassy field and went to have a look at the crossing. It was a wild and wicked-looking river, but it was a lot tamer here than it had been farther downstream.

"It doesn't look very deep, but it's far too swift to ford," father said.

Mac nodded. "I wouldn't put a raft in either. It'd take you miles downstream and you'd still be on this side."

Suddenly I could see us all going downstream like Spittal and the Monahans, all our provisions swept into the river.

"See that island over there?" Mac pointed to a long narrow island close to the far bank and less than half a mile downstream from where we stood. Between it and the bank was a shallow slough.

"There's a towpath on that island, and there's a longer one running down this side from where we are. Under the willows just along there I've got a dugout canoe. If you'll all help, I'll take your outfit across."

We towed the canoe to the upstream end of the path where the pack horses were waiting and loaded provisions aboard. Mac climbed in with my brother Dan and they started across, but hard as that big man paddled, they were still swept down to the farthest tip of the little island. There they unloaded the canoe. Then, with Mac standing in the stern, Dan took hold of the tow-rope and began towing it up the length of the island while Mac poled. Dan climbed back in and once more Mac began paddling furiously, this time to get back to our side of the river, but as fast as he paddled the current carried the boat downstream so that they landed nearly a mile from the place where we waited.

I ran down the towpath to meet them, grabbed the towrope and began pulling. Mac poled and I tugged and after a while we arrived back where the others waited to load the canoe again. On the second trip, Dan and Mac beached the canoe at almost the same spot they had landed the time before. We watched them climb out and start wading ashore with supplies on their shoulders.

Then suddenly from up the river we heard a strange sort of roar and around the curve came a waterspout of immense size, sucking the river up as it approached us. There must have been millions of gallons of water going up into the air in that twister. I glanced across the river and there was the canoe sitting its full length on absolutely high and dry ground. Then within thirty seconds, the water was back to its normal level. If that water-spout had come a few minutes earlier there would have been a couple of Donald MacDonalds sailing around the sky in a dugout canoe. It was some few minutes before anyone was ready to go back to work.

Dan and Mac finished unloading and brought the canoe up the island, but this time Dan did not get back in. Mac sat down, grabbed his paddle and started across, but in the middle of the river the canoe seemed to go straight up on end, then rolled over, pitching Mac into the water. But he had not survived thirty years on the trails and rivers of northwestern Canada just to be stopped by an accident like this. Within seconds he reared up out of the water with the paddle still clutched in one hand and grabbed the overturned canoe with the other. All this time both man and canoe were being swept downstream in the terrific current, though at least being pushed toward our bank.

Just beyond the end of the towpath on our side of the river a long, slender sweeper extended out over the water. Under this sweeper went the canoe. I saw Mac's head duck and vanish and then come up on the downstream side. Instantly he threw his weight onto the sweeper, clamping it to the bottom of the up-turned canoe. He had brought it to a halt. With his fast reflexes, cool head and quick thinking he had not only saved his own life, but also the all-important canoe and paddles.

The moment I saw the canoe upset I had hollered to the others waiting at the landing to come as fast as they could. They were at least half a mile away but they heard me; I guess the great set of lungs that Nature gave me were intended for this sort of emergency. Father, Angus and Stephens were there minutes after Mac arrived at the sweeper. Carefully, we worked our way out along the tree and caught hold of the towrope. Then father and I held on to Stephens while he got a good grip on Mac and pulled him out of the water.

While I towed the canoe up to the landing the others helped Mac to camp, stripped off his wet clothes and gave him a good stiff rubdown to get his blood circulating again. They got dry clothes from his pack and built up the fire so that he could toast himself. I made coffee and Stephens dug out the 35 overproof Hudson's Bay rum that he kept in his pack, so that we could finish off Mac's cure with a cup of laced hot coffee.

We were all glad that Dan had not been in the canoe as he would surely have drowned. Although father had taught us all to be resourceful, none of us had ever had to call on presence of mind to cope with a river in full flood.

The next job was rounding up the horses, herding them into the water and making them swim to the other side. For a while it looked as though they would never make it to the island for they were being carried farther and farther downstream, but the river was not as swift on the other side and just as we were becoming anxious, Jane angled up against the current. The others followed her, and minutes later they all struggled up onto the beach.

The next load was the pack saddles so I went along to begin catching and saddling the horses. Angus came with the next load, and father and Stephens came last. We were all very grateful to Mac for his kindness, even risking his life for a bunch of strangers. We wanted to pay him but he refused to take anything.

"I was glad to do it," he protested. "Besides, I had nothing else to do except sit here until my pack train catches up with me."

Everything we possessed was now on the island. I had saddled the horses and all that remained to be done was to load the pack horses. We wished our friend Mac the best of luck and headed off into the slough that separated us from the mainland. The vicious Athabasca was behind us. Mac set up camp on the island and would cross back to the other side when his pack train arrived.

After four hours' travel we came to a likely looking campsite — near a stream where there was plenty of horse feed and many signs of deer. While we made camp, Angus took the rifle and went looking for fresh meat. He was back in an hour with a small buck thrown across his horse. He told us that when he had shot the deer, he had flushed out a herd of mountain sheep on the hillside above him, but just watched them run away. We had all the meat we could use with that deer. As usual, we ate some of it fresh and salted the rest to smoke each night when we camped.

In the morning, we forded the stream easily and entered a beautiful meadow full of wildflowers. In the centre were the remains of a house, though just an outline of rotting logs and part of a stone fireplace were all that was left to show what it had looked like. The fireplace had been a work of art. Someone had made a frame of willow boughs plastered over with wet clay, then built the stonework around it; when a fire was built in the fireplace it had baked the clay and burnt out the willows, leaving their imprint in the clay forever.

We realized that this must be the remains of Jasper House, which had been abandoned in the early 1880s, and the meadow that we were standing in had been used to pasture the pack horses that the Hudson's Bay had kept here in the early days of the Yellowhead pack trains. The creek we had just crossed had therefore been the Snake Indian River, and our campground of last night had been close to the spot where a band of the Snake or Carrier Indians had been massacred by the Assiniboines around 1830.

We made good progress the next few days, for although we were climbing into the mountains, the grade was slight and there was little mud or brush to slow us down. The Snaring River was not too deep to ford and we plodded across without incident. Then, just as we were beginning to think about camping for the night, we came to a creek and looked across at the other side and the surprise of our lives.

Laid out there in the midst of the wilderness was a beautiful farm. Beside a large log house was a big vegetable garden and a wealth of hardy mountain flowers. There were fields of wheat and oats and hay, and twenty head of grade shorthorn cattle grazing in a pasture. The Durham bull that eyed us over the fence was a fine-looking animal. There were chickens scratching in the barnyard and a pen of pigs nearby.

The farm belonged to Lewis Swift. A tall, wiry man about sixty years old with a long snow-white beard, he lived here with his wife, a lady of mixed races, and their half dozen children. With his family's help, the industrious Swift had built a water wheel on the creek appropriately named after him. This wheel drove the grist mill which he used to grind his own flour and oatmeal. Remembering the terrible rivers we had crossed, we asked how he managed to bring his cattle and machinery in from Edmonton, and he explained that he brought most of it in during the winter over the frozen rivers and streams; the chickens and pigs had come in by pack train during the summer months.

The Swifts were expecting Mac MacDonald's pack train to arrive any day and we were able to tell them of his progress.

"We have a young man staying with us waiting for Mac to arrive," said Swift. "He's hired on as a packer and he's supposed to meet Mac here."

We looked around expecting to see the young man.

"He's out hunting," said Swift. "In fact, we're kind of worried. He was only going for the day but he's been gone since yesterday. He should have been back last night."

We set up camp near the creek, our thoughts on the young man out in the mountains. Father had told us about his adventures while prospecting alone so we had a fairly good idea of the dangers facing the packer in that rough and treacherous country. We would have liked to set off to look for him but even Swift had no idea which direction he had gone. Besides, it was growing dark and the sky had clouded over. It looked as if we might have a bad storm that night, but there was nothing we could do before morning.

We hung around until ten o'clock the next morning hoping that the young man would emerge from the woods, but everything remained silent. Then Swift called his oldest daughter to him. She was a strange creature and to us appeared somewhat retarded, but Swift spoke quietly to her, explained the problem of the missing packer and asked for her help. She nodded, walked over to the couch and lay down. She folded her arms under her head and closed her eyes. Within minutes she seemed to go into a deep sleep. We waited. I glanced at my father and brothers. They were obviously as uncomfortable and skeptical as I was. The Swifts were quiet and calm. Finally the girl sat up and looked around as if she was dazed.

"I saw a young man," she said. "He's badly hurt. He's near . . . Swift Creek . . . about six miles back in the mountains . . . he needs help . . ."

Swift had listened attentively and now he thanked her. "We'll have to leave right away, or it'll be dark before we carry him out."

Father, Angus, Dan and I followed him outside and saddled up our horses and followed him up the creek. We were able to ride for the first three miles; after that we walked. And all the time we were thinking, what are we doing this crazy thing for? Ahead of us Swift struggled up the mountain just as though he had a map showing where the packer was lying hurt.

After about two hours of climbing, we stopped on a ridge beside the creek and there in front of us was the young man. He had killed a yearling deer and while packing it out to where he had left his horse, he had come to a steep hill. There was no other way around it so he had attempted to climb down, slipped and smashed his knee. It was horribly painful, but he had not lost consciousness — he had tried crawling on his hands and one good knee but had had to give up. The terrain was just too rough. However, he did manage to haul himself over to the creek, and that was where we found him, soaking his knee in cold water, using his shirttail for a bandage. Though he knew exactly where he was, he had no idea how long it would take for his knee to get well enough so that he could hobble down the mountain to his horse.

We had come prepared with a big piece of canvas to use for a stretcher. We cut two poles eight feet long, fastened the canvas onto them and placed the man on the stretcher. We took turns carrying the stretcher and the deer hindquarters down to where we had left the horses. To get our patient onto his horse we had to bind his leg good and tight, then lift him stiff-legged onto his saddle. It was painful for him but he was made of tough stuff and made no complaint. At the farm, the Swift family took over his care. They were very kind, capable and resourceful people.

Afterwards, we often talked about the rescue and about Swift's daughter. We had no idea how she had known where to send us but we would never have found him by ourselves, I know that. Years later, Angus went back to that district to work. The Swifts were still there and the girl—who was a grown woman by now—was still astounding people with the remarkable things she did. Angus was not much of a one for believing "this psychic stuff," as he called it, but he was really impressed.

Fred Stephens left us at Swift Creek to head for the Smoky River district. We never saw him again. All of us, but especially father, missed his company because he was an excellent travelling companion.

The next hurdle to be crossed was the Miette River. Compared to the Athabasca or the McLeod River, it was very small but it was a mass of white foam and enormous boulders. Swift had told us that it came straight off the glaciers and dropped nearly a thousand feet to the mile.

"You'll never cross it down here," he had told us, "but if you follow the trail you'll find the fording place clearly marked. It's the only place you can get across."

So we started to climb up the trail beside the torrent of water dashing down over the rocks. The scenery was spectacular but it was hard going for the horses. When night came, we camped beside a little creek which tumbled into the river from the northeast. After dinner, Dan and I got out our fishing lines and began working our way up the creek, stopping to try for fish here and there, but we had no luck at all. Then clambering over the brow of a hill, we looked down on a beautiful little lake nestled in the mountains.

We scrambled down to it and put out our lines. As quickly as our fly hooks hit the water, they were snapped up. Soon we had almost too many fish to carry back. I have done a lot of fishing since then, but I still think most fondly of that evening fishing on an unnamed lake deep in the Rockies.

At noon on the third day after leaving the Swifts' farm we came to the ford. On each side of the river there was a post to mark the spot, and we could see that we would have to angle slightly downstream to arrive at the landing site on the west bank. But it was absolutely necessary to follow the line from the one post to the other because there were boulders everywhere else and the water frothed and foamed over them and around them. Our horses could easily lose their footing and be swept down into the Athabasca far below.

Father looked the situation over and decided to lead the seven pack horses over himself, one at a time. Even though we had learned a lot on this trip he still felt that he could not risk our lives with the line-up we usually followed on the trail. This meant thirteen trips across for him with us holding our breaths each time. As he set off with the last horse, he told us to follow in a direct line behind. We were very careful to follow his instructions exactly because we were scared to do otherwise, and each of us breathed a sigh of relief when we reached the west bank of the river.

The next body of water we came to was a small lake with a hand-printed sign posted nearby which read, strangely, "Cow-dung Lake." (It is known today as Lucerne Lake.) Its shoreline was very steep so that sometimes we followed the old Indian trail along the edge overlooking the water and sometimes the trail led us right into the lake. Here we rode on a ledge of underwater rock, almost deep enough to force the horses to swim.

We followed its outlet for a few miles until it emptied into another creek. This one was so narrow that we could have stepped across it easily. After a while, as we rode along beside it, I noticed that father was leaning over in his saddle to look at the water more closely. Then suddenly, he turned around and called back to me.

"Ervin, look at the stream! See anything wrong with it?"

I had another look at it but before I could say anything, he shouted again. "It's flowing west! This is the Fraser River that Mac told us about!"

I shouted the news back down the line to Dan and Angus, while up ahead father burst into "Comin' through the Rye." He was singing in Gaelic at the top of his lungs. I'm sure there wasn't a grizzly bear or a mountain goat that did not know we were on our way. We boys grinned and sang quietly along with him but never loud enough for him to hear us.

We had reached the summit of the Yellowhead Pass while hardly noticing the climb. The rest, as they say, was all downhill.

7

Cariboo

W E FOLLOWED the course of the Fraser for many miles, now and then fording small streams which emptied into it, until at last it opened into another lake. This was Moose Lake, and skirting it presented the same problems that Cowdung Lake had given us: some of our packs got a little wet this time, but there was no great damage done, and we certainly had the cleanest horses in British Columbia by the time we camped that night at the foot of the lake.

The next day we began following the Fraser again which was now a fair-sized river. We were on its north bank so that after a while we came to a wide, shallow tributary entering from the direction of Mount Robson; it had a clear gravel bottom, such a pleasant change from the muddy, swampy creeks that we had been crossing. We rode about half a mile up it to find an easy ford, and here we had a clear view of Mount Robson. Father was spellbound by the beauty of it, and as we rode on, my brothers and I could see that he was completely happy. The mountain air was working its magic on him again.

We arrived at Tête Jaune Cache on the Fraser River on the first of July 1907. For weeks we had struggled toward this point, expecting a town of considerable size, but there wasn't one darn building in sight. Just two tepees sitting in the middle of a clearing.

An Indian man abou. fifty years old emerged, two squaws around forty-five, three young women named Big Harriet, Mary and Annie, one sixteen-year-old boy named Samuel, and four or five young children. Of all of them only Samuel seemed to have an occupation, going out each day in his dugout canoe to catch spring salmon to keep this little colony supplied with fresh fish. There were two large smoking racks beside the river, and the women kept them loaded with the fish that Samuel caught and with wild game.

Since we intended to stay here a week or more, we set up a good camp beside a creek. It was a lovely spot; the scenery was truly magnificent and there was plenty of fine grass for our horses. We picketed one of the saddle horses nearby and settled down to take life easy for a while. When supper time came round I took my time establishing a fire and prepared sourdough biscuits with all the little children standing about watching every move I made. After a while, Big Harriet and Mary and Annie came to watch as well, which sort of pleased me because they were good-looking girls and it had been a long time since we had seen girls at all. But by the time we sat down to eat, all the Indians had come over, not saying anything, just sitting on the ground watching every bite we took, their eyes following our forks from our plates to our mouths and back to our plates again until we darn near choked. Finally, father jumped to his feet.

"For God's sake, Ervin, feed these poor hungry people!" he yelled and stalked off. He never could bear to see anyone go hungry. So after that night I always cooked up our biggest kettle full of salt pork and dried beans, and the next biggest with rice or sago and dried apples, and a huge batch of sourdough bread. Then I would sit the Indians down and feed them while across the clearing in front of their tepees sat racks of fish and venison and other wild game. When they had eaten, I would call my father and brothers to eat.

On our second day at Tête Jaune Cache, Mac MacDonald rode into the clearing accompanied by an American named Finch, the man who was to operate the store at the Cache. He was a small wiry man about fifty years old, who had only one thing on his mind: he had to get a building up before the pack train arrived with his supplies.

He buttonholed father as soon as he dismounted.

"Mr. MacDonald," he asked anxiously, "would you and your boys help build my store? I'll pay you well...."

This was really history in the making—and there is not a MacDonald alive who can resist finding his place in history.

"We'll be glad to help," said father and got his axe out of his pack. The store had to be built of logs, of course, so we headed for the small clusters of trees that grew here and there in the clearing. Mr. Finch, Angus and I cut fourteen- and eighteen-foot-long logs, the dimensions of the building, while father put our single set of harness on Sugar Billy, who was not too pleased to find that he wasn't going to get the same rest break as the other horses. Dan, who was a natural-born teamster, skidded the logs to the building site about a hundred feet back from the river. Father and Mac notched the logs and put them in place as fast as Dan could deliver them and we could cut them. The walls were up in three days, the ridgepole and other roof supports were in place the following day. Next the split timbers were put up for the roof and the joints between them chinked with moss. We made a stoneboat and hauled blue clay from the river, mixed the clay with water to make a thick paste and plastered it over the split timber to about six inches thick. We smoothed it down and left it to dry in the hot sun to make the roof watertight. Father made the door and the store counter of hand-hewn boards. We put a couple of small windows into the side walls and built shelves for the stock out of small poles.

Two days before the store was finished, the pack train arrived, so work came to a halt while we unloaded the supplies and covered them with canvas and tarpaulins. The population took quite a jump with the arrival of the three pack-train men, but there were more on the way: Bill Spittal and the Monahans arrived the next day and that night two more men joined us.

One of the latter was Bill Sprung, a real loner who told no one where he was going or why he was going there. He was an absolute mountain of a man with the smallest pair of eyes I ever saw. He had the strength of an ox but probably the same amount of intelligence.

He had teamed up on the trail with Ed Chappel, who was perhaps the same age as Sprung, somewhere in his forties we

137

guessed, but considerably smaller, about five feet eleven and 185 pounds. He told us he had ranched in Montana and sold out there to come to the Cariboo. He was happy to hear we were headed that way, too.

Father's eyes kept straying to Chappel's saddle horse, a first-class-looking dapple grey about sixteen and a half hands high, a tough, fast animal.

"A fine horse," commented father.

"Yes," said Chappel. "I wouldn't trade him for a million bucks!"

"One of Grey Eagle's strain?" asked father.

"You know Grey Eagle's horses?" asked Chappel. Sure enough, this was one of the Flathead Indian horses, just like father's old Frank, and Chappel and father traded stories of their mounts' abilities far into the night.

The opening of the first store in Tête Jaune Cache called for a celebration and we all decided that a feast was necessary. Finch contributed beans and bacon baked in a large Dutch oven, a ham, and dried fruits cooked with rice. Father shot a young buck deer and we barbecued the hindquarters along with the ham.

When the food was ready, we invited all the Indians and everyone else to feast with us. The food disappeared quickly and everybody had a good time, especially the Indians. I always marvelled at the enormous quantities that group could eat when white man's grub was put in front of them. Of course, it was early in the year and we were probably the first people to arrive in that part of the mountains with a good supply of grub, and maybe the only people willing to share it.

With the store open for business and the feasting over, Spittal and the two Irishmen headed downstream about twelve miles to what Angus dubbed Spittal Creek: it was here that Bill had made his strike. Father and Angus went with them. Having prospected so many years, father simply could not resist having a look.

They set up camp at the edge of the creek and wasted no time getting out their gold pans. The Monahans were new at the game but they caught on after father instructed them in the finer points of panning. Spittal seemed to know just where to look for gold there and settled to work methodically on a gravelly sandbar.

At the end of the first day there had not been a sign of gold and Spittal was in a vicious mood, snapping at everyone. It was not very pleasant around the campfire that night. The next day he headed into the creek still shovelling his breakfast into his mouth. The Monahans and MacDonalds followed a little later. Once again they finished the day empty-handed, and Spittal's temper was even worse than the night before. The Monahans, to escape his wrath, decided to go hunting in a nearby grove of trees from which they had heard movement during the afternoon. A bear, perhaps, they decided. Stealthily, they crept up and, sure enough, there was something big and black in the bushes. The older brother, the same one who had lost his boots in the McLeod River, raised his gun and fired. His aim was absolutely dead on. He had shot his fine black Irish hunter dead. Now he would have to ride one of the pack animals back to Edmonton.

I am sure Spittal never slept that night because he was in the creek panning before the others had rolled out of their blankets in the morning. As they ate breakfast they listened to him cursing every stone beneath his feet. After lunch, the younger Monahan, the one who was going into the priesthood, sat down on the bank despondently.

"Billy," he said, "is it sure you are that this is the right creek? It is possible that—"

Spittal assured him in rather colourful language that it was.

"Then," said Monahan, "is it sure you are that this is the right part of the creek? You see, Billy, my brother and I are thinking there's no gold here!"

Spittal exploded. "Damn it, I *know* there's gold here because I put it here!"

This blew the prospecting party all to hell, so Spittal and the Monahans headed back to Edmonton together. We never heard of the two Irishmen again, but two years later we heard of Spittal. Some Indians came into the 70 Mile House with a story about some white men starving up in the Clearwater country, and the police came through our ranch to look for them. Apparently Spittal had got hold of some ore samples and showed them to people claiming they were from a mine he had found up there. They paid him money to take them to it in the fall and got snowed in. The only thing that saved them from starvation was shooting one of their horses.

It had now been ten days since our arrival at the Cache and it was time to move on. Before leaving we had to replenish our grocery supplies because we had used a lot more than we had figured on. Of course, feeding the local Indian population had not helped at all. Our supplies had melted away like a snowbank in the sun. We were the first customers in the new store, and we bought a hundred pounds of flour, fifty pounds of sugar, fifty pounds of dried beans, fifty pounds of bacon, ten pounds of coffee and five pounds of tea. This, we figured, would get us through to the next store if we avoided freeloaders.

We expected prices would be much higher than they had been in Edmonton owing to the terrific cost of having to pack everything in over that long, dangerous trail, but we were still a little shocked when we saw the bill. Two hundred and fifty dollars! Flour was $1.00 a pound, bacon that we had bought in Edmonton for 25 cents a pound was 75 cents here, and sugar was $1.25 a pound. Luckily, Finch owed us for our construction work so we came out nearly even on the bill. Father decided that we would only need five pack horses for the rest of the trip because we had much less to carry, so we sold the Squaw Mare and Jackie to Mac for $150. Father was happy when Mac paid by cheque: he wanted to give him the horses for all the help he had given us, and never cashed the cheque.

Meanwhile, father had bought one more horse from the Monahan brothers, a little brown mare called Midget who had developed sores all over her back from having her pack sacks poorly placed and balanced. The Monahans had not deliberately mistreated her; they were simply ignorant about packing and about treating sores. We certainly did not need another horse, especially one that could not carry a pack or a saddle until her sores healed, but father could not bear to see an animal suffer. He began doctoring her up as soon as he bought her; on the trail she would follow him on a lead.

We had hired young Samuel and the old Indian to take our camping outfit and supplies across the Fraser River while we did our shopping. Now they loaded our newly bought groceries into the dugout canoe while we took our horses across. There was no dangerous current to deal with here but the river was deep, so we forded as far as possible, then slipped out of our saddles, grabbed the horses by their tails and were towed across. This method is the safest in swift water, for if you stay in the saddle you make the horse top-heavy and the current could quite easily roll the animal over. Once this happens, it is likely to drown before it can right itself.

It had been our intention to follow the Fraser all the way to the Cariboo, but Mac had convinced us to abandon that idea.

"The only way you can go down the Fraser is by canoe," said Mac, "and you'll pardon me for saying so, Archie, but I don't think you or your boys can handle a canoe good enough for that."

Father agreed, of course. Canoeing was one of the few skills he had never acquired, though I am quite sure he could have — the opportunity had never come up. The Indians at Tête Jaune Cache also agreed with Mac's verdict on the Fraser route, for they had a wealth of information about most of the routes and trails. Our best bet, they said, was to cross the Fraser, continue south to the Canoe River, then turn southwest to the North Thompson and follow it to Kamloops.

On the far bank of the Fraser we repacked our horses and headed south, away from the proposed railway line. The land we had camped on and ridden over would be worth thousands of dollars an acre once the railway came through. We could have bought it then for a song but we did not want it. Our eyes were turned to the Cariboo.

We travelled south for twelve miles on a wide-open flat, until it became flanked on either side by steep mountains. Here on the west side of the valley close to the base of a mountain range was McLennan River. The valley itself, we had been told, was called Starvation Flats.

Nine years earlier, a party of eastern Canadians heading for the Klondike had lost their way in the late fall. Trapped in this seemingly pleasant valley by sickness and injuries, heavy snow and bitter cold, they had run out of grub. Without snowshoes it was impossible for them to walk through the drifts. Having no idea how to fend for themselves in the bush, they became worn out and discouraged, and before spring all of them had died of starvation.

Father seemed particularly depressed by this area, remembering his own experiences in the Klondike; but in a deep draw on the west side of the valley we found a spring bubbling up in a grove of trees and made camp there. Father headed up the mountain the next morning to look for his elusive rainbow, but there was no gold or, for that matter, any other mineral. Except for the great coal deposits in the Pembina and McLeod river basins, this did not seem to be mineral country. In fact, I have never heard of any major mineral deposits being discovered in all the country we travelled through.

The Canoe River was swift and wide. Father looked it over with his expert eye and decided that we would make a small raft for our groceries and anything else that had to stay dry, and we would swim the horses with the remaining supplies.

When the raft was built and the groceries were loaded, father and Angus took the raft across, then came back to help Dan and me swim the horses. Everything went off without a hitch. We had done this kind of crossing so many times that we had become experts.

We camped on the bank of the river that night, though we were worried that the grass was so scarce. It was possible the horses would go too far in their search for more, so we took out our knives and cut all we could find and hauled it to them. As an extra precaution we tied up two saddle horses for the night.

We put up the tent and had supper while the horses ate the cut grass and grazed around the willow clumps nearby. Then as usual we settled around our campfire to talk. Just as it was getting dark, we heard horse bells heading toward the river, and we got a good look at Jane plunging into the water with the whole herd behind her. She had remembered the beautiful grass of Starvation Flats and was leading the herd back there.

Father shook his head. "No use trying to do anything about them in the dark. Let's roll in so we can deal with them in the morning."

We ate a hurried breakfast at the crack of dawn; father and Angus saddled up and swam back across the river to search for Jane and her followers. Though horses will usually head for home under such circumstances, there was no danger that these animals would because they had been moved so many times they no longer had any thoughts of home. Instead, they had stopped at the first good grass they came to, just as we expected. However, it was nearly noon before Dan and I heard the bells, and we could tell that the horses were coming on the run. Father and Angus were deliberately making them run as fast as their legs would carry them, hoping to give them a lesson they would not forget in a hurry. As each one came dripping out of the river, Dan and I caught and saddled them. Father and Angus ate a quick lunch and we set off.

We made up for lost time by travelling until it was almost dark, then camped when we found a good patch of grass. The two saddle horses that had been tied to the trees all night were by now badly in need of rest and feed. Jane and her gang behaved that night and there were no more unscheduled swimming lessons.

The next few days of riding were uneventful. We packed and unpacked horses, made campfires, mended harness, rode through rolling countryside, down valleys and through streams. At length we came to the upper reaches of the Albreda River, a small shallow stream that we could step across. We followed it for several miles, crossing back and forth hunting for the trail which was hardly marked at all. The stream grew bigger so that each time we crossed, it was deeper and wider until, at a point just above where it empties into the North Thompson River, it had become swollen and swift from other streams emptying into it. We forded for the last time and rode another mile or two till we arrived on the banks of the North Thompson. We were now on the point of land between the two rivers, only a couple of miles from their junction.

Here, camped on the bank of the river were Bill Sprung and Ed Chappel, who had left Tête Jaune Cache a few days before us.

"We're waiting for the river to go down," said Sprung anxiously. Neither of them had ever crossed a big river before without help.

"You'll have a long wait," said father.

The winter of 1906–7 had been a time of extra heavy snows in the Rockies as well as on the prairie, and June and July had been hotter than usual, making the runoff unexpectedly heavy. Even though it was now the third week in July, we could not expect the river to begin to drop for another week or two.

Father prowled the bank, then ordered, "Let's get busy! We'll make a good stout raft, big enough to carry all of us and our gear. It'll be quite a raft to handle, but there doesn't seem to be anything else we can do. Come on!"

Sprung and Chappel got to their feet and followed father and us boys up the North Thompson about two miles where we found plenty of dry trees. Our raft, father calculated, would have to be at least twenty-eight feet long and six feet wide, and it took the six of us all day to build. The placement of each log and the knots on every rope were checked and double-checked by father. This raft had to be stronger than any we had built so far.

Father sang as he worked and my brothers and I mumbled and hummed along behind him. As usual we did not know the Gaelic words he was singing but it made us feel good to hum the tune anyway. When the raft was finished, we were all quite pleased with it.

"Practice makes perfect," said Angus. Father grinned.

On the second morning after reaching the river, we loaded all our belongings and Sprung's and Chappel's onto the raft, then rounded up our horses and swam them across. From our side of the river father had picked out the spot where we were to land the raft. About a mile and a half downriver, a large cedar log nearly four feet across extended from the far bank. It was angled downstream and partially submerged, but two limbs, broken off about eighteen inches from the trunk, stuck up in the air like handles. Father wanted us to aim the raft for this log, snub it to the two limbs and use the log as a wharf to unload our supplies. When we reached the log Sprung and Chappel were to jump out first and tie the raft securely.

Just before we embarked, Sprung took off his boots and hauled a pair of knee-high rubber boots out of his pack.

"Not going to get *my* feet wet, he announced as though we were all fools not to wear rubber boots, too.

We climbed aboard and took our places.

With father and Angus manning the sweeps, Dan and I ready with poles to shove off from the bank, Sprung and Chappel clutching the ropes ready to jump at the right moment, father gave the signal to go. Down the driver we went, angling toward the middle then neatly slipping into the current running down the other side.

"Now when the time comes to move," father ordered, "move *fast!* Just like it's the last move you'll ever make!"

The raft struck the bank at exactly the right spot, and Chappel and Sprung moved fast. Too fast. They flung themselves toward the log but fell short, plunging into the water. Dropping the ropes, they grabbed for dear life on to the log, their arms up over it, their legs dragged underneath by the swift water. Fortunately, they were held firmly against it by the pressure of the water.

Angus and I, seeing their plight, jumped onto the log, grabbed for Chappel and pulled him out. Then the three of us got hold of Sprung's enormous bulk and, with much tugging, hauled him up. But just as we landed him, Angus's little black diary in which he had written faithfully every night popped out of his pocket and disappeared into the muddy river. Angus groaned out loud but there was nothing we could do about the loss.

I let out a groan, too, but it had nothing to do with the diary. I was looking at Sprung's rubber boots and realized why the river had been reluctant to let go of him—his boots were full of water.

By the time we got him out, Angus and I were both thoroughly wet, but we set off along the river bank at top speed following the raft. It had only touched the log then shot downstream as fast as if it had been sent for. Desperate, we scrambled over logs and dodged through brush until, almost a mile downstream, we came to a large sandbar created by a sharp right-hand bend in the North Thompson. Directly across from us was the mouth of the Albreda River.

We ran out onto the tip of the sandbar where we could see around the bend and there, to our delight and relief, was the raft tied up on the opposite side just slightly downstream from us. We could see father and Dan working like beavers getting out more ropes to tie the raft to some trees. Later they told us that the current along that side was so swift that they had been afraid the ropes would break and the raft would be torn loose at any moment. How they managed to stop at that spot long enough to tie up, I will never know. There were so many handicaps to overcome: the swift current, their lack of manpower, the steepness of the bank. It was so steep, in fact, that it was more like a cliff, and the cedar trees growing thickly up the face of it all had a bend in their trunks like sleigh runners. Father and Dan were forced to stay right there on the raft.

So there we were, all of us safe, but Sprung, Chappel, Angus and I on one side of the river and father and Dan on the other. We had the horses. Father and Dan had everything else—blankets, dry clothes, grub, and all.

"Are you all right?" we hollered.

"Yes," Dan hollered back. "We've got things under control."

Sprung and Chappel joined us on the sandbar.

"What's the ground like there?" shouted father.

"It's flat but there're lots of bushes and logs on the ground." Some of the logs must have measured four or five feet across.

"Go downstream after you get those men dried out. Find a good place to land the raft on your side and let me know how far it is."

We realized then that Dan and father could not see very far down the river so we knew there must be a wide bend ahead. We would have to scout for them. We headed into the brush and found a fairly decent place to camp. There were several large cedar trees in a group that gave some shelter from the sun and wind. Even without an axe, we had no trouble gathering up all the firewood we would require for a fire. With our pocket knives we shaved bits of dry cedar and heaped them in the centre of our campfire. But who had a match? We turned our pockets out. Angus had none at all. Chappel and Sprung had been so thoroughly soaked that the matches in their pockets had all lost their heads. I found a few in my pocket tangled up with some fishing line. Being the cook, I always had the job of getting a fire going as soon as we stopped for the night. Unfortunately, I had got wet rescuing the two men, and my matches were damp.

"Try one, anyway," demanded Sprung.

I had my doubts but I shielded it carefully and struck it across a stone. The head just rubbed off against it. There was no fire. I was afraid to try another and no one could think how to dry them.

Then suddenly I thought of my hair. If I could get it dry, I could dry the matches in it. I started rubbing my thick hair as hard as I could with my hands. After about five minutes of frantic rubbing, I drew the matches through it, then took a chance on striking one. Lo and behold, it lit! Carefully, I touched it to our pile of cedar shavings and soon we had a roaring fire.

We hauled some pieces of driftwood by the fire for seats and began to dry out our clothes. Chappel and Sprung had to take all their clothes off and hang them on an arrangement of sticks that we stuck in the ground close to the fire. Sprung stripped as soon as the fire was going but Chappel hesitated, slowly taking off his boots, then his pants. Finally, when his shirt came off, we understood why. He had a money belt strapped around his waist! Cautiously, he examined its contents.

"They're all wet!" he said.

"Lay them out around the fire," said Angus. "They'll dry quickly. We'll keep an eye on them."

I guess he figured we MacDonalds were honest so he laid the bills out on pieces of driftwood. We could see he was very nervous about having to do this. The money was mostly in big bills, fifties, one hundreds and five hundreds—I never did count it but it looked like an awful lot of money. Chappel sat there naked, not taking his eyes off it for a moment. On the other side of the fire, Sprung stared at it, too.

We kept our fire roaring and the clothes and money soon dried. When everybody was dressed again, we busied ourselves collecting wood: we would have to keep the fire going all night because we might not get it lit again in the morning with the few damaged matches I had left.

There was not a thing to worry about, we sadly told ourselves, no food to cook or tent to put up or beds to make. We were living a carefree life! The horses had plenty of grass, and by the sound of their bells we knew they were not too far away. Just before dark we used our pocket knives to cut slender cedar boughs to sleep on. They were not very comfortable, but none of us would sleep soundly anyway since we had to keep the fire burning.

All of us were very hungry, having had nothing to eat since six o'clock that morning, but I have never seen anyone as hungry as Bill Sprung. He moaned the night long that we would all starve to death, that he could feel himself dying already. Angus and I were not worried. Father would never let that happen.

All my hooks and my fishing rod were in the pack with our pots and pans so I could not even catch breakfast. I consoled myself that even if I had my fishing tackle I probably would not have caught anything because the river was too high and too dirty. I will never know whether this was true. There were no berries either because the timber and brush were too thick, though later we would find berries galore just downriver on the open hillsides.

Early in the morning, still moaning about his hunger, Sprung started off into the bush.

"I'm going to have a look at the horses," he announced.

Chappel watched him go, then as soon as he was sure that Sprung was out of earshot, he grabbed my arm.

"Ervin, I want you to wear my belt."

"Your belt?"

"My money belt. Bill Sprung can't wait to get his hands on it, but he'd never suspect that a kid like you would be wearing it."

I must have looked completely stunned because he then explained that this was all the money he had in the world. He had sold his ranch in Montana and had brought the cash with him to buy new property in the Cariboo. Well, I guess I was not very bright, and I most certainly did not realize the responsibility I was taking on, because I agreed to wear it. Though it was uncomfortable, by punching some new holes in it we were able to snug it up, and eventually I got used to the weight of it around my middle. It was a bit bulky looking, too, but since I was wearing bib overalls, it was not too noticeable.

When Sprung came back he was leading our little brown mare Midget. With the treatment we had been giving her sore back, she was improving quite fast and had become nice and fat. Sprung marched her down to the tip of the sandbar and started hollering at father.

"Archie!"

Father waved from the raft.

"Archie, where's your rifle?"

"Right here." Father reached for it and held it aloft.

148

Sprung pulled on Midget's lead and turned her broadside to the river. "I want you to shoot this horse. We're starving over here!"

Father put his gun down. We could see him shaking his head.

"Shoot her," bellowed Sprung.

"No," shouted father. "You can survive—"

"Shoot her!" thundered Sprung, "or our lives will be on your head!"

Father picked up the gun again, raised it and took careful aim. Then he lowered the gun.

"She's too small a target, Bill! Besides she won't make good eating with all those sores on her back! I tell you what, Bill. You go get that buckskin saddle horse of yours and I'll shoot him instead. He'll make a bigger target and he'll be damn fine eating."

When it sank into Sprung's head exactly what father had said, he suddenly lost his appetite for horse meat, and he forgot that our breakfast had been a few mouthfuls of icy cold water. He dropped Midget's lead and I took her back to the herd.

A few hours later, Sprung was back on the sandbar yelling at father again.

"Archie, throw me an axe!"

"A what?"

"Throw me an axe!"

We had no idea why he wanted an axe. We were getting all the firewood we needed. Perhaps the poor man was in shock from his mishap and had no idea what he was saying.

"That's impossible, Bill," father called back. "I can't throw that far. The river's too wide."

But Bill insisted, waving his arms around and bellowing ferociously. I guess father was pretty tired of all the nonsense by this time, and he dug into the supplies on the raft and pulled Sprung's axe out of his outfit. Then he stepped to the edge of the raft, took a good grip on the end of the axe handle, whirled the thing around his head a few times and gave a mighty heave. The axe flew fast and true toward the point on the sandbar where we were standing, but it fell about thirty feet short. There was a splash as it disappeared into the fast-flowing river. We hadn't a hope in hell of recovering it.

When Sprung had gone off to sulk, Angus and I told father

149

what we had found out about the land down the river. We had located a good landing place only about a mile and a half farther down. The river made a sharp bend there and the main current swept in close to the shore. We figured it would not be too difficult to manoeuvre the raft in there, though there was still the problem of it being undermanned.

Father had already considered that and decided he must get one more of us over to his side of the river to help. He and Dan would build a smaller raft, cross over to our side with some grub and take Sprung back. He was the right man to choose, for although he was certainly not very intelligent, he was as strong as an ox, and when father used his sergeant-major voice on him he usually did as he was told.

Father and Dan shifted aside all the provisions on the raft leaving a clear work space about eight feet square. They tied safety lines around their waists and worked their way up the cliff to fasten the other ends to trees near the top. If they had fallen into the river they would have had no chance of surviving that current.

Father chose a number of the cedars with the sleigh-runner curve in them since they could be used to advantage at the front end of the raft. They would tend to clear the water, making it easier to pole up the river. Each log had to be lowered to the deck with ropes so the new raft took more than a day to build.

At noon of the third day everything was ready for father to attempt the river. They slid the small raft into the water, tied a sack of grub and an axe onto it, and then father got aboard with a paddle and a long pole. Chappel, Sprung, Angus and I stood on the point of the sandbar, watching and worrying. There was not a thing we could do to help.

Father began poling upstream close to the river bank where the current was slack, heading straight for the mouth of the Albreda. When he figured he had entered far enough that he could cross the mouth without being swept away down the North Thompson, he gave one hard shove with his pole and propelled himself almost halfway across. He pulled the pole out and plunged it down a second time, to get the raft moving fast enough so he would have time to switch to the paddle. But the river was too deep here: the pole missed the bottom and father lost his balance, shooting over the side of the raft after his pole.

We let out a shout. He would never be able to get aboard. Across the river Dan stood frozen on the edge of the big raft, poised almost as though he intended to jump in and save him.

But as usual we had underrated father's abilities. In some remarkable way, he popped up beside the raft and slipped back onto it within seconds of plunging overboard. He grabbed his paddle and began paddling furiously across the mouth of the Albreda, heading for a shallow slough that ran behind a long island on his side of the North Thompson. Both island and slough extended upstream a mile or so ending close to the spot where we had first launched the big raft. Once he reached the slough, he poled with the paddle and made good progress.

After he disappeared behind the island, the four of us ran back up the river to the cedar log where we had tried to land the big raft. This was where he planned to land and he had told us to be ready to give him a hand when he got there.

From our grandstand on the log, we watched the river anxiously. He would be coming down at a tremendous speed and our fear was that he would overshoot the log. Our hearts were in our mouths as we saw him shoot out from behind the island paddling like fury. He would never make it! He was coming so fast that he would be carried past the log too far out to throw us a rope, and the current would carry him right back to Dan.

But as we despaired, suddenly he caught a crosscurrent which shot the raft toward our log. Father threw us the rope and we pulled him in.

We were so happy to see him safe and sound that we were talking all at once. Then, before he could get up off his knees, we almost lost him after all. Bill Sprung had only one thing on his mind—food! Grinning like an idiot, he jumped down onto the raft, all 300 pounds of him, yelling, "Did you bring something to eat?"

The raft was driven clear under the water, soaking father for the second time that day. The sack of grub was well tied on but got soaking wet, too. Father was so furious that he jumped to his feet and threatened Sprung with his paddle.

"Get the hell off here, you crazy fool," he yelled, brandishing the paddle over Sprung's head, "or I'll split your head wide open!"

He was just wild to think that after going through all that work and danger, this darn fool had nearly ruined everything.

Sprung scrambled off as fast as he could. He knew father meant what he said.

We cooked a meal right away, as God knows we were hungry enough to eat anything, soaking wet or not.

Before father set off with Sprung, we discussed the layout of the river below us and father gave us our orders. The two had no trouble returning because the current was just right, and Dan gave a hand tying the small raft alongside. Now that it was no longer needed they dismantled the small raft and balanced the load again on the big one.

As the day ended, we were three and three on each side of the river. Two campfires glowed in the dusk, and two dinners were cooked. For Chappel, Angus and I, it was a big meal, our first real one in three days.

The next morning, father, Dan and Sprung brought the raft across without a hitch. On our side, we three waited in the bend of the river to assist their landing. After four days' delay, we were able to unload the raft, round up the horses, put on their saddles and packs and set off on the trail again, with Chappel and Sprung added to the tail end of our train. The North Thompson was not the biggest river we had crossed but it certainly gave us the biggest headaches.

The horses were now in excellent shape after the rest and good grazing, which was just as well considering the country ahead of us. I am sure that not a living soul had been through that part of the country in years. The brush was almost impenetrable, and every few yards we would come to a log so big that no horse could possibly jump over it. Many of them were at least six feet across, and it would have taken days to cut through one of them with an axe. Even with a crosscut saw, we could never have moved the log once cut. So each time we came to one we had to find a way around it, and then chances were when we got around it, another giant log was blocking our path. Sometimes after hours of travel, hard work and sweat, we would end up not half a mile from our starting point.

The only thing in favour of that country was the high bush blueberries and huckleberries. As we rode along we could reach out and break off a branch loaded with these delicious berries and stuff them into our mouths until our hands and faces were stained a deep purple.

After hours of this difficult travel, we came to an open ridge and our spirits picked up. Just ahead we could hear a noisy river and as we came closer we found an old sign on a tree: Thunder River. It was certainly well named. There was little use trying to talk to each other in the noise it made dashing down the mountainside hurrying to meet the North Thompson.

It was very similar to the Miette River but was not as large, so we had no trouble fording it, and continued on our way over open benches and sidehills above the river. Unfortunately, the animals found little grass here and we had to search carefully for campsites. Then late one afternoon we approached a beautiful meadow, several hundred acres of lush green grass. As far as we knew these meadows had no name, but later learned they were called the Blue River Meadows. We camped for several days, letting the horses have a rest and a good feed, and taking time ourselves to mend equipment and relax.

My brothers and I liked the look of this meadow, and we wanted father to stay there and build up a ranch.

He shook his head. "It takes more than hay to make a ranch, boys. You need rangeland, and the timber round this meadow is far too thick for grass to grow. Here we'd have no summer range."

He was a whole lot wiser and more practical than we were, and we could see that he was right. But I think that for him there was something else wrong with the Blue River Meadows. They did not fit the ranch he had seen in his dream. Where was the beautiful lake? Where were the open fields sloping down to the shore? We would have to go farther. It was not time to settle yet.

Not long after breaking camp we came to the picturesque Blue River, a crystal-clear stream. Since it was not swift we were able to ford it easily and ride on in a leisurely way till we came to the Stillwater Flats. Lying along the North Thompson River, these flats were thick with brush and flooded at that time of the year. For miles the trail wound through sloughs. We fought our way through, fording the sloughs, pulling our horses out of mud holes, being eaten up by mosquitoes and frying in the heat. We had one heck of a time.

One day in the midst of this mess we came to a tumble-down log building that housed a huge cache of wire, glass insulators and equipment that looked as if it had been intended for a tele-graph line. We were completely dumbfounded, but later we were told that it had been brought there in the mid-1860s by the Collins Telegraph Company which had planned to build a telegraph line through Alaska and across the Bering Sea to Asia, beating out the people laying the Atlantic cable. But the cable people won, and Collins abandoned their project and their wire caches.

It took several days to work our way out of the thick bush and swampy flats. We had been almost eaten alive by the mosquitoes, and the horses were getting desperate for a real feed. We emerged at last from the swamps and bushland close to a small farm on the bank of the North Thompson. Ellingham, the owner, was an English bachelor around sixty years of age, not a tall man but huskily built. He wore a short, full, well-trimmed beard. He had lived in this isolated spot for many years, tending his fine little farm where he kept everything neat and clean. His house, his barn and his hay shed were built of logs. He had a good saddle horse, and a team that he used for farm work and for pack trips to Kamloops which he said was only 150 miles away.

We admired his excellent vegetable garden, his apple and plum trees, and the nice variety of berry bushes. In the pasture were a few head of cattle including a couple of milk cows, and some pigs and chickens. About the only things he ever needed from the outside world were staples such as flour, sugar and coffee, and the usual household supplies.

"Would you like to camp here for a while?" he invited us. "You and your horses look as if you could do with a rest!" He knew what a tough trail we had travelled over because he had made a few pack trips for wire from the cache to use on the farm.

I think he really wanted us to stay because he was lonely for someone to talk to, but whatever his motives, we were more than willing to camp at this lovely spot and enjoy his company. He gave us some new potatoes and other vegetables, the first fresh vegetables we had seen since stopping at Lewis Swift's farm in late June; they tasted unbelievably good.

All six of us—father, we three boys, Chappel and Sprung— thoroughly appreciated our stay at this kindhearted man's farm, but it was now the beginning of August and we had a long way to go to find our dream ranch. We thanked our host for his gracious treatment of strangers and climbed into our saddles. As a parting gift, Ellingham handed us a dozen eggs to carry with us, a marvellous luxury. He would take no payment for all he had done for us.

We were soon back into the old routine of making camp in the evening and packing up to hit the trail at first light. We crossed two small rivers in the next couple of days—the Mad and the Raft—and although they were flooded and swift, we were able to ford them without much trouble. Here and there as we rode along we began to see small homesteads. Our trip was nearing its end; we were returning to civilization.

Not long after leaving the Raft River behind, we started down a long hill that led back toward the North Thompson River. Suddenly, we heard a shout from Angus, and we brought the train to a halt. With no warning whatsoever, Old Dan, one of our German coach horses, had dropped in his tracks. He was dead.

It was a tremendous shock to us, for he had shown no sign of being sick. We took quite a few minutes to decide what to do, then Dan and I took his pack off while father led the little brown mare Midget along the trail to where poor Old Dan lay. With father's careful doctoring, her sores were all healed and she was ready to take a pack again. We loaded it onto her back and with our lasso ropes we snaked Old Dan's body downhill away from the trail.

About a mile farther on we came to a stream, and in spite of it being early to make camp, we had to rearrange our packs and decide what to do about our dead horse. Father wanted to try putting dry logs around the body in the morning, to see if we could burn it, but even before dark our problem was solved.

From one of the nearby hills came a mournful howl. Another howl answered the first. Timber wolves. I felt cold fingers of ice down my spine. They were giving their hunting call, and the answering calls were coming in from every direction.

"I think we've got our answer, boys. There won't be much left of poor Old Dan by morning. The scavengers of the wild are on the job."

So this was the end of a very faithful pack horse, a veteran of the terrible Yellowhead Trail.

We sat around the campfire for a long time that night, listening to the wolves fighting over their meal. Father could tell how scared we were.

"Don't worry," he said. "A wolf won't bother humans unless it's starving, and they certainly have plenty to eat tonight."

The horses were restless and jittery so we rounded them up and tied them. Loose they would have taken off as far as they could get from those howling wolves.

We left camp especially early the next morning.

In the afternoon we arrived at Mosquito Flats, where the trail led back across the North Thompson River since huge bluffs came right down to the water's edge making it impossible to go either over them or around them. However, the crossing looked much easier than our first had been, for even though the river was considerably wider here, the current was much slower. We set up camp, planning to cross in the morning when the horses were rested. Shortly after we had finished our chores for the night, we saw a man coming toward us along the trail. Over his shoulder was a contraption with smoke coming out of it. He was a queer-looking sight indeed. Not even father had seen anything like it before.

"What is that?" he asked.

"A smudge pot to keep the mosquitoes away!" he told us.

It certainly did the trick. We were surrounded by millions of the pesky insects yet he was not bothered at all. We had often sat downwind of our campfire to escape them but we had never thought of carrying a fire with us.

"How do you make one of those things?" Angus asked.

Our new friend, whose name was Will Wilson, joined us at the campfire. "Take a ten-pound lard pail, punch a few holes in the bottom and wire it onto a stick about three feet long. Put a little wood in the bottom of the can and some dry grass on top of that and set it on fire. When it gets burning good, put green grass on top. Soon you'll have smoke rolling out just like this without any flame. Then you just put the pole over your shoulder and go on your way. Whenever it burns down just add more wood and grass."

Father asked how long he had lived around there.

"I've lived in these parts nearly two years. Came from Addy, Washington. It's close to Colville," he said.

He was pleased to hear that we had come from Colville and that we knew many of the same people. In the course of the conversation, father realized he knew Wilson's parents. Around 1892 there had been a depression in the United States, what people had called a "panic." There was such a serious shortage of money that the government had trouble collecting taxes and hired extra people to travel around the countryside collecting whatever they could in cash or goods that could be sold to pay taxes. Father had taken on this job for a while and in his travels he had met the Wilson family.

"That farm simply wasn't big enough to support us," said Wilson, "so I came up here and pre-empted land, just down there near the river crossing.

"What do you mean 'pre-empted land'?" Chappel asked.

"A pre-emption," explained Wilson, "is a hundred and sixty acres of government land. Anybody over the age of eighteen can file a claim on it at the government land office. Filing that claim just costs you ten dollars. The land doesn't cost you anything."

"For ten dollars you get a hundred and sixty acres of land!" exclaimed Chappel.

"Well, there's strings attached, of course," said Wilson.

"What kind of strings?" asked father quietly.

"You have to prove up on your pre-emption inside of three years."

"What does proving up mean?"

"You have to fence in part of your land, cultivate it, build a house or cabin and barn on it and live there for at least six months out of each year for three years in a row. In other words, you've got to make a home there. At the end of three years, you ask the government agent to send an inspector to look around the place and if he approves your work, you get a certificate saying that you've proved up your land. You send that certificate to the government agent and he gives you a crown grant to your land and after that it's all yours, just like you bought it and got a deed of purchase for it."

"So I can claim a hundred and sixty acres," said father

thoughtfully, "and when each of the boys becomes eighteen he can claim his own pre-emption."

"That's right," said Wilson. "But once you've proved up your first pre-emption, you can pre-empt another hundred and sixty any time you like."

All this was entirely new to us and we peppered him with questions. We told him of our intention of going to the Cariboo to look for a ranch big enough to raise beef cattle.

"What's the best way to get there?" asked father.

"Your best route is over the old Cariboo Trail. It's an Indian trail over the mountains ending at the Hundred Mile House on the Cariboo Road. It got used a lot during the Klondike gold rush so it's pretty well travelled. You won't have any trouble finding it. Right where we're standing you're just about fourteen miles upriver from a place called Little Fort where the trail begins. But it's on this side of the river so you'll have to cross back again when you get down there."

What a relief it was to hear the words "Cariboo Trail." It made it sound as though we had almost arrived.

When Wilson stood up to leave, it was dusk. "By the way, I have a dugout canoe in the river. Can I take your gear across for you in the morning?"

We slept well with no wolves to disturb us, but before I dropped off my mind wandered to poor Old Dan. I wondered whether father, when he bought our ailing little Midget, had had a premonition that we would need her before the end of our journey. She was in perfect health now and had taken her pack like a seasoned trooper.

Wilson was at the river bank in the morning before we arrived, ready to load his canoe. We swam the horses first and they settled down to eat as expected on a piece of flat land with good grass. I went over with the first canoeload and found a campsite. I knew that everyone was hungry since it was taking longer than anticipated to get all our belongings across, so while the fire was getting hot, I put some setlines in an eddy close by, reputedly a good place to catch Dolly Varden.

Twenty minutes later, I went to check my lines and sure enough there was a dandy ten-pound trout. I cleaned it immediately, covered it in a casing of clay and buried it in the hot coals.

When the kitchen supplies came across the river, I prepared some of Ellingham's vegetables and a dessert. Within two hours the fish was baked and we were sitting around enjoying a hearty meal.

After lunch, each of us made a smudge pot and found it worked great. We put one of them in the tent before we went to bed, for the smoky atmosphere was a whole lot better than the constant swatting of mosquitoes that made it impossible to get any sleep.

The following day we washed clothes and cut hair. Angus was the barber, though a rather unwilling one; he refused to cut our hair very often. We also checked our pack saddles and equipment and made the necessary repairs, just as we had done on so many layovers. The day passed all too quickly but we felt more rested and I am sure the horses did, too. That evening we smoked the mosquitoes out of our tent again and had a fairly good sleep.

The land we travelled over now was flat and open, a welcome change from the sloughs and mosquitoes and rocks and fallen trees. We rode a little faster, eager to see the Cariboo just around the next bend in the trail. In the late afternoon when we began looking for a place to camp, we chose a five-acre patch of level land between a steep sand hill on one side and the river on the other. Downstream about three hundred yards was a neatly kept farm.

After supper, a man emerged from the farmhouse and came our way, curious to find out who we were and where we had come from. His name was Stan Williams and he worked for the owner of the farm, a widow named Genier. He explained that we were camped on an Indian fishing reserve.

"There's no restrictions on who camps here," he said, "just so's you don't do any fishing."

"You know anything about this trail to the Cariboo?" father asked. "Fellow named Wilson up the river a piece tells us it goes from Little Fort."

"Yeah, that's right. I never been over it but the Indians from Chu Chua use it all the time when they go to the Indian Reserve at Canim Lake. But you gotta cross the river again."

"So Wilson told us," said father. "We'll need to build a raft for that, I guess."

"Mrs. Genier's got a rowboat. I think I'm pretty safe in saying that her boy will take your supplies across for you."

When he had gone father said, "Well, boys, I think we'll take that Cariboo Trail instead of going all the way to Kamloops. It can't be any worse than some of the trails we've already come over."

In the morning we went to the farm and made arrangements with young Genier to take our supplies across. Mrs. Genier told us there was a store about six miles farther down the river at Chu Chua near the reserve so we decided to do some shopping first. We all needed new clothes: our shirts, overalls and other apparel were showing the abuse they had taken on the long trail through the mountains. We were threadbare, patched and repatched.

The store was well stocked with groceries, clothing and most everything country general stores carried in those days. But since the owner and manager, George Fennell, did most of his business trading with the Indians—there were still very few white people in that area—most of the stuff he carried was designed to appeal to their taste.

Young Genier rowed us and all our gear across the river the next day—the third and last time that we crossed the North Thompson. On each occasion it was wider and deeper but now the rowboat made our final crossing the easiest and quickest of all. By ten o'clock in the morning we had all our horses and belongings safely on the other side. Father offered to pay the boy but he refused to take anything. We were very grateful for his help.

Little Fort had been a Hudson's Bay trading post years earlier, but no sign of the post remained; we saw only one small deserted shack. The Geniers had told us that a murder had been committed there and several Indians had been questioned but nothing more had come of it. We camped nearby on the bank of the river and used the rest of the day to rearrange our packs, adding the supplies we had bought at Chu Chua, and prepared ourselves for the last lap of our journey.

Bill Sprung left us here, heading south for Kamloops sixty miles downriver, probably to pursue a logging job. As soon as he was gone, I whipped off my shirt, unstrapped Chappel's money belt and handed it back to him. I breathed a big sigh of relief to be rid of that cumbersome thing at last. We never saw or heard of Sprung again so we never did find out whether he was the kind of man who would have stolen Chappel's money.

The next morning the five of us began the long hard climb out of the river valley to the plateau above, nearly three thousand feet above sea level. But once we were up there, the trail led over flat, rocky country, covered in jack pine. There were occasional creeks and several clear sparkling lakes.

At nightfall we arrived at a large lake, easily three miles long, with several small islands rising out of its still waters, a perfect setting for our camp. Angus christened it Island Lake and it is still known by that name today.

The trail was bad the next day. We hit mud holes and fought our way through thick brush. In some places the ground was terribly rocky, making it hard on the horses' feet, so we had to slow down and let them pick their way with care. At noon we slid out of our saddles beside another lake to rest and eat our lunches. A little way along the shore was a large beaver house, so we dubbed this lake with its present name, Beaver Lake.

After a good rest we struck out again. The trail climbed for a ways, crossing a sidehill covered with large fir trees. Then for about two miles we dropped down onto a jack pine flat. We had covered almost twenty-five miles since leaving Little Fort and it looked as if we were in for a hard ride to the 100 Mile House. Then all of a sudden, we came out of the pines onto a sidehill covered with tall, waving grass of every kind. There must have been several hundred acres of it. And at the bottom of that sidehill was the most beautiful lake with the clearest blue water that we had ever seen. It was breathtaking.

We stood absolutely still, taking in the fantastic scene. It was father who broke the silence.

"Boys, this is it. This is the place I saw in my dreams months ago and hundreds of miles away."

But we knew before he spoke. We could almost see the tail of the rainbow overhead.

8

Ranch and Trapline

FOR NEARLY FOUR months, without the aid of maps or compass, father had led us three boys over the roughest and most difficult trail imaginable in search of the piece of ground that now lay spread at our feet. On that late August afternoon, it was hard to believe we had arrived. We rode slowly down the hill through heavy grass so tall that only the ears of our horses rose above it. After a mile or so, we came to a log cabin on the lakeshore. Nearby was a small barn with a lean-to shed, and a fence enclosing a little vegetable garden. But not a living soul came out to greet us.

We rode on along the shore and set up camp, sure that whoever owned the place would not object to our camping there and, with all those acres of grass, would not begrudge the little bit that our horses ate.

The lake was so long that we could not see the end of it but estimated that this part was at least five miles long and a mile wide; we learned later that the whole thing was eight miles long. About halfway across was a small island, and on the south shore opposite the island were a high rock cliff and heavily timbered hills. On the north side where we were, the land sloped back for a mile or more. It was mostly open with small bunches of willows and poplars, and the tallest, thickest carpet of grass that we had ever seen. The valley ran west to east, giving the south-facing grassy slope full exposure to the sun all day long.

Grazing along the slope above the lake were about fifty head of grade shorthorns—big red and red-roan cows and calves, and a dark red shorthorn bull with all the markings of a thoroughbred. And every one of them was so fat it seemed to shake when it walked.

After supper we walked up to the cabin. The door was padlocked but beside it a notice announced, as if meant for us: "I am putting up hay in the meadow about eight miles south." The meadow had to wait till morning, and after breakfast father started saddling up Frank. "I'm going to find the owner. There must be a trail of some kind." We knew father would find it if there was one.

Shortly after he left, Ed Chappel saddled up, off to look for land for himself. We boys fixed up our camp and then took another look at the surroundings. On the lake we found a small raft fitted with oarlocks and homemade oars. Once out from the shore we had a wonderful view of the landscape behind our camp and down the lake—a fabulous prospect of green sidehills and lake water as clear as glass. We didn't know the name of the lake, of course, but we decided to call it Long Lake.

We lay on the raft and, shading our eyes, watched fish swimming fifteen or more feet below us. We had known there would be lots of fish because of the number of loons around. They are such attractive birds with their snow-white breasts, black heads and black wings, and their wild, weird, lonely call. We watched them dive and swim underwater and made bets where they would reappear. When we tried answering their calls, some of them were attracted close to the raft, perhaps to see what kind of loons we were.

We paddled to shore about four o'clock just as father and another man rode in. This huskily built, middle-aged rider was Jack Demming, the owner of the land here on Long Lake and another 160 acres of natural hay meadow eight miles to the south. Since it was time for me to start making supper, our host told me to get any vegetables that I wanted from his garden, and so I cooked a big meal for all of us. While we were eating, Demming told us he had found this place just two years earlier, and had pre-empted 320 acres and bought 160 acres of meadow for five dollars an acre. He kept a little store here at the main ranch, mostly trade goods which he exchanged for furs from the Indians. Some parts of this country were very good for furs, he told us, offering beaver, otter, mink, muskrat, weasel, marten and lynx—in fact, almost every kind of fur-bearing animal native to Canada.

At the end of the meal, we leaned back, trying to look nonchalant. How would father persuade Demming to sell us this ranch, we wondered—because all of us knew this was the place where we were meant to live. We watched Demming pull out his pipe and light it.

"I'd like to sell this place," he said casually. "My rights to this here pre-emption on the lake and that there hundred and sixty acres of meadow. I'd like to sell the whole thing."

"Your cattle, too?" asked father.

"Yup. It's too big for one man way out here fifty miles from anywheres. Can't get hired help for love nor money!" He shook his head sadly.

"Well," said father, "I might consider making you a proposition but I'll have to talk it over with my sons." Father stood up, and we followed him to the door saying goodnight and walked back to our camp. Of course, there was nothing to talk over. My brothers and I were more than agreeable. In the morning, the two men settled on a price and we became the owners of the ranch on the big lake and the meadow eight miles away.

Father and Demming would have to go to the government office at the little town of Clinton on the Cariboo Road, a distance of eighty miles, in order to transfer Demming's pre-emption rights. Ed Chappel had found some land that he liked so he would go with them, and since the nearest store was also at Clinton, Dan would go to help pack home our winter supplies. Consequently, a couple of days later the four of them set off on horseback with all the pack horses except one; Old Molly was too old and worn out by the trip to go any farther. Angus and I were left on our own, and while this was not a new experience for him, I felt lonely before they were even out of sight.

While they were away we were expected to start cutting the heavy crop of grass on the hillside for winter feed for the horses and calves. There was no mower or any other farm equipment at the home ranch on the lake, so it appeared we would have to cut all this hay with hand scythes, but I quickly realized that Angus had no intention of slaving that way.

"Why should we do all that work by hand when there's a perfectly good five-foot Frost and Wood mower and a rake over at the meadow?" he asked me. He knew because he had heard father and Demming discussing them.

The big problem was how to move them to the home ranch along an eight-mile trail. With only old Molly for horsepower, we had a bit of a problem. However, we still had the single set of harness that we had used to haul raft logs so we decided to give it a try. Early the next morning we left leading Molly with the harness on her and a small pack containing two axes, wrenches, bailing wire and wire pliers. It was a mile and a half to the head of the lake where the trail forked. We had never been to the meadow but we knew it was to the south, and since the Cariboo Road was somewhere to the west, we took the fork that seemed to head in a more or less southerly direction. Pretty soon we could make out the tracks of two horses where father and Demming had ridden a few days earlier. It was a very poor trail with quite a number of small logs lying across it, but we had come over a lot worse ones in the last few months.

After three hours we came out of a thick wood of jack pines into a lovely meadow with a small lake at one end. We picketed Molly and walked out into the field, flushing out great flocks of mallard ducks and big Canada geese along the edge of the lake. There were plenty of deer tracks, too, and we realized that we had landed in a hunter's paradise.

On the upper edge of the meadow we found a log cabin and a corral made of poles where the mower and rake sat. We began to dismantle the mower, taking off the cutting bar and the tongue, then attached a pair of makeshift shafts. We cut two handspikes — poles about two and a half inches in diameter and six to seven feet long — and tied them onto the mower. At noon we went to the cabin intending to make tea to go with the lunch we had brought with us. The inside of that cabin was quite a shock: a bunk made of poles with a pile of swamp hay on top for a mattress, a few old clothes hanging from wooden pegs driven into the wall, a sheet-iron camp stove in one corner and a small table made of hand-hewn slabs; a packing box nailed to the wall above the table contained a few pots and pans, tin cups and such like, just the barest and crudest necessities. One small window faced the lake. It was impossible to believe that Demming had really lived in that shack part of each year, and as soon as we made our tea we got out into the fresh air again.

After lunch we hooked little Molly to the mower and started for home, Angus pushing from behind when necessary. Whenever we came to a log across the trail, we let her step over it, then we put handspikes under the mower, lifted it up and called, "Get up, Molly!" She would pull the mower over and away we would go until we came to the next one. Once or twice we had to chop a log or tree out of the way. But it was the big rocks that were most difficult because the wheels of the mower were brittle cast iron and could crack if they hit a rock too hard. So what with lifting and pushing and gently easing around boulders, we made it back to camp in seven hours—a bit more than a mile an hour. We figured it was well worth our work and trouble, however.

In the morning, we headed back to the meadow with Molly. Success had gone to our heads! If we could move the mower, said Angus, why not try getting the rake over? This would be a much more difficult project, since the rake was nine feet wide, too wide for the trail. But Angus was undaunted. He showed me how to remove the teeth, then set about taking off the tongue and wheels and stripping the rake down to its frame. We constructed a stoneboat frame slightly longer than the width of the rake and to it attached three crosspieces, one at each end and in the middle. These projected about six inches past the frame on each side so that we could put the handspikes under them. Next we loaded the frame of the rake onto the stoneboat, fastened it in place, then loaded the loose parts and set off for home. Our progress was slower this time. Whenever there was grass for the stoneboat runners to slide on, we made good time, but much of the trail was bare, dry ground causing the stoneboat to drag harder. Therefore, for most of the trip we helped Molly by pulling with ropes tied to the crosspieces.

When we arrived at the ranch we turned faithful old Molly

loose. That was the last work she ever did: for the rest of her days she was free to enjoy the green fields of grass.

In the morning we reassembled the mower and the rake and had them ready to start cutting hay as soon as father and Dan got back with the horses. Demming had told us that the return trip from Clinton would take about ten days so we still had plenty of time to turn our attention to the cabin at the home ranch. It was pretty dirty and took some elbow grease to clean up. Demming had built roughly the same setup here as at the meadow, though this cabin was larger and in a little better condition. There was a Yukon heating stove with a drum oven on the stovepipe which Demming had used for all his cooking. There were two good-sized bunk beds made of poles, a hand-hewn table and some wall shelves. A few of Demming's personal things were still hanging on pegs but he had said he would be back for these later. We moved all our belongings up from camp as soon as we had the place scrubbed out. After camping for so long, we found it was a most welcome change to have a real roof over our heads.

The day after we moved in, I tried to bake sourdough bread in the oven but it was impossible. The oven was a double-compartment affair and the smoke and the heat went both through and around the compartment where the bread was cooking. This meant that the only way to control the oven temperature was to control the heat of the fire and that was almost impossible because of the different kinds of wood we were using.

"It's no use, Angus," I said, "I'll have to go back to cooking over a campfire if I'm going to get it right."

"I've got a better idea," he said. And he did. Together we gathered rocks and blue clay and built a stone oven outdoors just like the one we had seen in the ruins of Jasper. We built a fire inside and outside of it and kept it burning until the clay was baked hard. When it was cooled enough to touch, we cleaned away the ashes and inspected our masterpiece. It looked pretty good to us. Then since it was still hot inside, Angus kept a small fire going while I mixed up a few loaves of bread and a pot of beans and bacon. The bread was baked in an hour; the beans took about six hours. But both were just perfect!

Shortly before dark on the tenth day since we'd been left

167

alone, the pack horses started to string in. As each arrived, Angus and I took off the pack and saddle, and suddenly Angus said, "Hey, what's going on here? There's seven here already and here come two more. That makes one too many!"

He was right. Father had bought one of Demming's horses since it was an ideal teammate for Pete, the remaining German coach horse. Father was very pleased that we had found a way to get the mower and rake over from the meadow because now we could do the haying much faster and have more time for the other work necessary before winter.

Ed Chappel had filed on a piece of land on a nice open sidehill that was as near to being a natural hay field as you could find in all the Cariboo. Near the north end of the meadow there was a large spring of clear, cold water that was never known to freeze over, and at the south end was a lake about a mile and a half long which we christened Montana Lake in honour of his home state. He set up camp there and began to cut logs for his house and barn. We saw him now and again since we had to go by his place to get to our meadow, but with all the work that had to be done before winter, none of us had much time for socializing.

Father had bought one set of harness from Demming and another in Clinton, so we could put one team on the mower and two of the biggest pack horses on the hay rake or on the hay slope, which was simply a lightweight hayrack on fourteen-foot runners used to haul the hay from the field to the stack. With the four of us working from dawn to dark, and the weather holding good, we had two stacks of hay built in two weeks.

Our standard of living had picked up. We had bought all of Demming's shorthorns so we separated from their calves two that looked as if they might make fair milkers and broke them to milk, providing us with plenty of milk and more than enough cream for butter and cheese. Quite often we shot a deer for fresh meat—in that country, big fat mule deer which made excellent eating. And there were so many vegetables in Demming's garden that we had to build a root cellar to store them.

Since we worked such long hours, we ate three hearty meals a day, but there were no coffee breaks. Breakfast at five in the morning consisted of mush with cream and sugar, sourdough pancakes, bacon and eggs. Sometimes the meat was venison, moose meat, pork or beef steaks. Frequently, there would be hot sourdough biscuits or toast, and nearly always fried potatoes. We drank coffee and lots of milk.

For our noon meal we ate rice or potatoes, meat or fish or poultry, baked beans, vegetables, bread, and desserts such as custard, bread or raisin pudding, or cooked fruit. We always had some kind of dessert. Our evening meal was a repeat of the noon meal, and we finished the day with a big snack before bed. Every Sunday I made a huge batch of sourdough bread, enough loaves to last the week. Churning butter was also a Sunday job as was cheese making.

One day in late September on his way to the meadow, father dropped in to see Ed Chappel. The place was deserted. Only a partially built barn showed that anyone had ever tried to settle there. We never did find out why or where Chappel went, but we figured he may have left because he was too lonely and the job he was undertaking was just too enormous. It took a strong back and a lot of determination to carve a home out of the wilderness all alone.

In early October, father prepared for a second trip to Clinton and down to Ashcroft. The first time he had been unable to file on the property because the record of Demming's relinquished claim had to be sent to the government land office in Victoria, when the land would be listed as open and available for pre-emption again. Now that Angus had turned eighteen, he would be able to pre-empt 160 acres of his own and therefore would accompany father on this trip. They took the pack horses and left us the saddle horses so that we could look after the cattle and cut wood in the meadow. We would need a good pile over there as someone would have to spend the winter at the cabin feeding and watering the cows.

Dan and I watched the pack horses vanish down the trail. The two of us, at sixteen and fourteen, would be all by ourselves fifty miles from nowhere for the next ten or so days. But father rode off without an apparent care or worry in the world. He had perfect confidence in our capabilities. He had raised us to be responsible and independent, and expected us to carry on just as if he were there. And we did.

Six days after father and Angus left, Demming rode in just

before dinner time, leading two pack horses. He had come to pick up his things. After supper he got his packs ready for a very early start the next morning and settled down in the bunk that Angus and father used. In the morning after he left, while making up Demming's bunk I found a bulky little canvas sack, and in it a great big thick roll of money. I was just dumbfounded to see all those greenbacks in a plain old canvas bag, and when Dan came in from milking I showed him the sack of money.

"It must be Demming's," I said. "We'll have to go after him."

Since Dan had already been over the trail, he rode out to try to overtake Demming. It was about three o'clock in the afternoon when he got back. He told me he had caught up to him on an open flat near a big lake that the Indians called White Fish Lake, six miles out.

"Have you lost anything?" Dan asked him.

Demming looked worried and searched through all his pockets. "My god," he said, "I've lost all my money!"

"Any idea where you might have lost it?" Dan asked.

"No, it could have been anywhere. I've had nothing but trouble with these danged horses. Been bucked off twice, and them pack horses have been bucking too. Had to stop back there and repack the whole works. It's just been one dang thing after another!"

Dan held out the sack to him. "Is this yours, Mr. Demming?"

"By golly, yes! Where did you find it?" he asked.

"My brother Ervin found it when he was making up the bunk you slept in last night. I started out as soon as he found it but you had a two-hour lead on me, and I was a little afraid I'd have to follow you all the way out to the 70 Mile," Dan said grinning. "Maybe you better count the money to see that it's all there."

When Demming finished counting, he held out his hand to Dan. "You're a very honest boy. I want to give you something for your trouble." Dan looked down at his hand; he was holding a ten-cent piece.

Now, my brother Dan was always the kindest and best-natured of us three boys, but this was just too much for even him.

"Keep it," he snapped. "That's a damned insult! Better to offer me nothing at all than a ten-cent piece!" And he turned his horse and rode off.

The next morning, Dan and I began cutting fence rails for a pasture for the calves that were to be weaned away from their mothers. We scarcely noticed the time go by, then suddenly it was the afternoon of the twelfth day and there were father and Angus riding up from the lake, their pack horses loaded with supplies: groceries, winter clothes, footwear, tools and nails, spikes and wire for fencing. Father told us he had met Demming at the 70 Mile House when he and Angus stopped there on the way home.

The 70 Mile was a stopping place for the freighters, the stage-coaches, and any wayfarer who wanted a night's lodging and a good meal. It was owned by Mrs. Boyd, whose husband had died only a short time before we arrived in the Cariboo, but she carried on with the help of her daughter Tottie and her four sons, Jim, Bill, Jack and Ira. The Boyds had a telephone and the telegraph office as well as the post office for the whole district. Like most of the stopping places, or roadhouses as they were generally called, the 70 Mile sold liquor by the bottle or by the glass, and in the evenings the travellers gathered in the big public room and swapped tales of the day's doings and the news of the countryside in general.

There was a pretty big crowd in the 70 the night that Demming decided to tell father about losing his money at the ranch. "Your boys are honest enough, MacDonald," he said, "but they sure don't got any manners! Your son Dan swore at me and told me what I could do with the ten cents I was going to give him!"

"You offered him ten cents reward for riding all that way to give you your savings?" asked father. "Mr. Demming, you're the one without manners! Any man who'd be so tightfisted as to offer ten cents to a boy who had returned all that money to him is frankly beneath contempt."

That was the last we ever heard of Demming.

The trip that father and Angus had taken to Ashcroft had been successful. Father had drawn enough money out of the bank to pre-empt the 160 acres on Long Lake where the home ranch was located and to pay $2.50 an acre for the 160 acres adjoining it. Angus had pre-empted the same amount of land at the head of the lake and had bought 160 acres on the north side of it.

Now after only a few months in British Columbia, we had a total of 800 acres of land— 640 forming the main ranch at Long Lake, and an additional 160 forming the meadow bought from Demming. Three years later, father and Angus pre-empted another 160 acres each adjoining their properties after they had proven up on their first pre-emptions.

Although we had been calling the beautiful lake at the main ranch Long Lake, when we got a map a few years later we found it had already been named Lac des Roches, probably by some French-Canadian trapper who had been impressed by the high cliff on the south side. However, we had got used to calling it Long Lake so we continued to do so. Very few people in the district, in fact, ever called it by its true name.

With father and Angus home again, the pace of work increased. We finished the pasture fence so the calves could be separated for branding and weaning. The first few days we could hardly put up with the uproar as they and their mothers bawled all day and all night for each other. Fortunately, they gradually calmed down and the cows began to stay away from the calf pasture for longer periods, until finally they forgot all about their offspring. We intended to keep the calves at the main ranch for the winter because there was better hay; the rest of the stock would go to the meadow where they could feed on rip-gut, otherwise known as slough hay.

In early October, while we were cutting wood at the meadow, we had found an even bigger meadow and another lake just south of it into which our creek flowed. So when father was in Clinton, he had leased the lower meadow from the government for two years until Dan turned eighteen and became eligible to pre-empt land, giving us 360 acres of good hayland in one block. However, there was no barn at either meadow, and the cabin was unfit to live in, so father decided that he and Angus and Dan would stay over there for the winter while they built a good log house, a barn, sheds and corrals. I was to stay at the home ranch to look after the calves, the horses and the two milk cows.

When the first of December came around, we drove the cattle to the lower meadow which was covered with thick, heavy slough grass. The stock was able to rustle out there till almost spring because the winter of 1907–8 turned out unusually mild, making a great saving on our hay supply and on our time since we didn't have to haul feed out to the animals. All that winter, father and Angus were able to work on the buildings while Dan took care of the cooking, cut water holes in the lake ice for the cattle to drink at, and acted as a general roustabout.

Game was plentiful and they had no trouble getting several fine, big mule deer to dress and hang up. These froze solid and so kept in good condition. After the small lakes at the meadow froze over, Dan cut holes in the ice and caught plenty of silver trout (kokanee landlocked salmon) and rainbow trout.

Alone at the home ranch, I watched the weather get colder. Now and then there was the odd skiff of snow. Several mornings I woke to find Long Lake partly frozen, but as soon as the wind came up, the big waves would smash up the ice. But day by day as the temperature of the air dropped, the warmer water in that big lake steamed like a huge kettle, the wind churned up bigger and bigger waves, and the water got colder.

About the first of January, I woke one morning to find the air exceptionally cold and clear. The surface of the lake was like a giant mirror, a smooth, level, glittering sheet of ice stretching for miles. This was the beginning of my first experience with a freeze-up, and though I watched it happening many times in the years which followed, the terror I felt on that first occasion will always stay with me.

The new ice contracted and expanded with the changing temperatures, exploding like thunder or splitting with the crack of artillery fire. Sometimes it went on cracking and banging all night, leaving me wide-eyed and scared out of my wits as I lay in bed. In the daytime I would hear a sharp snap from the lake, then a long whistling sound, and turn to watch a crack in the ice travelling right across the lake. After days and days of this, the giant mirror of smooth ice was completely covered by pressure cracks running in every direction, and along the shore a pressure ridge had formed nearly three feet high. Finally, the ice grew too thick to crack any more, and when the snow fell it hid all the cracks and ridges. I watched the whole process in amazement, not understanding how and why it was happening because there was no one to give me an explanation. I was only a young kid living alone miles from anywhere.

Meanwhile, every day I milked the cows and poured the milk I didn't need into large, shallow milk pans and put them outside to freeze. My father and brothers had no fresh milk over at the meadow and no oven in which to bake bread, so I baked extra loaves in the rock oven that Angus and I had built, and once a week packed the frozen milk and bread over to them. We put the frozen milk in the clean snow on the cabin roof, and whenever they needed some they chopped off a piece with a hand axe.

I was able to make the round trip to the meadow in about six hours, including stopping long enough for a meal with the others at noontime. I sure hated when it came time for me to ride back, for I was very lonely at the main ranch. I lived in a completely silent world. The ice on the lake had stopped snapping and banging, and on the clear, frosty nights, I could hear the Northern Lights crackling. Sometimes, I would stand outside the cabin at night to watch the colours in the sky, and now and then I'd give a few loud yells just to make a sound. When the timber wolves answered back, I was reassured that there was still some sort of life in the world.

One day about the end of January, an old Indian came to the cabin. He had two very large dogs with him, each one carrying a pack. They were big, yellow mongrels with heavy bodies, something like mastiffs, and could carry up to thirty pounds apiece on their backs. The Indian was about five and a half feet tall and strongly built, though I think he must have been nearly sixty years old, and he wore heavy mackinaw clothing and moccasins. He could speak better English than most Indians, and told me that his name was Cashmere. He was very disappointed not to find Mr. Demming at the cabin because he wanted to trade some marten and mink skins for some grub. Of course, I had no idea what his furs were worth, but I invited him to stay for supper with me; while we were eating I explained that Demming had sold all his land to us and had left the country. I told him about father and my brothers. He asked if he could stay with me for a few days and I was pleased. It would mean a break in my lonely routine.

I was in for a valuable education from this old Shuswap Indian. He proved to be a remarkable fellow and very intelligent. He had, on occasion, acted as a guide for the RCMP when they were travelling around the country investigating trouble or looking for lawbreakers. He had also been a guide for timber cruisers, hunters and prospectors. He was a past master at camp cooking, and he showed me how to fasten bannocks and biscuits onto willow sticks and cook them over a heap of hot coals, and how to attach trout to a split piece of timber with wooden pegs. He knew all kinds of short cuts for cooking without pots and pans.

When I asked about his snowshoes, he helped me make a pair just like them and taught me how to use them. He said they were much better on the dry, powdery snow of the Cariboo country than the factory-made ones that the white men used. Then he explained how to set traps for all the different kinds of fur-bearing animals, how to recognize their tracks in the snow, and how to tell the difference between a good fur and a bad one. I knew nothing about these things so I absorbed every word he said.

Much later, as I learned more about Cashmere, I realized that he was a real confidence man, or as close to one as an Indian could be. He had a fine piece of gold-bearing ore that he carried around in his pack, as perfect a specimen as you could find anywhere: you could see the gold in it with the naked eye, and with a magnifying glass it showed very rich indeed.

Old Cashmere knew how to get the most mileage out of his chunk of ore and soon "Cashmere's Mine" became the talk of Kamloops and the settlements along the river. Whenever the old man saw two or three prosperous-looking men together, he would sidle up and show them his ore specimen. Then he would sit back and wait for them to come begging to see his claim; he would size them up and decide which one to take into the mountains to see it. He would furnish the horses, demanding an exorbitant price by the day, while his victim would have to supply all the grub, the camping outfit, the prospecting equipment and a sizeable cash deposit. When everything was ready, Cashmere would lead his man into the mountains for a week or ten days.

He always managed to reach some fine fishing lake by the time they were ready to stop for their noonday meal, or when Cashmere decided that the horses were "too much tired maybe. Maybe much better camp." Sometimes, if their noon camp turned out to be a really good fishing spot, they would stay there all day while the horses recovered their stamina. In this way, Cashmere killed time, all the while getting well paid for his horses and his guiding services. At other times, it was simply amazing how that brilliant old woodsman could lose his way and stumble into such thick jungles of brush and windfalls that it would take him hours to find the way out, just in the nick of time to camp an hour before sunset by a little lake of clear water with plenty of fine rainbow trout for the taking and lots of good grass for the horses. There would be a nice place to pitch a tent overlooking the water and a thick cluster of spruce trees for a background. The victim soon forgot the last few hours of fighting through the jungle. But as soon as they hit the trail the next morning looking for that gold mine, old Cashmere would become confused again. He would say, "Me not too sure, everything look different. Maybe this time we find. Maybe over thataway, maybe. Me getting to be an old man. Maybe soon go *mimaloos* [die]. Maybe now we go thisaway."

And so the old man would stall around, having a good fishing trip and earning good money until it was time to go back to Chu Chua with another very disappointed prospector. If any of these victims ever got wise to the fact that they had been taken on a wild-goose chase, they were generally too ashamed to admit that an old Indian had just been a little too smart for them. A lot of people had doubts about Cashmere's mine and some of them said flatly that it didn't exist at all. But Cashmere had a gold mine all right, even if it was just in his crafty old brain.

A couple of days after Cashmere arrived on his first visit with me, a terrific blizzard came up. It wasn't safe to travel, so he stayed two more days while the storm blew itself out. On the third day, though the temperature had dropped to thirty degrees below zero, the sun came out and the whole outdoors was changed to a fairyland, the air thick with frost crystals sparkling like diamonds. There wasn't a breath of wind, just a bright, snow-covered silent world, beautiful beyond belief, the evergreen trees covered with dazzling snow.

It was time for my visitor to leave. He prepared his packs indoors, then got his dogs from the barn where they had waited out the storm and tied them to a tree. He explained that he never let them see the packs beforehand because they would run away and he would never be able to catch them. They resented being made into pack animals, he said. He thanked me for letting him stay through the storm and then, with his new groceries safely loaded onto the two big dogs, he hit the trail.

I was alone again with a lot of work waiting to be done. Besides my regular chores, the blizzard had made extra work: everything was covered with snow, so I had to dig out the cabin and the barn, shovel the drifts from the water holes on the lake, cut the ice where the stock watered, dig out the woodpile and uncover the rock oven. I fired up the oven and put in several loaves of bread and a kettle of beans to bake, and life began to look a little brighter. You develop a big appetite in such severe weather and it takes plenty of food to fight the cold.

The next day I set off for the meadow with bread and frozen milk but it was tough going over the drifted trail; many trees had fallen in the storm and I had to either chop them out of the way or go around them. My trip was two days later than usual so father and my brothers were very glad to see me, though I was never quite sure whether it was me or the food that was most welcome. They had had no bread for a couple of days and were eating baking-powder bannocks cooked in a frying pan on top of the stove.

After that, the weather stayed clear and cold till about the middle of February when we had another snowstorm and sub-zero temperatures. When the weather cleared again, I started out on my new snowshoes to set a few traps. Demming had kept a good assortment of traps to sell to the Indians and left a supply of them in the cabin as part of the deal when we bought the place. Following Cashmere's advice, I set weasel and mink traps along the lakeshore where I could see their tracks in the snow. I also set a few traps and snares for the big Canadian lynx where I had seen the large round tracks they left while hunting snowshoe hares along the edge of the spruce swamp.

One evening about this time, I had my second visitor, a tall man riding a big bay horse. I had been around saddle horses most of my life so I knew a good one when I saw it, and this was without doubt one of the best. That animal had been ridden about thirty miles across country through three feet of snow that day, but he still had plenty of steam left.

Although Ike Simmons must have been about the same age

as Cashmere, from my fourteen-year-old vantage point he seemed too strong and virile to be considered old. He told me that he and his three brothers were starting a horse ranch on a meadow on the South Bonaparte River, just south of us, and that he had met father at the 70 Mile House in November. Father had told him we'd be happy to see him whenever he was in our neck of the woods, and since he had time on his hands for a few days, he had set off to see the country and meet his old friends and some of the newcomers.

I was glad to have him stay as long as he wanted; besides, no one was ever refused shelter in the wintertime in that country. Simmons pitched right in and helped me with the chores and the cooking, then came along while I worked on my traps and pointed out my mistakes in setting them. He showed me how to make wooden stretchers for my furs by cutting pieces of spruce the right length for the different skins. Spruce generally has a very straight grain so that it splits easily, making it ideal for the three-piece wedge stretchers over which weasel, muskrat, marten and mink skins are drawn. Beaver and bear have to be stretched on a flat surface, or the beaver skins can be sewn onto round hoops made from a willow, the most practical way when out in the mountains.

After a week, Simmons announced he had to leave and went along with me when I took milk and bread over to the meadow, which was near the head of the South Bonaparte; he could go home the last twenty miles that way, visiting with father, Angus and Dan for a few days first. We found that since the days were now getting longer and warmer good progress had been made on the new buildings at the meadow. But I could only stay a few hours before heading back to the home ranch and my regular routine. I really missed Simmons's company now, but I knew I had profited from his visit in many ways. He had explained how to make skis and I got busy making a pair. Those first ones were quite crude, but they were a lot of fun, and in time Angus, Dan and I were able to make skis that served our purposes much better and gave us great pleasure, too. The biggest problem was the best kind of wood to use. We tried jack pine but it was soft and wore out too fast on crusty snow. Then we tried spruce, and although it was lightweight and easier to shape, it was so soft

178

that it wouldn't hold the sharp curve of the ski tip. Douglas-fir was too brittle and it made the skis too heavy. Finally, we found that birch wood was just right and there was an ample supply all around us.

We cut a birch tree about six or eight inches in diameter with a good straight trunk and free of limbs for about nine feet, and took it to our whipsaw pit to cut into boards eight feet long, an inch and a half thick and about four inches wide. Then we settled down with a drawknife and spokeshave and plane to shape the boards into the proper form. Finally, we would stand the boards tip down in a five-gallon can filled with water and set it to heat. As a rule we built the fire outside, but sometimes we set the can on the kitchen cookstove. We kept the water boiling for an hour or two until the wood was well heated, then put the boards into a press we had made to bend them in an even curve. It took several days for the wood to dry thoroughly and take on a lasting curve. Next we sanded the bottoms until they were velvety smooth and attached a harness we had made out of old horse harness. There were heavy leather pieces across the toes and straps looped around the ankles so that it was possible to twist our feet out of the harness easily. We waxed the bottoms with paraffin to make them slide smoothly and set off over the frozen lakes and the deep-drifted snow.

Occasionally, we had accidents with them. Once when I was skiing down the hill in front of our house, I got travelling so fast that I lost control: the tips of my skis hit the gatepost and came to an abrupt stop, but I didn't because the harness broke and I flew headfirst through the gate, landing about thirty feet away in a huge snowdrift. I was shaken up though unhurt, but the points of an especially good set of skis were broken right off. I had to get busy making a new pair.

Near the end of February, I began to see coyotes and timber wolves travelling on the lake ice, and sometimes in the early mornings a giant moose would trot right across the lake. There was never too much fresh snow on it as the high winds swept it pretty clean, leaving just a thin covering frozen fast to the ice. This made a great highway for the animals to travel on. I liked it fine, too, because I could walk without snowshoes along the lake edge to look at my traps.

A small stream came down a draw at the east end of our property about a mile from the cabin and the beaver had built a dam where it emptied into the lake, creating a large pond behind it. There was a big beaver house there, but I couldn't set traps for them because for several years it had been closed season on beaver. However, where the water spilled over the dam to the lake was a fine place to trap mink and otter because I could see their tracks in the snow along the edge. I also had traps for weasel along the edge of the pond itself.

Whenever I went to check these traps, I took a 30–30 carbine rifle with me and once in a while shot a coyote or a wolf. Though their fur didn't bring much money, I could collect the government bounty; at that time it was thought these animals killed too much game.

One morning when I headed down the lake as usual to visit my traps, out on the ice I could see rabbit tracks that went out for about forty yards and suddenly stopped, yet there was no rabbit. I was curious and walked out to investigate, but all I found were light marks about twelve inches from either side of where the tracks stopped. I stood there puzzled, but finally the answer came to me: these new marks had been made by the tips of a great horned owl's wings where they had brushed the snow. One of the silent grey-ghost hunters of the night had swooped down on that rabbit and in one continuous movement hooked his talons into his midnight supper and carried it away to his hoot-owl retreat.

When I arrived at the open water at the beaver dam that morning, I saw fresh moose tracks. Our supply of meat was getting low so I decided to follow them. The animal had headed for a thicket of reed willows which were a favourite food of moose, so I slipped back to a low ridge and worked my way along behind it till I thought I was about opposite the willows. Creeping up to look over the ridge, I saw the head and neck of a moose; it was feeding off the tops of the willows. Resting my rifle on a limb of a small spruce tree, I took careful aim on the biggest part of its head near the ears. I fired, and it dropped like a stone. I ran down into the thicket; it hadn't moved.

It looked about two years old, a healthy young bull moose. Now my only problem was how to get it to the cabin. I ran all the way home, harnessed the team, got a long strong rope, a log chain, an axe and a singletree, and started back to get my moose. I tied the rope around the head, hooked up the horses and pulled the moose out of the thick bush. Then I exchanged the rope for a chain. Once I got the carcass to the lake most of my troubles were over as the horses were able to walk along easily.

It was noon when I got back to the cabin and found father, Angus and Dan waiting for me. I was just as surprised to see them as they were to see me coming up from the lake with the team dragging that moose, but they could see how proud and pleased I was with myself.

Over lunch, father casually asked, "Ervin, do you know what day it is?"

"No," I said. I had no idea. I had lost all track of time because every day is the same when you are alone.

Then he grinned and said, "Happy birthday, Ervin!"

It was the first day of March 1908 and I was fifteen years old. And I had shot my first moose! What a day for me and one that I will always remember. Father and my brothers had come over from the meadow especially to wish me a happy birthday. I was so glad to see them.

But there was still work to be done even on my birthday. We dressed and quartered the moose and father estimated that we had about four hundred pounds of fresh meat. It was supper time before we had finished and done the chores. Father had arranged things at the meadow so that they could stay all night. Long after the others were asleep that night, I lay in my bunk thinking of the events of the day.

Early the next morning, they helped me to hang some of the meat about eight or nine feet from the ground on a strong pole fastened between two trees down near the lake where it would freeze for as long as the weather was cold. The rest of the meat was to go over to the meadow where it would be hung in the same way.

In warmer weather we hung meat up in a flyproof safe that we had built under a cluster of trees at the lakeshore. Moose meat and venison soon got a hard crust on the outside and the meat on the inside kept fresh and sweet for two or three weeks. Probably one reason for this was that the nights were always cool. We kept beef and veal in the same way, but we never butchered pigs in summer because we found out that pork would not keep. We intended to build a proper icehouse when we had the time, but other jobs were more pressing.

After the meat was hung, father and Dan headed back to the meadow for another six weeks' work on the buildings. Angus stayed on with me to cut fence rails. Already the days were getting longer, but we were all so busy that the time passed very quickly and spring took us by surprise. One morning I woke up to find a warm south wind blowing. The snow began disappearing under our feet and water ran everywhere. Like magic the ice along the shore of the lake melted leaving long strips of open water.

By mid-April, flocks of geese and ducks were flying high in the sky; robins and other birds had reappeared. The grass was beginning to grow again and the trees burst into their new, tender, green dress. I couldn't believe that anything could be so beautiful.

At the meadow, the buildings were finished. We brought the cattle home and turned the cows with their new crop of calves out on the summer range. During the winter we had drawn up plans for a new house and a big barn at the main ranch, and father had worked it out that for the house we would need sixty logs about a foot across, twenty-five and thirty-four feet long. The main thing to remember in building with logs, he told us, was to select straight, uniform trees. "Always walk around each tree and take a good look from all directions, as a tree is like a woman, she keeps her prettiest side toward you!" How right he was. When Angus and I set off to find the trees for the house, we often saw one that looked just right at a distance, but when we got close and sized it up from all angles, it turned out to be crooked and worthless. Since we intended to build the house out of peeled logs, we had to start cutting immediately while the sap was running. Once the trees had been felled, trimmed and cut to the right length we hauled them out of the bush and placed them on skids, or long platforms, for peeling. The logs were not hard to peel because the fresh sap loosened the bark, and as they were off the ground on skids we were able to keep them nice and clean. By working twelve to fourteen hours a day we had all the house logs ready within two weeks.

Next, we began selecting logs for the barn. In the meantime, father and Dan made a trip to Clinton, taking all the pack horses because they would have a big load of supplies going both ways. Going to town, they carried the furs we had trapped. Angus and Dan had taken about two hundred muskrats on the lakes at the meadow, a few dozen minks and weasels, and a coyote or two. Added to the pelts I had taken, they made a good-sized bundle, and when father sold them to the fur buyers in Clinton, they paid for all our purchases. This was our first indication that trapping was going to be a big financial help in our struggle to build up a ranch.

Father and Dan were gone for eight days, but they came back with everything we needed to get on with our work. Among the packages were garden seeds: we had seen what a beautiful garden Demming had cultivated and we thought we would try our luck with one. Father inspected the work that Angus and I had done and announced: "You've done a good job. I am really pleased." This was rare praise from father, and Angus and I grinned at each other like a pair of conspirators at the memory of the fishing we'd managed to squeeze in.

By now all the ice on the small lakes had melted, but the main body of ice still sat in the middle of Long Lake, though we could see it was getting darker in colour and water-logged and there were large cracks across it. Then on 15 May, a wind from the west started to blow and very soon the ice began to move, slowly at first, but gradually building up speed until the whole mass was moving, grinding and crashing as it broke into pieces. The first open water appeared at the west end of the lake, and in a few hours the ice was all gone. We stopped work to watch the last of it disappear and the return of that huge body of sparkling, clear blue water. Within a week, trout were jumping all over the lake, as if celebrating their freedom after being locked under the ice for four and a half months. About a week later, the bluebirds came back, and the loons returned with their wild, lonesome calls. Spring was here for sure.

One of our first projects that spring was to build the line fence around our property, and one day when we had worked our way to a point in the woods nearly half a mile from the house, we came across a big female mule deer lying on the ground. Her back was broken although she was still alive. Most likely she had been struck down by a grizzly bear that had been scared off by the noise we made chopping and falling trees. The doe would never be able to regain her feet so father shot her to end her suffering. Since we could see that she had been nursing young, we started to look for them in the thick brush. We weren't having any luck when we heard father beckoning. He was standing in a cluster of willows and he pointed to a spot under the trees: two tiny fawns lay there, but it was almost impossible to see them because they were so still; they were so well camouflaged they seemed to be part of the earth itself. They were alive, but we knew they wouldn't live more than a day or so without food. When we got them to their feet we saw they were no more than one or two days old—still wobbling on their long, spindly legs. One was a buck and the other a doe. We carried them back to the house and fed them two parts milk and one part water, thinking that straight cow's milk might be too rich for them. They learned very quickly to drink from a bottle through a nipple made from the finger of an old leather glove.

Right from the start, however, the tiny buck seemed much weaker than the doe, and within a week he died. But the doe which we named Queenie was strong and lively, and had an appetite like a little pig. She became a great pet, matured quickly and soon had the run of the ranch. To make sure she would not be shot by some hunter, we fastened a little bell around her neck. She soon became fast friends with our big greyhound pup, Swift, and they would race each other all over the ranch. However, if a strange dog arrived, Queenie would put one ear forward and the other one back, her hair would stand on end, making her look twice as large as she actually was, and she would charge the intruder. She would spring up into the air and, drawing all four feet together, come down onto the dog's back with all her weight and tremendous force, trying to break the animal's back. With this technique she could put the run on any dog in the country.

The one thing we didn't approve of was the way she also put the run on our calves and cows. She would rear up on her hind legs and strike at them with her front feet to keep them away from her favourite haystacks. It didn't take them long to learn to keep out of her way. She would round up all the calves, as if she were a cowboy, and head them toward the lake hitting them with her front feet to keep them going. We had dug a twenty-foot-wide, forty-foot-long trench sloping to the edge of the lake for the cows to reach the water, and Queenie would herd them down it whether they wanted to drink or not. Then she would buck and dance around, completely pleased with herself. We just had to be grateful that she never bothered the horses or the pigs and chickens.

Queenie gave us a real education in the ways of deer. If she saw one of us inside the house, she would simply jump through the window and join us. This was a nuisance as window glass could only be bought in Ashcroft or Clinton, so we nailed slats over the bottom part of the windows. She would follow all of us around like a dog, though she seemed to have a particular fondness for father. Many times, in good weather when we had the doors open, we would find her sleeping on father's bed when we came home. If we wanted to go anywhere and didn't want her to follow us, we had to lock her up in the barn. We tried everything to keep her out of the garden, but she refused to be kept out because she just loved the cabbages and carrot tops. Sometimes we gave her tasty crusts of bread.

She always chose the highest spot she could find to sleep. Usually it was the highest haystack, but if there was no haystack close by she would get on top of a shed, or the barn or chicken house or some other high building. On winter mornings, we would find her sleeping on her chosen spot, completely covered with snow, but when she heard us she would stand up, shake off the snow and come running, making a mewing sound. She always came when we called her name.

Queenie liked very few people who came to our house. She would rear up and strike out at whoever she disliked with those quick-as-lightning front feet of hers. She took a great liking to Bill Banning who lived on Bridge Lake about ten miles away and who sometimes worked for us. Quite a few times she followed him home, even starting out a day or two after he had gone, and if his door was unlatched, she would push it open. Poor Bill would come in from his chores to find her fast asleep on his bed.

Frequently she would follow me on my trapline, sometimes showing up two or three days after I had left the ranch. It was almost uncanny the way she was able to track me even in deep snow. She would just put her nose down and go. The first time she showed up I was just getting a lynx out of a trap: she struck at it to kill it by rearing up and coming down on it with those powerful front feet. Then she danced around and mewed as if to say, "Just see how helpful I can be!"

There was considerable sadness in our household when in the fall of her second year her mating instinct called and she left us. We often wondered just what became of her, but we consoled ourselves that we had given her two years of life which she would have missed if we had not taken her home with us the day her mother was struck down.

In that first spring in 1908, father had his heart set on having our new house built before haying time, which meant that we had to work quickly. But even when he worked fast father was such an expert axeman that the dovetailed corners on the house were simply a work of art. For the time being, the house would be just one big room with the sleeping quarters at one end and the living and cooking area at the other. An attic provided extra sleeping room. The house was capped with a shake roof. As a rule, shakes are cut from cedar trees, but since there are no cedars in our neck of the woods, we cut ours from fir trees. The floor was puncheon, that is, jack pine logs about eight inches in diameter split in two, then smoothed with an adze. The split logs were fitted over log stringers; when carefully laid, they make a reasonably even floor. We made the doorjambs and window frames from hand-hewn timbers and the doors from whipsawn lumber. We bought windows in Clinton which my brothers packed in from the 70 Mile House without breaking a single pane. By the middle of June, we had a roomy house and gratefully we moved from the little dark cabin where we had lived since our arrival.

We had finished our house-building with a few weeks to spare before haying time, and father decided he would use it to buy a wagon and one more mower, and a decent cookstove for the new house. I think he was tired of eating burnt food: I was doing the best I could, but it was very difficult cooking on a heater because it got far too hot. Mowers and wagons could only be bought in Ashcroft, and getting them home would be an even bigger problem because there was no wagon road from the 70 Mile to our ranch. However, when father made up his mind to do something, he didn't waste any time, so one morning at breakfast he announced that he was riding to Clinton to see about getting a wagon road built. When he returned a few days later, he announced, "Boys, it's all settled. We can go ahead and build the road!"

We had not much time left before haying, so for the present, as long as the road was passable we weren't going to fuss over it. For the first ten miles from the ranch, it was easy going with little slashing necessary, but about eight miles along we came to the creek that connects White Fish Lake with a long, narrow, winding lake that we had named Crooked Lake. Here we spent three days building a good log bridge that would withstand the traffic of wagons. The land near the outlet of the creek was a favourite camping place for the local Indians when they were on hunting and fishing expeditions. They often stayed for weeks at a time, so when we began building there, they came to watch us. Those who had never seen a bridge before were greatly impressed with this invention of the white man. As soon as we finished, they began riding their horses back and forth over it; like children with a new toy, they were fascinated. They began calling the creek "Bridge Creek," and they renamed the lake "Bridge Lake," and that is how lovely Bridge Lake with its twenty-seven islands got its name.

Two miles beyond Bridge Creek was a swampy place where we had to make a corduroy road: we cut logs and placed them side by side to make a cover over the swamp which took another two days. There was a crystal-clear lake nearby which we named Crystal Lake. For two miles along its shore we had to do quite a bit of slashing, but half a mile from the end of the lake we came out onto an open hillside with a long, narrow meadow and a small lake at its lower end. There was scarcely any clearing to do along here. We were now about fifteen miles from our ranch, travelling along the headwaters of the North Bonaparte River.

At the far end of the meadow we found about two hundred head of sheep guarded by a young man and a dog. The young fellow was Dal Price whose father had pre-empted the meadow about two weeks earlier.

"We came in with two other families," he told us, "from south of Spokane, Washington. We cut a makeshift road from the Seventy Mile as far as the Bonaparte River so we could bring in the wagons." Dal had been sent on alone with the sheep while the rest of his family figured out some way to get the wagons to their pre-emption.

We were pleased to know we were getting neighbours, especially since they wanted a road as badly as we did and would be only too happy to help us slash one out. Father rode on to enlist the aid of Mr. Price and the other men, and as a result we soon had a passable road built. Some of the hills were quite steep and the sidehills gave us trouble but none of us could take the time to do any grading. Where there was a real danger that a wagon could upset, we solved the problem by carrying a pole about twenty-five feet long with a five-inch butt and two inches at the top; on the steep sidehills, we would tie it securely crosswise on the top of the wagon box with the small end projecting up the hill. A short rope was tied to the small end and one man walked along the sidehill above the road, holding on to the rope and keeping his weight on this long lever. This method was consistently successful in preventing upsets.

When a hill was so steep that the team might have trouble holding the wagon back, we cut a tree with lots of limbs on it and chained it by one end to the back axle of the wagon. Dragged against its branches, the tree made quite an efficient ruff-lock and prevented the wagon from crowding the horses. Whenever any of us or the Price family had time, we worked on the road and gradually improved it.

Father and Angus had the honour of making the very first trip over the new road to buy the wagon, mower, stove, and a good stock of groceries before haying got under way. They also intended to buy a heavy team of horses, as most of the pack animals were too light for hauling a heavily loaded wagon over the new road. They took one of our old teams out with them but on the way stopped at the ranch of Henry Atwood, who lived on the west side of Green Lake not far from the 70 Mile, and bought a nice team of mares. Continuing on to Ashcroft, they made the rest of their purchases.

On the way home they stopped in Clinton at Archie Mac-Donald's General Store. "Silent Mac," as he was known, was also MLA for Lillooet District in those days, but for the people in the surrounding district and north of Clinton on the Cariboo Road and right into the Chilcotin country, he was the man they came to for pins or harness, rifles or blankets, clothing, dry goods, groceries, or anything else you could think of. On the very first trip that father made to Clinton in 1907, he bought a 30–30 carbine rifle from Silent Mac for $17.50, and ammunition at 95 cents for a box of twenty shells. It was an exceptionally reliable gun and I brought down a lot of game with it over the next twenty years.

Father and Angus had an enormous load on their return trip but they had hitched all four horses to the wagon. What a treat it was to have a real cookstove after making do for so long with a campfire or a heater! The new stove was made of cast iron and had an oven with doors on two sides. Now I was able to make really good puddings and when I had the time, I even tried my hand at pies and cakes like Lavena had baked for us long ago. We never used the old rock oven again because our new house was about a quarter of a mile from the old cabin.

Haying began in the second week of July and we made fairly good time with our two mowers and using a bucking pole. To speed things up even more, we hired two young Indian men to help, but though they were good workers, they wouldn't stay with the job for more than two weeks at a time. Then they took their wages and headed for the reservation where they spent their money or gambled it away. When it was all gone, they would come back and work for another short spell. This really annoyed father because we had to get as much hay into stacks as possible when the weather was fine.

Then one day, Will Wilson, the man who had showed us how to make smudge pots at Mosquito Flats the year before, showed up with his father, a big one-armed man about sixty years old, and Will's three brothers, George, Charlie and Albert, who had come up from Washington looking for land to pre-empt. They all

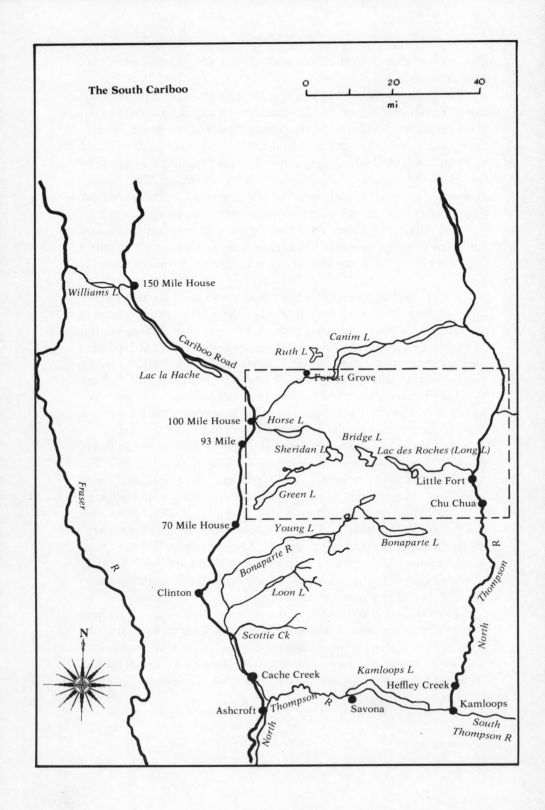

The South Cariboo

0   20   40

mi

150 Mile House

Williams L

Cariboo Road

Canim L

Ruth L

Lac la Hache

Forest Grove

100 Mile House

Horse L

93 Mile

Bridge L

Sheridan L

Lac des Roches (Long L)

Fraser

Green L

Little Fort

Chu Chua

R

70 Mile House

Young L

Bonaparte L

Bonaparte R

N

Loon L

North Thompson R

Clinton

Scottie Ck

Kamloops L

Cache Creek

Heffley Creek

Ashcroft

North Thompson R

Savona

Kamloops

South Thompson R

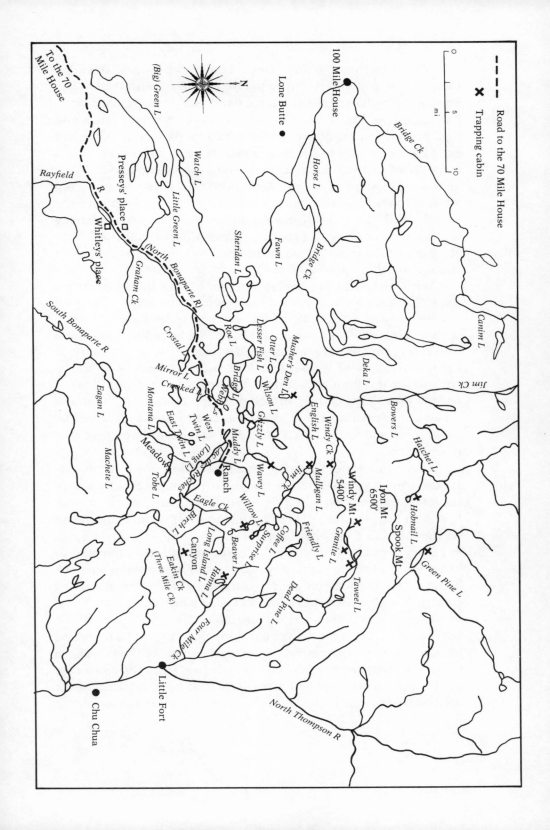

To the 70
Mile House

Rayfield

(Big) Green L.

Watch L.

Little Green L.

Presseys' place

Whitleys' place

(North Bonaparte R.)

Graham Ck.

R.

South Bonaparte R.

Crystal L.

Mirror L.

Crooked

Eagan L.

Machete L.

Montana L.

East Twin L.

West Twin L.

Meadow

Tobe L.

Birch L.

Eakin Ck.
(Three Mile Ck.)

Long Island L.

Hanna L.

Canyon

Beaver L.

Willow L.

Eagle Ck.

Surprise

Four Mile Ck.

Little Fort

Chu Chua

North Thompson R.

Sheridan L.

Fawn L.

Lone Butte

100 Mile House

Horse L.

Bridge Ck.

Bridge Ck.

Roe L.

Bridge L.

Lesser Fish L.

Otter L.

Musher's Den L.

Wilson L.

Webb's

Muddy L.

Long L.

Lac des Roches

Ranch

Grizzly L.

Wavey L.

English L.

Coffee L.

Friendly L.

Jim Ck.

Mulligan L.

Windy Ck.

Windy Mt.
5400'

Granite L.

Iyon Mt.
6500'

Taweel L.

Dead Pine L.

Green Pine L.

Spook Mt.

Hobnail L.

Hatchet L.

Bowers L.

Jim Ck.

Deka L.

Canim L.

Bridge Ck.

N

stayed with us for a few days, found land they liked and staked it; then George and Albert stayed to give us a hand with the haying. They were both experienced farm hands so we made good time, putting up the balance of 200 tons of hay at the main ranch and then moving our outfit over to the meadow. By this time, we had used the damp days to slash out a proper road, so now it was just a matter of loading the machinery onto the wagon and hooking up the team. All of us except Dan moved over to the meadow. My job was to cook for the gang and in my spare time help with the haying. With the two Wilsons on the mowers and Angus driving the rake, we made fast progress. When Charlie returned from filing their claims in Clinton, he pitched right in too, and we soon stacked another 150 tons of hay.

With the haying finished, it was time to start building our big barn. The logs we had peeled had been sitting on the skids all summer and were now bone dry. They were very easy to work with and the barn went up quickly. It had a large loft which held nearly fifty tons of hay and provided wonderful sleeping quarters for the overflow of grub-line riders and travellers who stayed with us by the hundreds during the years we ranched there. I used to love sleeping there myself during the summer, and it was especially pleasant to wake to the sound of rain falling on the shake roof and know that I wouldn't have to get up early that morning.

About this time, the government sent out word that home-steaders must get their land surveyed to establish exactly where the lands they had bought, pre-empted and leased were located. It was up to us to hire a government land surveyor to come in and do the job, so on October first, father and Angus took the four-horse team out to Clinton again to see about hiring one and to buy supplies for the coming winter. In ten days they were back home with a big load on the wagon, and behind them came two strangers with a team and democrat. One was Neville Smith, the surveyor, and the other was his chainman, Neil McCall. We three boys went with them into the bush as axemen to cut the trees and brush away from their survey lines. Father wanted the lakeshore to be our southern boundary, so we started from the southeast corner post which we had already placed by the lake a short distance below our house. From here our land was surveyed, the first in the entire district to be done. It took several days to do the ranch and the meadow, but we didn't mind. Neville and Neil were lively, jolly fellows, always playing pranks on each other and chuck full of jokes. My brothers and I had so much fun while they were with us that we were sorry to see them leave.

There was a lot of good land in the Bridge Lake district and father figured that if it were surveyed and properly staked, it would be more attractive to new ranchers, which would mean more services for the area. He contacted the government agent in Clinton, Mr. Soues, to see if he would send in a survey crew. He also asked him to try to get the government to reserve a point of land on Bridge Lake as a future park site, preserved from land speculators for everyone to enjoy. As a result of father's concern, Neville Smith came back the next year with two survey crews and worked in the Bridge Lake district for two seasons. When the land he surveyed was mapped and made available to the public, many more settlers took up pre-emptions, and thus the prosperity of the district was increased.

We were much better prepared to meet the winter of 1908–9 than the previous one. We now had a good house, barn, sheds and corrals at the home ranch as well as at the meadow. And we had made preparations to do a lot more trapping, having learned a great deal about it the winter before and now knowing the lakes, streams and the surrounding country.

On his final trip to Ashcroft in October father had bought another cookstove and a large heater that would take a stick of wood four feet long, allowing us to take the smaller cookstove and heater over to the meadow. Our new stove was a real dandy: a six-hole modern range with a large oven, a warming oven and a reservoir for heating water! After that, I found it much easier to cook for the large numbers of people who often sat around our table.

Our ranch was now at the end of the road from the 70 Mile House and at the beginning of the old trail to Little Fort on the North Thompson River, so it became the most convenient stopping-off place for anyone making that trip. We often entertained government men and transients as well as the local people coming and going. For those on the way into the country looking for land, we were a source of knowledge about the district and the land open for pre-empting. Actually, our house almost became a hotel—a nonpaying one. Father refused to accept a penny from anyone for a meal or for staying the night, even when they stuck around for a week or more. Horse feed was free, too. I'm sure he gave away a fortune in our years on the ranch, but father wouldn't have it any other way, saying it was repayment for the many acts of kindness he had received during his long years of wandering. Though I occasionally accepted board money for the extra work that guests made, father would have been extremely angry to hear of it.

It was decided that Angus and Dan would take turns running the operation at the meadow that winter, and around November first we moved the cattle and most of the horses over there: grass was still available on the sloughs and potholed meadows where the cattle could rustle until the snow got too deep. Whoever looked after the cattle at the meadow would also trap on the lakes and streams there, and I would have someone to help on my trapline at the home place.

With the snow and cold weather, Angus and I blazed out a trapline and set our traps. Since it was a long line, we built a cabin at Wavey Lake which would save us having to come back to the ranch in bad weather. We made more snowshoes, having found them better in the brush than skis, then started to trap in earnest.

Around the first of November father had bought six heavy brood mares from Mr. Lee and Mr. Hamilton, proprietors of the 59 Mile House, one of the stopping places for the freighters on the Cariboo Road. Since there was quite a demand for draft horses for freighting on the road, father thought it would be a good investment to raise horses for sale. One of the teams he bought was black Percheron, weighing 1,800 pounds apiece. He had paid $1,000 for the two of them and they were well worth the price. The other four horses cost $350 apiece.

When father was at the 59 Mile, Lee and Hamilton had told him about a big English shire stallion for sale by a man named Heatherbray at Heffley Creek on the North Thompson, about fifteen miles from Kamloops. This horse, so they said, weighed just under 2,200 pounds. Father kept thinking about this animal until finally he made up his mind to go and find Heatherbray and his wonderful horse, and if it was as good as they said, he would buy it. We had long since learned that whatever father wanted he usually managed to get, whether it was horses, cattle or pigs, and he always wanted the first-rate animals.

About four o'clock one morning in January, he started out fearlessly on one of our mares who was very good on her feet in the snow. Father would be seventy years old that year but neither Angus nor I tried to stop him. When he made up his mind to do something, he did it. He knew there was a hard trip ahead of him and deep snow over the mountains but that didn't frighten him. By this time the ice on Long Lake was strong enough to travel on and there was little snow on the surface, so he was able to ride about seven miles on the lake and avoid breaking trail through the snow over the mountains. When he left Long Lake, he had to wade through half a mile of snow to reach Birch Lake, where he could travel a few miles to its outlet. From there he plowed through snow again to the ice of Beaver Lake, but after that he had to take the trail which no one had travelled since the first snowfall. It was pretty tough going until he dropped down the hill to the North Thompson River valley where there was very little snow. The weather was always milder there than where we lived at 4,000 feet above sea level.

Angus and I knew just how much father would have to contend with on his trip because our trapline trail followed some of the same route, but all we could do was hope for the best. The wintry days passed one by one and every day we looked for him, consoling ourselves that father could look after himself. Then one night, when we were home from our trapline and had just finished fixing the fire in the big heater for the night, Angus said, "Ervin, I think I heard someone holler!"

We stood listening and then I heard shouts, too. We rushed for the door, both of us saying at once, "It's father!"

Outside, we could see right across the lake in the brilliant moonlight. It was very, very cold, nearly forty below. And there was father, riding one horse and leading another up from the lake. We could hardly believe our eyes. The mountain of a horse he was riding looked so immense that he couldn't be true. The animal was covered with hoarfrost and every hair stood out silvery white. Up on his back sat father in his great buffalo coat that came down below his knees, and it too was covered with frost. And as big as father was, he was dwarfed by that huge horse. In the clear frosty moonlight, the figure they made was so big and so ghostlike that Angus and I stood there in shock for maybe a minute before we were even aware of the intense cold.

Father slid down to the ground. "Boys, give the horses a good rubdown and be sure you blanket them well. They've had a very hard day." It was typical of father that although he'd had a very hard day too, he didn't mention himself.

When we had taken care of the horses, we hurried back to the house, and I soon had father sitting down to some hot grub and a pot of tea, for he was about famished. When he was warmed up and fed, he told us his story. It had taken a whole day to make a deal with Mr. Heatherbray; it is apt to be a long contest when two bullheaded Scotsmen try to outdeal each other. Heatherbray had not wanted to part with the stallion but because his fine young mares from the big horse were growing up, he had to make a change of stallions. It was evening before the deal was finally settled, so father was obliged to stay over and begin his return journey in the morning. The two men parted friends with a lot of respect for each other's bargaining abilities. Father rode our mare along the valley to Little Fort, but the new stallion the rest of the way because he was able to wade through four- and five-foot snowdrifts without the least bit of trouble.

The stallion's registered name was Sir Walter Raleigh, but we called him Walter for short. He was a pretty bay colour with white feet and a white star on his forehead, nineteen and a half hands high at the withers (in other words, over six feet tall at the shoulders). But big as he was, he was as quick and light on his feet as many horses hundreds of pounds lighter. He was as gentle as a lamb, and when he was loose in the pasture we used to just hold up his halter and call his name and he would trot right up and shove his giant head into it ready to be led away.

One day shortly after father's return with Walter, my old friend Cashmere came to the house to tell me that he had decided to give up his trapline because he was getting too old to go out into the cold any more, and he knew he would soon be going to the Indian's last hunting ground. As we had been so good to him, he wanted to give me his trapline. I felt sad for the old fellow yet I was very pleased for myself. Having a good trapline, and a long one, of my own was really something. He suggested I go with him so that he could show it to me—a matter of seven days, he told me, because he could travel no more than twelve or maybe fourteen miles a day.

Indian-like, he had no cabins, just brush lean-tos to camp in at night before an open fire. He showed me how he could survive even when the temperature registered forty or more degrees below zero. He would put an old wool blanket over his shoulders and lean back against a large tree to which he had attached a bunch of spruce or balsam boughs on a pole frame. Then with a little fire between his outstretched legs, an armful of dry wood on one side and green wood on the other, he could sleep for an hour or so, wake to put some green and some dry wood on the fire, and take another snooze. This way, he was able to sleep fairly comfortably off and on all night.

When I took over the line, I built cabins to stay in, locating them about ten to twelve miles apart, depending on the lay of the country and where wood and water were handy. Most of them were on the edge of good-sized lakes so that we could find them easily even on dark and stormy nights since we usually travelled along the shore ice. I think this foresight saved my life several times when I had broken through the ice and got soaking wet; Angus had similar narrow escapes.

In the years that followed, Angus and I built seven rather special log cabins. We made the walls only five feet high, then balanced three logs lengthwise on them to support the split-pole roof. We chinked the cracks in the walls and roof with moss and grass. Inside we dug out the dirt floor to a depth of thirty inches and shovelled the dirt onto the roof. The doorway, which faced the lake or, if there was no lake, the trail, was only twenty-two inches wide and three feet high to keep down heat loss; we entered by crawling through it. For light we used candles, and we packed in a small stove on our backs to provide heat. Our bunks were made of strong saplings covered with spruce or balsam boughs and we made a shelflike table out of split logs. We kept a good supply of dry wood on hand for our own use and for any trapper or hunter who was lost. In winter these cabins would be almost completely covered with snow which made them very warm and free from drafts. In fact, we usually had to keep the wooden door flap open when we had a good fire going.

Where it was necessary to make a loop in the trapline to reach some important group of lakes or streams, we built a larger cabin at a convenient junction since we would be using it for several nights in a row. At these main cabins we skinned the pelts and put them on stretchers. When the pelts were thoroughly dry we could take them off the stretchers and take them home to store until spring.

During the first spring after our arrival, Mr. and Mrs. Pressey and their five daughters and two sons had come into the Bonaparte Valley from the southern United States. Their preemption lay along the North Bonaparte River about twenty-three miles from the 70. Mr. Pressey built a roomy house there for his large family. They had brought in twelve head of milk cows and made cheese and butter to sell to the stopping places along the Cariboo Road. Mr. Pressey was a woodsman, hunter and trapper par excellence. His furs always brought a good price, paying the taxes on the property and other expenses. Presseys grew a big garden and so they fared quite well what with the wild game and fish to be had for the taking.

When father saw what fine people they were, he asked Mr. Pressey if we could stop there overnight when we had to make a trip out to the 70 for mail or on other business. "Certainly," replied Mr. Pressey, "come and stay just as long as you want. My house is always open to my friends!"

"I appreciate your kindness, Mr. Pressey," said father, "but we wouldn't think of staying without paying for accommodation and meals."

"I don't want pay! You can come and stay as neighbours and friends!"

"I can see your point all right," replied father, "but since we need somewhere to stay and your place is the only one in the right location, you must allow us to pay you or we can't stay with you. You have a large family to feed and clothe and we wouldn't feel right taking from them. We'll have to camp out if you won't take pay."

"Well, all right then," said Mr. Pressey. "The charge will be a dollar."

There was no use father arguing any longer, for Mr. Pressey was just as generous as he was himself. Consequently, whenever any of us stayed there, the charge was always a dollar whether there was just one of us in the party with one saddle horse, or three of us with a four-horse team.

By the fall of 1908 we had already discovered how inconvenient it was to ride the fifty miles out to the 70 to collect our mail or post a letter, so on one of father's trips to Clinton he investigated the possiblity of getting a post office closer to home. He talked to Mr. Soues, the government agent, and to Archie Mac-Donald, our MLA. A weekly stage and mail service would be a tremendous help to the settlers who were opening up our district, he told them. As a result of these talks, in the late fall of 1908 the government commissioned the Presseys to operate a post office and weekly stage from their home. Their eighteen-year-old son Henry took on the task of driving the stage to the 70 Mile House, a distance of twenty-two miles. He would leave home on a Saturday at eight in the morning with all the mail, express and any passengers. The road was still very rough with a great many large rocks and stumps that had to be carefully avoided, so the trip was slow and tiresome. It was always with a sigh of relief that the weary driver and his passengers stepped down at the Boyds' roadhouse around six in the evening.

Whenever we took something to the Presseys' post office we would leave home on a Friday morning for the thirty-mile ride and arrive by evening. Then because Henry would not return with the mail until Sunday evening, we would stay until Monday morning unless we were anxious to make the all-night ride home.

Early one Friday morning in mid-March of 1909, I saddled up my horse, loaded a pack horse with a bundle of furs we were shipping express to buyers in Vancouver, and headed for the post office. The March nights were still cold and I certainly did not relish the idea of riding all night, so our kind friends didn't have to do much talking to get me to stay the weekend. After a hearty breakfast on Monday morning, I loaded our own and our neighbours' mail onto my pack horse and set off on the new road we had made up the Graham Hill and over the high jack pine flats to the Price meadow: I had some mail for the Price boys and this was the shortest route to their place. As I came to the south end of their meadow I saw a coyote in a trap that one of the Price boys had set. They had been having a lot of trouble with coyotes killing their sheep, and for bait they had used part of a sheep that a coyote had killed. I stopped long enough to kill the animal and reset the trap, carefully covering it again with pine needles. A coyote is a very sharp customer and everything has to look very natural if you hope to trap him. I tied the carcass to my load and continued on my way. As I expected, Port Price, his two younger brothers and a neighbour, Roy Eden, were working on the new log house they had begun before Christmas.

Having given the Prices the coyote and their mail, I was invited to share noon dinner with them. We all went into the little cabin they had put up for a temporary home. No more than ten feet square, it was made of jack pine logs about a foot in diameter with split log puncheon for the roof. On top of this was a layer of slough hay, then about ten inches of clay. A door and a two-foot-square window were the only openings, so it got very warm inside that little cabin. In the far corner there was a double bunk, and between the door and the window was a large cast-iron cook-stove. There was just room enough behind the stove for some narrow shelves on which the Price boys had piled necessities like dishes and pots and pans and a couple of boxes of shotgun and rifle shells. Against the opposite wall was a small table.

One of the younger Prices had cooked the lunch and all five of us crowded around the table to eat. And was it ever hot in there with that big stove going full blast from cooking the meal! Of course, the huge logs of the walls and the low roof all helped to hold the heat in. The lunch looked good but I never did get to taste it. Just as I was raising the first forkful to my mouth, something went zinging right past my ear and hit the wall with a thud! For a split second, we just sat there thunderstruck, then the room exploded around us. The shotgun shells had been set off by the terrific heat from the stove. Like lightning, all five of us dived headlong for the door, with our arms up over our heads to protect our faces from the flying shot. Once outside, we hid around the corner of the cabin and listened to the shells exploding. Pretty soon the rifle shells joined the barrage so that it sounded like a full-fledged war going on inside.

After the last explosion we waited a long time before we got up courage to go back inside. Everything was shot to pieces. The dishes, the bedding, the pots and pans, everything in the room was either completely ruined or badly damaged. Even the remains of our lunch was full of buckshot and shredded pieces of shotgun shells. The real miracle was that we had escaped without wounds ourselves, and only sustained minor damage to our clothes. When I told father the story he nearly had a fit to think that anyone would do such a crazy thing as to store ammunition in a place like that.

In the summer of 1909, haying time began with our usual hired help problem; then one day a young fellow came riding over the trail from the east and stopped at the ranch to talk. He seemed to be in no hurry to get back to his home in Little Fort, so father asked him if he would stay and help finish the haying. He was willing, and we were well satisfied with his work. He told us that he had come from Missouri a few years earlier, and that folks just called him "Missouri." He was a tall, lean whipcord of a man with narrow hips, a slim waist and broad shoulders. But for such a big man, he had a very small head with huge ears that stuck nearly straight out like a pack rat's. His voice was high and sort of squeaky like that of a five- or six-year-old child.

When the haying was finished on the home ranch, the crew moved over to the meadow to put up the hay there while I stayed home to look after things. A couple of times a week I made the trip to the meadow with milk, butter, bread, vegetables and homemade cheese. I got pretty good at making cheese, but it tasted so good when it was fresh that we seldom had any left over to ripen properly.

One afternoon on my way back to the ranch I saw a young bear, probably about a year and a half old, climbing a jack pine. On the spur of the moment I jumped down grabbing the Winchester carbine from its scabbard on my saddle and walked around the tree looking for a spot where I could get a close shot through the branches. The bear was about sixty feet up, but I lined it up in my sights and fired one shot that brought it tumbling down. It was nice and fat from living high on the huge huckleberries, blueberries and saskatoons to be found all over the jack pine flats.

As I tied the bear onto my pack horse I could already taste

those delicious bear steaks. At home, I dressed the meat and hung it up in our flyproof safe to cool. Chops from a young bear are somewhat like pork chops so I waited impatiently to cook it. The next day I fried up a big pan of the chops for my noon meal. Scrumptious! As usual, I had cooked more than I needed for one meal, so I left the rest on the back of the stove in a big frying pan covered with a tight lid, intending to warm them up for my supper.

In early afternoon, I rode to the east range to check on some cattle and was gone about five hours. When I returned I found Angus and father in our blacksmith shop repairing a piston rod and blade from one of the hay mowers. But the first thing they had done when they arrived was to look for something to eat, for they had worked all afternoon and had not stopped for a meal before leaving the meadow. Spotting the frying pan at the back of the stove right away and being very hungry, they set to work on those fat, tender chops. They were feeling pretty contented when I got home, but father had a question.

"Ervin," he said, "where did you get those pork chops? They were so juicy and tender!"

"Did you really like them, father?" I asked.

"Yes," he replied. "That's the best meat I ever tasted!"

I didn't know what to say. It had never occurred to me that father would come along and eat those bear chops, especially since I had heard him say so often that he had never eaten—and never would eat—bear meat as it was not fit meat for eating. Now here he was demanding an answer to his question and there was no way around it but to tell him the truth.

I walked over and stood by the open door to be able to get out of there fast. "Father, just remember I didn't cook those chops for you to eat. They were for my supper, so it's not my fault you ate them, is it?" He looked terribly stern but I plunged on anyway. "They were bear steaks, father. I shot a bear yesterday."

I was poised ready to run, but he took it well since the damage was already done. And he had to admit that it was good meat. But he never ever ate bear meat again, although he really liked other wild meat such as venison and moose.

In mid-August, the haying for the year was finished and father decided to have a look for a route from our ranch to the

North Thompson River as a possible road. Missouri volunteered to go with him, wanting to see the country and do a little prospecting along the way, so they packed a light camp outfit and grub supply and headed northeast from the ranch. Father had been over the first ten miles of their route, but from then on it was all new country to both of them. Several times he had talked to the Indians about the possibility of following the creek from the east end of Long Lake down the canyon to the river, but they said it would be impossible because even their best hunters could not get through that way; but perhaps, they said, if a man went northwest to the headwaters of Jim Creek, then along the lower end of Taweel Lake, and cut over to the headwaters of Four Mile Creek down to the North Thompson, he might make it. But they emphasized the word "maybe."

The first ten miles was easy going: open rolling country and a string of lakes with clear, sparkling water. It was a sportsman's paradise—trout and other fish, ducks, Canada geese, deer and bear were plentiful. There was mile after mile of waving grass, and pea vine, lupine, vetch, wild rye and fireweed, with clumps of willows and poplars dotted over the hills. It was the finest cattle range anyone could imagine. But after a couple of hours' travel, the countryside suddenly changed. They had come to the beginning of immense stands of virgin timber as thick as it could grow, eighteen to thirty inches on the stump and at least a hundred feet high. To work their way through it, father and Missouri had to chop the windfalls and brush out of the way, but they kept going, hoping to come out into open country once more. From time to time they came to a little lake, some only a few acres in size and others half a mile across; they had to chop their way around each one.

At six o'clock in the evening when they arrived at another small lake, father decided to camp. In more than seven hours of hard travel they had come no more than five miles from open country; they would do better with a fresh start in the morning. The lake covered no more than twenty-five or thirty acres but it had a bit of grassy meadow near its outlet where the horses could feed. After supper, with still a couple of hours of daylight left, Missouri picked up one of the light hand axes and headed out of camp toward the unexplored timber ahead.

"I'm gonna have a look at that there timber," he said in his squeaky voice.

"Careful you're back before dark," father warned.

"Don't you worry none. I'll find my way back. I'm gonna blaze a trail as I go along!" And he grinned and waved the axe in the air.

Just as daylight was fading he returned as he had promised and reported that the timber was just as thick up ahead and the travelling just as tough. Then he added, "But I done something to make it easier going, I think!" And he grinned again and winked at father.

Father was puzzled, but since Missouri obviously meant this "something" to be a surprise, he didn't ask any questions. They rolled up in their blankets and soon were fast asleep. They needed a good rest for the tough trail ahead.

Early in the morning as they were saddling up, father suddenly noticed a big cloud of smoke rolling up a mile or so to the east, directly in line with their proposed route. He knew at once that they were faced with the worst danger a man can face in heavy timber: a forest fire. For a moment or two he stood beside his horse, undecided on the safest course of action, when suddenly a hot blast of air nearly took his breath away. Missouri immediately panicked and jumped on his horse, prepared to try to outrun the fire, but father grabbed the bridle and hung on.

"It's no use, Missouri! You'll never outrun it! When the fire crowns in that timber, you won't have a snowball's chance in hell!"

But he spurred his horse. "I ain't gonna die here!"

"We'll get into the lake, Missouri! It's our only chance!"

Finally, he allowed father to lead him toward the lake.

Of course, father was right. Once a fire like that burns its way up tall timber, it creates a terrible draft that spreads the flames across the treetops. In a matter of minutes, the fire has travelled miles.

Father told Missouri to get his wool blankets out of his pack, then they rode out into the lake leading their pack horses until the water came up over the animals' backs. There they dismounted, soaked their blankets in the water and draped them over the heads of their horses and over their own heads. Within minutes, fire ringed the little lake, and the heat became so intense that the blankets dried out almost immediately. Again and again, they dipped them into the water, but even with this water treatment, the heat from the fire was almost too great for them and their horses to bear.

By nightfall, the fire in the treetops had burned out, leaving only smouldering tree trunks and snags and logs. However, though father and Missouri were exhausted from standing in the cold water and inhaling smoke, they still couldn't leave the lake because all the soil that had been built up over the centuries from moss and needles and decaying timber was being burned off right down to the bare rocks. Although the main fire had moved on, the ground was still too hot to walk on; they had to stand in the water all that night and most of the second day. On the second evening, they led the horses out of the lake and made camp where the little meadow had been at the lake's outlet: the ground there was damp from seepage so it had cooled off more quickly than the surrounding land. The horses had nothing to eat, but father and Missouri were able to get some sleep on the blackened ground.

They packed up early the next morning and headed home, dodging hot spots on the ground and going around burning logs. Fortunately, the fire had changed direction so that when they got back to the grassy meadows they found them untouched by the flames. Near Jim Creek, they stopped awhile to let the horses feed on the good green grass, and they cooked themselves a bit to eat. Then they headed home, glad to be alive.

Father often speculated on just how that fire got started. There had been no sign of smoke the evening before and no thunder or lightning at all that day. Did Missouri drop a cigarette butt when he was blazing his trail the evening before? Or had he started the fire on purpose to burn the underbrush to make travelling easier? Having been raised in settled country like Missouri, he probably had no idea how dangerous a forest fire could be. He could have put a match to an old log or a stump which would have smouldered through the cool, damp night and burst into flame at sunrise.

We would never know for sure as father refused to ask him right out, but as we got to know Missouri better, we learned not to put anything past him. He was a very bad customer and a horse thief of the worst kind. (He even stole horses from us!) For his crimes, he spent several years in a penitentiary.

The forest fire burned off and on until the heavy snowfalls of winter finally put it out. In the meantime, whenever the weather was wet it would just smoulder along in the ground and in the peat moss of the spruce swamps, but a dry spell would set off the flames again. Then we could see great clouds of smoke blotting out the sky to the northeast. It was impossible to fight such a big fire because there were far too few men in the district, and it would have been almost impossible to reach without the aid of modern airplanes and helicopters. So before winter came it had destroyed tens of thousands of acres of fine forest, and God alone knows what the cost was in wildlife.

9

Visiting

ONE DAY IN June 1910, five men came over the trail from Little Fort. They were on foot and each carried a pack on his back; behind them came a single pack horse loaded down with their tent and camping outfit. Four of the men were six-footers weighing around 200 pounds. The fifth fellow was shorter and slighter, perhaps 150 pounds and a scant five feet seven, a little Irishman by the name of Paddy Boyle. They had all been loggers and railroad tie makers working along the North Thompson where the new railway, the Canadian Northern (later the Canadian National), was being built through to the coast. But it was no life for a man, they said, and they had made up their minds to pre-empt land in the famous Cariboo. They immediately took a great liking to our ranch and decided they should look for land in the same area.

Father invited them to pitch their tent down near the lake just inside our line fence where the cattle would not bother them, and in the evenings they would march the quarter mile up to the house to chat about land that was open for pre-emption. By now, we owned a map of all the surveyed land, and father offered to show them where the corner posts were located. They could take note of the post numbers and then go to Clinton to file on the land. It fell to Angus and me to show them around, but what a

207

strange company we made! Since they were lumberjacks, they refused to ride horseback, and Angus and I had no intention of walking, so they trailed along behind while we rode from corner post to corner post. It was slow travelling: we had trouble holding our horses to a slow walk and settled instead for forging ahead, then resting until the others caught up. Finally, all five of them found land they wanted and then made a second choice in case someone had already pre-empted their first choice.

Paddy was chosen to go to Clinton to file on their claims. They each sent him off with the ten dollars required for a claim as well as travelling money, then settled down to enjoy life for a few days. They borrowed fishing tackle from us and did some fishing, and they gave us a hand with the fencing to make up for the time that Angus and I had spent showing them around. After eight days had passed, we all began to look for Paddy to emerge from the trail along the lake. But there was no sign of him that day, or the next day or the next. Now we began to worry because even if he had been forced to walk every step of the way to Clinton, he should have been back. Two more days passed and still no Paddy. By now, the four big loggers had run out of grub since they had not come prepared for such a long stay, so naturally our kindhearted father told them they were welcome to eat with us. This meant I was cooking for eight men instead of four, and those big loggers had huge appetites. The fresh mountain air made them ravenous. It was just like shovelling coal into a line of blast furnaces and I found myself looking forward to Paddy's return more than they.

When the little man had been gone a full two weeks, the loggers decided to head for Clinton to see about their land and try to find out what had happened to Paddy. After breakfast they went to break camp in the pouring rain. About half an hour later I noticed that one of the men had gone off without his jacket so I tucked it under my arm and ran down the slope, but just as I approached their camp, I heard one hell of a rumpus going on inside their tent. I turned around and ran back up the hill as fast as I could to get father.

By the time we got back there, we found Paddy with his hands tied behind his back and a long rope around his neck. The four loggers were wrestling him toward a big cottonwood tree nearby, but he had obviously put up a good fight because his attackers were pretty bruised and bloody-looking.

Father was enraged. He let out one war whoop and jumped into the middle of the melee with his fists swinging, knocking men over left and right. The loggers were completely stunned by this assault and let go of little Paddy. In a flash, father had the rope off his neck and untied his hands. In the meantime, my brothers and I had grabbed sticks of firewood and held the loggers at bay while father completed his rescue.

"All right now," said father, "just calm down and tell me what the hell is going on here. No matter what this man has done, you got no business hanging him! That's called murder in this country and you'd all hang for it!" He turned and started up the hill with the bruised and shaken Paddy. "All of you come up to the house and we'll get to the bottom of this!"

At the house, Paddy told his story, that is, as much as he could remember of it. He said he had walked to the North Bonaparte post office at the Presseys' house on the first day. He stayed over and took the stage the next morning to the 70 Mile House, where he bought a ticket on the BX Stage to Clinton. Unfortunately, he had half a day to kill before the stage departed so he bought a quart of whiskey. He was very dry (or so he assured us) and he had not found any whiskey growing on the poplars and spruce trees along the way. He had a drink or two, and then a few more, and that was the last he could recollect clearly. He had no memory of arriving in Clinton or, in fact, of anything he had done after he got on the stage. He had a very dim remembrance of an Indian, a saddle horse, a bottle of whiskey and some money changing hands, but just what he did all the time he was gone was never cleared up.

Father took charge of the situation. "I'll be leaving for town in a day or two to get supplies. You men can come along with me to check up on your pre-emptions, and if you want to come back with me you can. I'll be needing men to help with the haying if you want jobs."

For a little while after that, Paddy was a very subdued man, hardly saying a word to anyone, but it was impossible to keep him down for long because he was naturally a happy-go-lucky fellow, always singing Irish songs, telling comical stories and playing tricks on everybody.

"Mr. MacDonald," he said, "I'd like to stay and work for you. I'm broke and need money badly. When you're in Clinton, please check with the government agent and see if I filed my claim. And if I didn't, would you advance me ten dollars on my future wages and file for me?"

Father agreed and he and the others left the next morning. At Clinton father went straight to the government office and found as he suspected that Paddy had not filed on any of the claims, so filed as he had requested. Two of the loggers filed but the other two went on a big drunk and that was the last we ever saw or heard of them. The two who filed stayed around that country for a while and one came back with father and worked for us through the haying season. His name was Bill MacDonald and he had been born in Northern Ireland. A slender man, he was all muscle and rawhide, and proved to be a real worker. With him and Paddy to help out, we had a first-class haying crew that year.

After the hay was put up, father and my brothers took our hundred or so mature steers and dry cows to Ashcroft to be sold. Big Bill went along to drive the chuck wagon, planning to continue on to Vancouver for the winter. Paddy stayed behind and borrowed a team of horses to haul logs for his new cabin. His pre-emption was about halfway between the ranch and our meadows, on East Twin Lake, one of the two lakes separated by a ridge of land and which we had named East and West Twin. Every year after that, Paddy came to work for us during haying season, until 1915 when he joined the army. He came back from the war without any wounds but he was a sick man and spent a long time in the Kamloops hospital. There he fell in love with one of the nurses and they married. He brought his bride back to his little ranch but she stayed only a month; being a city girl, she may have found it too lonely. Paddy stayed on there alone for a number of years and then one spring he packed up and left the country; we lost all track of him.

When the cattle drivers reached Ashcroft, Bill proceeded to get "drunk as a lord" and wound up in a poker game. Two days later when father and my brothers were ready to set off for home,

Bill showed up asking to come back with them. He had no money to go anywhere else. Father put him to work feeding the cattle at the meadow for the winter so that we boys could have more time for trapping. This worked out just fine until close to Christmas when Bill began to get thirsty again. He drew what money he had coming, put his belongings into his packsack and headed out on foot over the trail to Little Fort, where he planned to get the train to Kamloops. Another one of our friends was gone, never to be heard from again. But that's the way it was in that country in those early days. It was so big and empty that men just seemed to vanish into space.

Dan went over to the meadow to take Bill's place, and from time to time I rode over to take him supplies and give him a little company. He got pretty lonesome with nobody to talk to day after day, and of course he had no telephone or radio or television to break the monotony of his own thoughts. One clear, cold thirty- or-forty-below day when I was over there, we got the sudden idea of going down to Eagan Lake, about eight miles away, to visit a neighbour, a young bachelor by the name of Bill Hollandbach who had a small ranch along the lakeshore. No one had been over the rough trail between our meadow and Bill's place all winter so we planned to use our skis.

We made pretty fair time, taking turns breaking trail, but at one point, we had to cross a small river that had frozen solid to the bottom, forcing the water to flow over the top of the ice. With our skis over our shoulders, we stepped from one big rock to another across the river. We were nearly to the other side when Dan slipped and landed ankle deep in icy water. On the far bank we quickly built a fire and stripped off his wet moccasins and socks. By the time they were dry it was late afternoon and we arrived at Bill's place near dark.

Bill was surprised to see us but he was tickled, too, for he got very few visitors. We were grateful to get inside his nice warm cabin, slide out of our coats and moosehide moccasins, and pull chairs up to the stove. It was a big cast-iron cookstove but it was all that was needed to heat that little cabin. He had set it about three feet out from the wall so there was plenty of room for a person to work right around it; it even had two oven doors, one on each side, with a reservoir on one end for heating water.

Well, poor Dan was still feeling the effects of his icy ducking, so he put his chair in that three-foot space behind the stove, tipped his chair back and dozed off while Bill and I got supper ready. Bill had cured his own hams. He cut thick slices of ham to fry and put on a pot of the inevitable beans. He asked me to mix up a batch of my famous baking-powder biscuits. I made sure the fire was burning just right, then popped the biscuits into the oven. Pretty soon, when the ham and beans were ready, I opened the oven door to take out the biscuits, only to find that the darned things hadn't started to cook. I piled more wood on the fire, but twenty minutes later they were still the same as when I put them in the oven. What on earth was wrong? More wood went on the fire.

"Let's start without them," said Bill. We woke up Dan and told him to come to the table.

"No biscuits?" said Dan. I explained that they wouldn't cook for some reason.

"Oh," said Dan sleepily, "maybe if I close this door at the back, the oven will get hotter!" For the last hour he had been sitting with his feet in the oven with my biscuits!

In March of 1911, father began making preparations for his usual spring trip to Clinton and Ashcroft to buy supplies and sell our winter's catch of furs. On the three previous spring trips, either Angus or Dan had gone with him, but one morning at breakfast he suddenly said, "Well, Ervin, you've never been anywhere since we arrived here. I'm going to take you with me if you'd like to go. I think it's time you made your debut into civilization!"

Would I like to go? Since the day we left Lac Ste. Anne in April 1907, I hadn't been near civilization. I could hardly remember what a town looked like. Though I was ecstatic, I fought my excitement down and pretended to be very calm. Of course, I didn't fool anyone because I was beaming from ear to ear. My turn had come at last. I'll see stores, I thought, and railway trains, and restaurants. I'll see Clinton and Ashcroft and the 70 Mile House that I've heard so much about. I'll eat meals that I haven't had to cook, and I'll sleep in a real bed with springs like I've seen in the catalogue. And probably I'll see more than ten or twelve people at the same time. And I might even see girls!

When the day came for us to leave, one of our two black Percheron driving mares was too heavy with foal to make the journey, so we took the other, Minnie, and Sir Walter Raleigh. Giving Minnie an inch advantage on the doubletree would even up the pull on the way home. Along the way, everyone who saw our big stallion stopped whatever they were doing to take a second look. They just couldn't remember seeing such a giant horse before.

When we reached the 70, as usual a gang of travellers and freighters were there and our team caused a sensation among them. That night I had the privilege of eating Mrs. Boyd's excellent cooking and I had to agree that it was everything father had said, and so was the fine bed I got to sleep in.

In Clinton, once again our stallion was the centre of attraction. If he had been human he would have been getting very conceited by this time. My mind was on other things, however. I was terribly disappointed at the size of Clinton, expecting it to be something like the towns in Alberta; but there was only one hotel, a blacksmith shop, Archie MacDonald's general store, a couple of Chinese businesses, the government office and the barns where the government teams and road equipment were kept. Around them were scattered a few dozen homes.

The Cariboo Road itself was much more interesting than the town—by far the best road I had ever seen. It was smooth and hard, no mud, no stumps and no big rocks, just a darn good gravel road. Any rocks on it had long since been smashed to dust by the six-inch steel tires of the big freight wagons.

The next night we arrived in Ashcroft. This was a bigger, busier town than Clinton because it had both the railroad business and the Cariboo Road freighting business. Of course, we had hardly stopped in front of the hotel to see about getting a room and putting up our team in the feed stable out behind before a crowd of people had gathered around our horses. How many hands high was our stallion, they asked. How much did he weigh? How old was he? Ashcroft being a horse and cow town, these people had seen a lot of good horseflesh, but Walter was still a standout.

It took us a little while to get our team through the crowd and around to the stable. To celebrate my being eighteen years old and having my first trip to town, father took me into the hotel bar and treated me to a glass of port wine. I was now a man.

Father had business to attend to in Kamloops and the next day he left on the train while I stayed behind to look after the horses and amuse myself. He was gone four days but it seemed like a week of Sundays to me. Either that unaccustomed glass of port wine or the water or the strange food had made me very ill, and for nearly three days I lay in bed. What a way to celebrate!

As the freight and cattle-shipping headquarters for the whole of the Cariboo, Ashcroft always had a bunch of teamsters, cowboys and horsemen hanging around, and they argued continually about the pulling abilities of their own and other drivers' horses. And since there were freight wagons being loaded every day for the long trip up the road to Barkerville, the teamsters were in the habit of settling their arguments by wheeling two of the big freight wagons, hooked one behind the other tandem style and loaded with freight, out onto the hard, level gravel in front of the hotel. They set the brakes on the wagons, then hitched up the big "wheelers" which are the two horses closest to the wagon in a four-, six- or eight-horse team. A mark was drawn on the street in front of the wheels, then the horses' capabilities were put to the test. A competing team of wheelers was hitched in turn to the same rig and measured against the mark made by the first team. And all this was done against a background of bets and side bets being made by everyone in town.

With the arrival of our big Percheron mare and our huge stallion, the old arguments flared up anew. Could the big wheelers belonging to the present champion outpull MacDonald's team? After a bunch of the teamsters had a drink or two, the argument got so hot that there was only one way to settle it and that was to see our horses in action. With father away, they came to me to ask if I would let them make their test. I wasn't too sure that father would like the idea since he always treated his animals with great care, but I was too ill to resist their arguments for long.

"All right," I said, "you can make your test, but I won't be able to drive because I feel too sick. You'll have to find someone else, but it will have to be someone I approve of."

"Matt Botterill's your man," they said. "There's no one better than Matt."

The day we arrived I had noticed a man in the crowd who stood out from the rest. He was one of the best-looking men I had ever seen, close to six feet tall and of an athletic build. He had just looked on with an amused smile while the others were arguing over the horses. This was Botterill, and it was arranged that he would drive our team as a disinterested party.

Toward noon the next day, two heavily loaded wagons in tandem were pulled out to the street, the brakes set and the champion wheelers hooked up. Each team would get two tries in that they were allowed to lean into their collars to get the feel of the load, then step back, settle themselves, and at once lean into their collars for one mighty heave.

Two or three hundred people had lined the street on either side, eager to watch the show. They had seen dozens of these contests before but they never tired of them. The first team, which was familiar to everyone watching, did very well, moving the wagons four feet in one heave, which was a wonderful pull since there were nearly five tons of freight on the front wagon and four tons on the other. The crowd cheered and clapped, and those who had bet on the old champions congratulated themselves. No team could possibly beat that performance.

Then it was our team's turn to be hooked up and my heart was in my mouth. I had stipulated that Botterill was to use the doubletree from our own wagon because it was adjusted to give Minnie an inch leverage on Walter, which kept him from pulling her back against the wagons; without this adjustment the pull would be lopsided. Everyone accepted my condition since experienced teamsters always use this device when there is a weight difference in their teams.

At last, Botterill and the horses and wagons were in place ready to attempt to outdo the first team. I watched the horses step into their collars, get the feel of the load, then step back and set themselves for the pull. I was so nervous that I could barely stand still. I watched Walter's hindquarters strain, his belly nearly touch the ground. Then suddenly, the wagons shot ahead more than five feet. What a pull!

A terrific roar went up from the crowd. They cheered and clapped wildly. While the teams and wagons were taken away, all the men crowded into the barroom to settle their bets. The little town had never seen such a marvellous exhibition of horsemanship and pulling, and it would be the chief topic of conversation for weeks after we had gone.

I was delighted to see father when he returned from Kamloops for it meant we could start for home. I wasn't really impressed with civilization. Some of my disenchantment could be attributed to my not feeling well, but in fact I had learned that being in the woods suited me much better than being in town. I had seen all the things I had hoped to see—I had even seen a few girls, but was too sick to talk to them—and now I was ready to go back to the ranch.

I told father all about the pulling contest and how our horses had outpulled the best team the Cariboo had to offer. He was pleased. Then I had to tell him how sick I had been and that another man had driven our team, but he approved when he learned it had been Matt Botterill. We bought our supplies and headed out, taking five days on the road because of the weight of the load, but I didn't mind as long as I was going home. It was good to get back to familiar surroundings and out of my Sunday-best clothes, and I was glad to be working again. The garden had to be planted and the horses and cattle were waiting to be driven out onto the summer range.

Shortly after our return, when father was out on his faithful horse Buck checking the stock on their range, he found a big three-year-old roan shorthorn steer lying dead, apparently killed by a grizzly bear. At home he announced that he and I would ride back there early in the morning with rifles to see if we could get a shot at it. Once a bear starts killing cattle, it usually keeps it up. After first light, an hour's ride took us to a spot a quarter of a mile from the grassy slope where father had found the dead steer. We tied our horses to a tree and circled on foot so that we would come up over a little ridge above the place where the steer lay. We took our time, crawling carefully up the slope until finally we were able to peek over the top, and much to our surprise there was no steer and no bear. Nothing to be seen at all. We got to our feet and went to examine the spot, close to a small cluster of willows.

"This is the place all right," father said. We could see where the new grass had been crushed down and found some blood, but the steer was nowhere in sight. And it had not been dragged away because there was no telltale trail of trampled grass.

"Grizzlies sometimes bury the rest of their kill, don't they?" I asked, though I knew the ground here was too hard for a bear to dig a large enough hole. We looked around, trying to figure out where the carcass could have been buried. We had heard stories of grizzlies carrying their kill away, but it was hard to imagine a bear big enough to carry an eleven- or twelve-hundred-pound steer.

"The swamp," said father. "He must have carried it down to the swamp to bury it under a layer of spruce needles."

I nodded, but my heart was beginning to race a little. I knew that once a bear covered its prey, it would hide close by to guard it. A grizzly is at its most dangerous at this time, so a man has to shoot fast and true if he wants to live to a happy old age. But father was the fastest and most accurate man with a rifle I ever saw. And by this time I had had four years of trapping and hunting experience, so I was pretty capable myself.

We worked our way cautiously toward the spruce swamp, our rifles ready, watching for the slightest movement among the trees ahead. But we were still a good fifty yards from the nearest trees when the bear roared and came charging straight at father. He was prepared. His rifle came up and fired all in one smooth motion. At that range and out in the open field, he had a perfect target.

I was about the same distance from the bear but to father's left so I shot for the spine just above the kidneys, knowing that the surest way to stop a charging animal is to paralyze its hindquarters. My shot hit exactly where I intended but that darn bear still struggled toward father, dragging himself with his front feet. The agony and rage of that huge beast was terrible to see, and in the end it took two more shots in the head before he lay still.

When we examined him we found that father's shot had hit

the base of the neck and ranged down into the lungs, though it had not slowed down his charge. I don't think that even a shot through the heart would have stopped a bear like that from killing father. We felt badly that we had to kill such a magnificent animal but when grizzlies start attacking domestic stock, nothing else can be done. We were lucky to have got him before he went on a real killing spree. He was a 700-pound male and made a prime pelt. About two years later we sold it to a big game hunter from Texas for seventy-five dollars, breaking even on the loss of the steer.

When we found the steer carcass in the spruce swamp it was well covered with moss and needles. We left it there for the scavengers to clean up. The lake near the swamp didn't have a name but after that we called it Grizzly, and it is still known by that name—a very pretty round lake of about three hundred acres, well stocked with Kamloops trout.

That spring, father started to get the old prospecting fever again. He was longing to get out into the hills with his pick and gold pan, and it wasn't the first time since we had come to the Cariboo. In the summer of 1910, Cashmere had come to tell father that he would show him the place where he had found his ore sample. The old Indian knew it would not be long before he crossed the great divide and he wanted to give father his mine because he had been so kind to him, so they loaded up a pack horse and rode northwest from the ranch. This time Cashmere had no trouble finding the ledge of ore; as we had always suspected, he could have found it easily any time he wanted.

The ledge was on our trapline, on the bank of a lake we called Otter. The ore was there all right and it looked very good, but there was one drawback. It lay on a high plateau on the lake edge and there wasn't any lower ground nearby. If father wanted to sink a shaft, the only direction he could go was down, and as soon as the shaft got below the level of the lake, all the water would come pouring in. It would be just too expensive to drain the lake first. Sadly, father explained this to Cashmere, and the two old men gave up their dream of a rich gold mine and rode home again. Soon after that the old Indian went to the place where the lakes are always blue and full of fish and the trails are always shaded. We knew father believed that time was running out on him, too, and he was sad because he still had not found his rainbow. So, we were not really surprised when one fine May morning in 1911 he announced, "I'm going to look for minerals. They've got to be out there someplace. Dan, how about coming along with me?"

My brothers and I were glad he wanted Dan's company because he was, after all, seventy-two years old that year. Dan saddled up their horses, put a light camping outfit and small grubstake on a pack horse, and off they went. Angus and I were smiling as we watched them go because we knew father had actually never been completely happy doing anything but prospecting. He took real pride and pleasure in the ranch, but it had really been the pot of gold at the end of his sons' rainbow, and he had never stopped dreaming of his own. This trip was just the first of many prospecting trips he made in the next few years, but although he found a number of mineral outcroppings, the rock formations were so badly broken up that none of them could be developed.

While they were gone on that first trip, Angus and I built a twelve-by-twenty-foot log blacksmith shop to replace the old makeshift one we had inherited from Demming, and made up a list of equipment we would need from Clinton and Ashcroft: a forge, a blower, an anvil, pinchers and fire tongs, charcoal, horseshoes, iron bars; and the list grew as Angus thought of things he wanted to build at the new forge. On his return father began making plans for a trip to Ashcroft in June.

This was to be a very special trip because Lavena, her husband Jim Case, and their young son were pulling up stakes in Washington and coming for a visit, and they were bringing our little sister Ruth with them, arriving in Ashcroft in late June. By now the road to the 70 Mile House was in good shape and one man could handle a wagon on the sidehills without any help, so father made the trip alone. Meanwhile, our house, which had been just one large room until now, had to be partitioned so that we would have two bedrooms for our visitors. Father would sleep upstairs and we boys would bed down in the big, airy hayloft above the stable. But when we had finished our remodelling, we realized that the rooms were rather bare for our most welcome guests.

"It would be nice," said Angus, "to have a few more pieces of furniture, but we don't have time to make any." This was true, of course, because we had to prepare for haying. Then quite by accident, we heard about a family who was leaving the Cariboo: Angus went to see them and bought some pieces of furniture. But the prize among the things they were selling was a White sewing machine. Angus was enormously pleased with this find. He had been wanting a sewing machine for a long time so we wouldn't have to patch all our clothes by hand, but most of all he wanted it to make our shirts, mackinaw jackets, gloves and deerhide moccasins. That old White sounded just like a threshing machine but it was in good condition and it only cost five dollars! In the years that followed, Angus certainly got our money's worth.

En route to Ashcroft, father stopped long enough in Clinton to buy a bag of candy at Archie MacDonald's general store, saying to the clerk, "I'm going to meet my older daughter and her family and my little girl Ruth in Ashcroft, and I want to have some of her favourite candy for her. I haven't seen her since September 1906!"

Long before the train arrived, he was at the CPR station in Ashcroft, telling everyone what he was doing there. He just couldn't keep his good news to himself. Finally, the train pulled into the station and the passengers began to step down on the platform.

"Where's my family?" father demanded. "Yes, there they are!" He hurried down the platform. "There's Lavena and Jim! And that's young Eddie! But where's my little Ruth?" She hasn't come, he thought, and his heart fell.

Just then he noticed a beautiful young lady dressed up in the latest fashion. She was talking to Lavena. Could that be Ruth? No, he thought, Ruth is just a little girl! But it *is* her, and she looks exactly like the lovely girl I married so long ago. I should have known her right away.

Ruth had been only eleven years old when father last saw her and he had forgotten that time doesn't stand still. Her new appearance was quite a shock to him, but like the old warrior he was, he carried on. Suddenly he remembered the bag of candy he was carrying. I can't give it to her now that she's grown up, he thought, and hid it behind his back as he went forward to greet them. But Ruth noticed this little movement.

"What have you got there, father?"

He was sure embarrassed but he surrendered the bag to her.

"Oh, my favourite candy," she said sweetly. "How thoughtful of you!" She was as sensitive and tenderhearted as he was and would never hurt his feelings. Besides, she enjoyed that candy even at sixteen.

Father's attention now turned to his first and only grandchild, Eddie Case, and the two greeted each other solemnly: Eddie was four years old, father was seventy-two. The next morning when all the supplies had been loaded up, they began the long trip home to the ranch. Because the blacksmithing equipment was very heavy, the team could cover only twenty miles a day, making a full five days on the road. At Clinton, where father purchased a few more supplies, he proudly introduced his family to his friends.

It was an exciting day for Angus, Dan and me when they finally arrived at the ranch and all the family was together again. But unfortunately, our old taskmaster, haying, was calling us back to work. Lavena took over the cooking. Ruth helped her when she was available but most of the time she counted herself as one of the haying crew and worked right alongside me doing the stacking. In the evening she brought the milk cows in to the barn, riding one of our gentlest saddle horses. She really loved riding. Jim helped us with the haying and the chores. We all knew by the look on father's face how much it meant to him to have his whole family under his roof once again. I think it helped to compensate him for that still-so-far-away rainbow.

With all the equipment we needed for our new blacksmith shop, we soon had our forge in operation. Father had put in so many years doing his own horseshoeing, and sharpening picks and drill steel for his prospecting and mining, that he was able to teach us just about everything we needed to know. But Angus seemed to have a natural bent for it so he did most of the work. Besides being able to do our own horseshoeing, we could now do welding and other iron work, make light sleighs such as cutters and bobsleds, and repair our mowers, hay rakes and wagons.

However, there was one drawback to equipping such a fine

shop and having someone as expert as Angus to run it: all our neighbours started to come to our place to get their iron work done. Besides taking up our time and using our charcoal and iron, they usually stayed for a meal or two, but father refused to charge anyone or even accept money when it was offered to him.

Angus didn't mind these demands on his time. He truly enjoyed the blacksmith shop, and being so handy, he probably saved us as much money over the years on our repairs as we lost on the neighbours'. Whenever ranch work wasn't too pressing he would spend hours out there just tinkering and making things. I remember one time he even made a violin, copying from one that father had bought for Dan who was the musical member of the family.

When the haying was finished, Lavena, Jim and little Eddie left us, but they weren't going all the way back south. I took them by horseback to Little Fort and from there they went on the mail stage to Kamloops where they thought of settling. Jim was an experienced cook and it wasn't difficult for him to find a job. Within a few days after their arrival he got work cooking at the Colonial Hotel. Later on, he and Lavena took over the management of the hotel, though Jim remained head cook.

Ruth stayed on with us though it was a bit lonely for her. There were only three girls her own age in that country. Tottie Boyd lived fifty miles away at 70 Mile House, and the other two, Pearl Whitley on the North Bonaparte and Lizzie Wilson on the South Bonaparte, were twenty miles away. However, they didn't let distance deter them and they became great friends. There were more than enough young men around. For some strange reason, all the cowboys and homesteaders in that country suddenly found that the best way to get from one point to another was by way of our ranch, no matter if it did take them fifty miles in the wrong direction!

Ruth was certainly a popular girl. She was lively, full of fun and very good-looking, the image of our dear mother, or so father said. She loved to ride horseback, especially if there was a dance at the end of the ride. She encouraged us to step out, too, and many times the four of us would ride to the 70 or the 100 Mile House for a dance, fifty miles each way. It wasn't long before we three boys really looked forward to social events.

Ever since our first winter on the ranch one of our favourite pastimes was skiing, and we had just about the best ski hill in the whole district, a mile and a quarter run from a mountaintop above our hay fields right down onto the lake, a drop of at least a thousand feet. We got a lot of fun out of coming down a mile a minute, even though it took a good half hour to climb back to the top. Quite often we were joined by the three Burns boys who lived about eight miles away, and sometimes other neighbour fellows would join us, but the winter that Ruth spent with us, we had more young fellows on that hillside than ever before. Sometimes on a clear moonlit night, each skier took turns, starting our runs a minute apart. It was thrilling sport.

Another place where we skied a lot was just above our house. This run was only about four hundred yards long and not very steep—but it had a "hazard" which added to the thrill. Our house had two doors, one facing the ski hill and the other directly opposite facing the lake. Uphill from the house was a gate directly in line with the doors. We used to open both doors and the gate, sprinkle a good layer of snow on the floor, and then go to the top of the run. Down we would come through the gate, into the house and out again, and down onto the lake. It was great fun and by some miracle none of us ever got hurt. Of course, we only used this run when father was not at home, for we knew perfectly well how he would react.

When Ruth came to stay, we ran into a little problem because she didn't think much of this practice. She didn't like snow in the house and she didn't like freezing while the doors were open. So one day after we had prepared the house for an afternoon of skiing, she closed the uphill door and piled all our chairs behind it. When we came speeding down, we didn't see the closed door until the last moment; we only had time to throw ourselves sideways, one after the other, piling up neatly right beside the house. We untangled ourselves and stomped into the house where Ruth put iodine on our cuts and bruises. It did us no good to get annoyed with her, for she just laughed at us, but she cured us of skiing through the house. We never tried it again.

Our old bachelor home certainly did come alive with Ruth there. There were always young people around and plenty of social life. All the young fellows vied for her company, more than one fell in love with her, and one even named a lovely little lake near Canim Lake in honour of her. But she treated them all alike.

When she left us in the fall of 1912, it was father who missed her most of all. He was a different man when she was around, not always hiding his feelings as he did with us boys. She never complained but I guess it was a pretty lonely place for a lively young girl to find herself. About a year later she married her old sweetheart Ed Sizemore back in Republic, Washington. After that, they used to come up to visit us every couple of years. Because Ed loved fly-fishing, he was in heaven when he came to that Bridge Lake country.

Sometime in 1909 or '10, a bachelor by the name of Frank Rossi had taken up a pre-emption on a piece of open benchland about five miles from our place on the road to the Prices' ranch. Rossi had been born near the French-Swiss border and had come to Canada as a young man. Now he raised horses on his 160 acres. Whenever someone came along to buy one, he would round them all up so the would-be buyer could take his pick, but as soon as the man made his choice, Rossi would exclaim, "Good God, man, you don't want to buy that horse! It would kill you! There is not a man living who can drive a high-spirited animal like that except me. All my horses are so fast they would tear you to pieces!"

He spoiled every sale. The truth was he simply could not part with any of his dearly beloved animals, though he desperately needed money to pay the taxes on his property and buy grub and clothes. He wore other people's castoffs patched with canvas and bits of cloth of all shades and colours. God knows what he lived on. Every year in haying time, father would hire him and his team and mowing machine for two or three weeks to make sure he earned a few dollars, but outside of that I'm certain he had no income. But it never seemed to get him down. He was always happy-go-lucky, and he would tell the most incredible stories of cooking for Queen Victoria when he was young and taking care of her horses. We never learned whether there was a shred of truth in his stories but we listened all the same.

In the summer of 1912, when father was returning from a trip to Clinton on horseback, he stopped at the post office to pick up our mail and as usual collected the mail for everyone whose homes he would pass. On this occasion, there was a letter for Frank Rossi.

It was about dinner time when father arrived on his doorstep, and Rossi insisted that he stay and eat with him. The invitation took father by surprise because he knew the man seldom had enough grub to feed himself let alone share with anybody else. Father was reluctant to stay since he was so close to home, and he didn't think he would fancy Rossi's cooking any too well, but couldn't think of a good reason to refuse. Anyhow, Rossi just wouldn't take no for an answer.

"Mr. MacDonald," he said, "I'm so lonesome for company, you've just got to stay. Besides, I've got a lovely roast in the oven and I sure would like to share it with you."

Father was puzzled. Rossi was no hunter so what could this roast be? In the two years he had lived in the Bridge Lake district, though it was one of the finest game areas on the whole continent, no one had ever heard of Rossi shooting a single deer. He told great stories of killing game but we never saw any proof of his hunting skills. He even told us about his fine hunting cat which placed a rabbit on his doorstep every morning just in time for him to cook it for breakfast, but we never saw any of these rabbits. Once he entertained us with a tale about shooting the heads off ten ducks with one shot from his rifle, an old 45–90 Winchester with an octagon barrel. It was a little hard to believe, especially since the gun weighed a good fifteen pounds and the hole in the barrel looked like the tunnel of a coal mine.

"How did you manage to make such a wonderful shot?" Angus asked him.

"Ah, it was like this," said Rossi. "I was out hunting one morning near the upper end of Crooked Lake when I saw ten mallards walking along the road in a straight line, one behind the other. I knelt down and took a fine bead on the first duck's head, thinking to pick them off one by one. I pressed the trigger and to my amazement, all ten ducks dropped dead. I had shot the heads off them all!" Angus just shook his head.

While father waited and worried about what Rossi had cooked for dinner, Rossi set the table, and when at last everything was ready he opened the oven door and pulled out his fine roast. Oh no, said father to himself, not that! It was a roasted groundhog, and though it was nicely done, Rossi had left its head on: when father saw those big teeth grinning at him, he was absolutely horrified. How was he going to get out of eating that animal without offending his host? For a moment he sat in horror staring at those teeth, then all of a sudden he jumped up.

"Gosh, I'm sorry, Frank," he said, "but I just remembered that Si Hyman, Pat Burns's cattle buyer, is supposed to be at our place this afternoon to look over our beef steers. I just can't stay any longer. I have to send the boys out to the north range to bring them in." He grabbed his hat and was out of the door as though shot from a cannon. He got his horse from the barn and rode off like a wild man. I'm sure it was six months before he went near Rossi's place again.

Ross Bowers was about thirty years old when he came into the district and settled on Fawn Lake. He was a likeable fellow with a great sense of humour, and he could compose a poem to suit any occasion without pausing to collect his wits. A former light-heavyweight boxer, he was determined to become a trapper, so he often came to us for advice and in the wintertime stopped by on a short cut to his trapline, which was north of ours. A couple of times when a bad storm came up, he stayed over with us until the weather cleared, and often he stopped overnight in one of our trapline cabins.

We told him how old Cashmere had taught us to sleep out-doors during the cold winter months with no tent or even a tar-paulin. First we would find a cluster of evergreens so that their branches would protect us from heavy snowfalls, then cleared the snow under the trees and lit a fire to warm the ground. When the fire burned down, we moved the ashes aside and laid green spruce boughs to make a "mattress." Angus and I each carried half of a four-point Hudson's Bay blanket, about four feet by six feet, in which we rolled ourselves up for the night. With a fire burning near our feet, we got a pretty good night's sleep, and if a spark happened to fall on the blanket, it wouldn't cause much damage since wool only chars a little.

Ross adopted this method of camping out most of the winter. However, on one of his trips he must have been careless about clearing away the ashes beneath his mattress, for while he was sound asleep, fire erupted under him. He was able to put the flames out before he got burned, but his trousers suffered—the next time we saw him, they were patched with pieces of rabbit fur here, there and everywhere, making a most unusual costume.

On the way to his trapline, Ross would leave our ranch early in the morning and on the first night out sleep out in a grove of spruce trees near an unnamed lake. In the winter of 1911–12, Angus and I decided to lay a few more traps in that area, so early one morning we set off on snowshoes with our usual seventy-pound packs. We had a tough day breaking trail in fresh snow, but toward evening when we arrived at the lake where Ross usually camped, we decided that since the location met all the requirements, we should build a cabin. We could see the spot where Ross usually slept. Nearby we cleared the snow away and built a fire to thaw the ground. All night by the light of the moon and the campfire, we cut trees. It was much too cold to sleep anyway, so we drank coffee and ate and kept on working. By the next evening the cabin was finished, and we settled in for a good sleep.

On our next trip to the cabin we could tell that someone had used it, for there was a different pile of kindling wood near the door. Inside we saw that someone had peeled bark from one of the wall logs and written on it. We lit a candle and found a poem which went like this:

> When to this cabin I first came,
> I swore by gum I'd give it a name.
> I applied my talent for a moment, and then
> Decided I'd christen it the Musher's Den.
> I looked in your cellar and all around
> But none of your champagne I found.
> What I christened it with you'll never guess,
> 'Twas a whole pot of Lipton's Best.
>
> > Your friend and fellow trapper,
> > poet, prospector and propositioner,
> > Ross E. Bowers

Angus added:

> But one thing we'll say by gee
> 'Tis a whole lot better than
> Sleeping under a tree.

So the new cabin had a name, and after that so did the lake: Musher's Den Lake.

10

Hard Times

BY THE SUMMER of 1912, we had fourteen head of fine, blocky three- and four-year-old colts and about the same number of one- and two-year-olds coming along, all of them the offspring of Sir Walter Raleigh and our brood mares. We had visions of selling them for a good price to the freighters on the Cariboo Road. Some of the older ones were already broken to work which was not much of a job since they were all very gentle animals, but we were particularly careful not to overwork them because they were so fat and heavy.

One day in August when we went out to the pasture, we found that four of the young colts and two of the older mares were sick; ten days later all the sick ones were dead and four more were down. None of the cayuses and lighter-weight horses were sick. Whatever the disease, it only hit the heavy draft animals. Father was pretty good at doctoring horses and cattle but this terrible sickness had him stumped. He had never seen anything like it: the fatter and healthier the animals looked, the faster they got sick and died. It was heartbreaking. Father tried to get a vet to come in but there were just not enough of them to serve that vast ranching country. While we waited for a vet to come, the disease raged on and the horses kept dying. No one else in the district experienced the terrific losses we suffered, and we were the only people who had heavy draft-type horses.

September came and went and the weather got colder. Winter was on its way and we began to give up hope of a veterinarian coming in that late in the year. All during October and November, the horses died one by one. December rolled around and we knew that any day the full fury of winter would be upon us. Father had been holding off on a trip to Kamloops but he had important business to transact that couldn't wait any longer, so one morning around the middle of the month he set out. The weather was fairly good, and even though he was now seventy-three years old, he went off alone riding his favourite little buckskin mare, Buck. He went by way of the South Bonaparte River, Young's Lake and Scottie Creek. He left Buck at a feed stable in the town of Savona on the CPR line and took the train to Kamloops, arriving there on the third day.

When he had completed his business in Kamloops he returned to Savona for his horse and started home, but this time he took a different route, first to Loon Lake and the farm of a friend. He got an early start the next morning to the 59 Mile House about twenty-five miles away. There had been a fresh snowfall overnight leaving about eighteen inches on the ground, so he was forced to break trail all the way. At the 59, Hamilton, one of the roadhouse partners, told him that a government veterinarian had left in a cutter for our ranch the day before to check our horses. Father was now very anxious to get home and he asked Hamilton to lend him a fresh horse because Buck was just about played out; regrettably, he didn't have a single horse to spare. Father was disappointed but he had a good meal and a short rest, then set off for the 70, eleven miles farther up the road. He was almost certain to get a horse there. Unfortunately, Jim Boyd had sent all their saddle horses over to the Flying U Guest Ranch at Green Lake, seventeen miles off. There was nothing for father to do but eat, have a little rest and keep on riding toward home. The Whitley place was about twenty-three miles from the 70, a matter of about four hours' ride. Father felt sure that Whitley would have a horse to spare. He was very tired as he rode now, but Buck was even more tired so from time to time he would dismount and walk for a mile or two to give the poor animal a rest. On and on they plodded until it was after dark when they arrived at the

Whitleys. Supper was on the table and they insisted that father put his horse in the barn and stay for the night. But he could not take the time and explained to his good friends why he was so anxious to go on that night.

He explained how far he had come without a change of horses or a rest. "Do you have a horse you can spare for a few days?" he asked. Whitley shook his head. He had sent his horses to winter at a meadow several miles away.

Father gave Buck a rubdown and let her rest while he ate supper, then they headed out on the last twenty-seven-mile lap. Sometimes he rode, sometimes he led her, breaking trail all the way. It was a test of endurance that would have conquered many a man far younger than father. No doubt Buck was just as pleased as her rider to see the lights of home, for they were both completely exhausted, having ridden eighty-six miles in twenty-two hours.

The vet had diagnosed a virus disease in our horses. He inoculated them all and left drugs and medical instruments so that we could keep treating them ourselves. We were thus able to save the few we had left, but our fine heavy herd was virtually wiped out.

It was a terrible financial loss to us, and our hopes of raising and selling these fine animals were gone with the wind. We decided to raise only smaller horses suitable for ranch work in the future because we couldn't be sure the virus wouldn't return. These horses apparently had better endurance. There was not such a big demand for heavy draft horses now anyway: the Grand Trunk Railway had been built through the Yellowhead Pass to Prince Rupert and most freight to the northern mining areas was by rail. By some miracle Sir Walter Raleigh had escaped the illness that killed his offspring; we sold him to one of his admirers, a partner in the Ashcroft Hotel, and bought a smaller stallion.

Early in the spring of 1913, father heard that Henry Atwood intended to retire and wanted to sell his herd of range cattle. We boys agreed with father that we should buy the whole herd to build up our stock. We had lots of hay and unlimited summer range. Henry's stock had been brought in from the same place in eastern Washington as our own original herd and were grade shorthorns. Father looked them over and made a deal to buy them all.

On the last day of February, father, Angus and I went to drive our new herd the forty miles home. We took a four-horse team and a big sleighload of hay so that we would be able to feed the stock along the way.

We arrived at Henry's place feeling very sad, for one of our favourite stopping places whenever we were out riding after cattle or on some other business was bachelor Henry Atwood's home. He had a long, low log house. The roof was made of split jack pine logs with a covering layer of clay. It was always warm and cosy and a fine place to spend the night after a long cold ride, and Henry was always glad of the company.

However, if riders came to his door before taking care of their horses, he would meet them with a blast of cusswords that would curl their hair. "Why in hell don't you look after your animals before you come to my door?" he would yell. "They're more important than you are! Without your horse you'd freeze to death or get lost in the bush!" Once the horses were rubbed down, fed and watered, Henry would calm down. Sometimes there would be three or four young cowboys there for the night, but Henry was always up to the job of looking after them all. He would give everyone a chore to do and before long he would have a big feed on the table. Sometimes there was moosemeat stew, and sometimes a pot of beans and salt pork, but always there was a big pan of sourdough biscuits.

After everyone was well fed and the dishes washed up, we would swap stories about hunting and fishing, though most of the time we talked about cattle drives and bucking horses. Once in a while old Henry would challenge someone to a wrestling match. He loved to wrestle, and in spite of his seventy-odd years, he was very good at it. Though not much more than five feet tall, he was built like a block of granite, very powerful and long in the arms. The fellows who wrestled him found it hard to get a firm grip on him because of his build and because he was as full of different holds and tricks as a pet 'coon. He gave all of us young fellows a good lesson in the manly art of wrestling.

Because he was so short and broad and thick, it was very difficult for him to mount a horse, so he had a six-foot length of rope spliced in a circle which he threw over the horn to pull himself up into the saddle. It was rather amusing to watch but it worked, and that was all that mattered.

Henry was a master at making sourdough pancakes, which he always cooked for breakfast on a special soapstone griddle that he had shipped in from Spokane. His sourdough jug was his pride and joy. He boasted that it hadn't been washed for forty years because washing would spoil it for a good sourdough batter. I was probably the only person around there who agreed with him, but that was probably because I considered my sourdough pancakes something special, too.

Shortly after Henry retired, he hired an elderly Irish woman to keep house for him. She had a mind of her own about how to run a clean, orderly house, and one of the first things she did was throw out Henry's precious sourdough jug. This nearly finished the old fellow. He had lived and slept by that jug for over half his life and it nearly broke his heart to part with it, but he submitted in order to keep his housekeeper happy. However, after about four years the old lady died, and it wasn't long before Henry had his jug back on the job, and became his old happy self once more.

The first day of March 1913 was my twentieth birthday, and the day to start driving Henry's herd of cattle to our ranch. Although there was still a lot of snow on the ground, the weather was warm and sunny with a south wind blowing. We considered ourselves lucky to have such a fine day. After a hearty breakfast of Henry's special flapjacks, we moved all the cattle off the feed ground and, behind father leading with the sleighload of hay, we strung the cattle out onto the road. We had no trouble because the animals were quite willing to walk in a double file following the sleigh, between high snowbanks.

We had a hundred head of yearlings and two-year-olds and about sixty cows that would soon be calving—a long string to drive, so the going was pretty slow. Soon they got warm from the sun beating down on their heavy coats of winter hair and started to lag even more. Finally, in order to speed them up, I went ahead and split the drive, slipping in behind the first eighty animals. Angus followed with the same number and this way we were able to keep them moving faster.

As the day wore on, the sun got warmer and the south wind

melted the snow until there was water everywhere. We made twelve miles that day and stopped at the home of Bob and Sam Graham, a pair of crusty old Scottish bachelors. We herded the cattle into their big holding corral and gave them a good feed of hay. The Grahams had a large meadow there and another one at their main ranch on Big Green Lake, some eighteen miles from the 70 Mile House. They and the Boyd family were the pioneer ranchers in the Green Lake district.

The next day was just a repeat of the day before, except that before noon our sleigh runners were cutting through the soft snow to the bare ground, and we stopped for the night at Alec Burns's ranch on the lower end of Crooked Lake, our neighbour for the last year. There were only twelve miles to go. By now the snow had disappeared from the road and it had become a sea of mud, forcing us to leave our sleigh and hayrack at the Burns place. Father borrowed a saddle horse and we turned the draft horses loose, heading them toward home ahead of the cattle. We split the stock into three groups and made much better time. As the snow melted, the trail had widened, so the cattle spread out more and moved faster.

At last we came to the top of the hill from which we could look down into the valley where our ranch lay, but there was bad news ahead. Storm clouds were building up on the northeast skyline. We were still about three miles from home and it would be dark before we got there.

"I'm going on ahead, boys," father called to us. "I'll help Dan haul out hay! Keep 'em moving as fast as you can!"

Angus and I herded the last of them into the feed ground just before the storm broke and darkness fell. Less than an hour later a howling blizzard was blowing. I had seen bad ones on the prairies and one or two in the Cariboo but nothing like this. The weather changed from warm, sunny and springlike to bitter winter in less than an hour. The snow was a solid wall driven before a terrific wind, and we had barely found our way to the house in the sudden dark. It'll be over in an hour, we reasoned, because as a rule a severe storm blows itself out quickly, especially this late in the year. But not this one. It howled all night and most of the next day. When it finally died we were back in midwinter again: snow was piled up in big drifts over everything and the temperature had dropped to thirty-five below zero.

Out in the feed ground, our new cattle had come through the storm very badly. Being on strange terrain, they hadn't found the dense spruce thickets that our old stock used for bed grounds and shelter. Because the storm had hit them before they knew their way around, they had drifted ahead of the blizzard and were trapped against the fence.

We hauled huge loads of hay for them, but the damage had already been done. Such a drastic change in weather was just too much for them. For the next two weeks, the temperature ranged from twenty below in the daytime to forty below at night; our new cattle got pneumonia, and stood running with sweat in the below-zero weather. Soon they were dying like flies. Many of the cows calved but the calves only lived for a day or so. In spite of all we could do for them, in two weeks' time we had lost two-thirds of our new herd.

The final blow to our finances came later that month when we sent our furs to market. Prices had dropped drastically from the previous years, not even paying enough to cover our taxes. All our beautiful horses were gone, and so were our cattle, which meant we had no way to raise money that year. The tax money was most urgent and since we didn't have it, Angus and I went out to work on the Cariboo Road, leaving Dan and father to run both the main ranch and the meadow.

We got work at the government camp seven miles south of the 100 Mile House where rock was crushed for road repairs. Here we met a hard-boiled old-timer by the name of Joe Marland. He had been one of the original members of the North West Mounted Police, having come west to serve on the prairies and later at Fort Steele in the East Kootenay. Though retired for quite a few years, he was now working at the crusher camp levelling gravel on the road.

Angus's job was driving a team of horses hauling the crushed rock. The wagons had been specially built with hopper-shaped boxes and gates in the bottom that were opened by the teamster as needed. When a load of gravel arrived where old Joe wanted it dumped, he had the driver release the lever that controlled the gate. Joe would holler, "Let her go!" and the driver was supposed to keep the team in motion as the gravel emptied out, spreading it evenly along the road.

Well, the team that Angus was driving had been an old freight team and I guess they were afraid that someone would holler "Whoa!" and they wouldn't hear it, because at any sound that resembled it they stopped instantly. Joe's "Let her go!" sounded like "Whoa!" to them, so they stopped immediately with the result that the load of gravel spilled out in one big heap, giving Joe a lot of hard work spreading it with a shovel. Angus tried to tell him to just give a hand signal for his team, but Joe wouldn't listen. No young twenty-four-year-old smart aleck was going to tell him how to handle his job!

One afternoon when father had business with Captain Watson, the owner of the 108 Mile House, he decided to come to the crusher camp to see Angus and me. As he passed by the place where Joe was working, Joe looked up from the gravel and met father's stare. They recognized each other instantly even after a lapse of forty-five years. They had both been raised in the Ottawa Valley and had sat across the schoolroom from one another during father's brief month of formal schooling. Joe was four years younger than father and had worked for him as a young man, cutting timber and rafting it down the river.

Father stayed in camp that night to have a good visit with Joe. They reminisced about the logging camps of the Ottawa Valley and talked about what they had done since then — father's years of prospecting, searching for his "rainbow" in hopes of becoming wealthy, and Joe's years in the Mounties. After so much time, here they were meeting again at a rock crusher plant in British Columbia! Life was certainly strange, they agreed. All the crew gathered around to listen to their stories. Joe told about father's ability as a bull of the woods, and his outstanding skill with a broadaxe, and how he kept order in the camps and on the river drives.

"I remember one first of July in Ottawa," said Joe. "Archie and his crew had just arrived after delivering a raft of timbers in time to take in the big celebration. There were a lot of promoters and gamblers in town from New York and they had brought in a couple of professional foot racers with the idea of cleaning up a lot of the local money. We didn't have any great runners let alone a professional, but Archie had a pretty good reputation as a runner, so a bunch of us wanted him to run against one of the Americans. Archie refused. He said he'd been logging all winter and on the river all spring, so he wasn't in any condition to run a fast race. We wouldn't accept that excuse because we were confident he could outrun any racer that the Americans could put up. After a lot of urging Archie finally said he would do it.

"'All I can promise is that I'll do my best,' he told us.

"So the race was arranged and the bets made. The distance was five miles which suited Archie fine as he figured he would have a better chance in a long race where endurance was more important than speed. But he was worried about his feet; he wondered if they would stand up to the test because he had been on them constantly all winter and spring. We Canadians insisted on some odds in the betting. 'After all,' we said 'our man isn't a professional!' After some discussion, the Americans agreed to our terms, and the race began.

"Well, Archie had no trouble outrunning the renowned American and he even had a little time to spare. There was a happy bunch of Canadians around town that day, for as well as winning the race, Archie had maintained Canada's prestige and earned us a good pile of money!"

When old Joe found out that Angus and I were sons of his boyhood friend, we became friends of his for life. From that day on, Angus couldn't do a thing wrong, and Joe quit yelling "Let her go!" and used hand signals instead.

A lot of the men in that camp delighted in playing tricks on each other and sometimes they even teased old Joe. Then, if he was "feeling good," he would retaliate by challenging them to a fist fight. He always insisted that fights had to be governed by the Marquis of Queensberry Rules. The men got a big kick out of that. But they liked the old ex-Mountie and enjoyed hearing his stories of whiskey runners and other adventures in the early days of the west. I think the old fellow enjoyed the attention he got from all of us.

The meeting between Joe and father gave us a better idea of father's early life and showed us why he was such a capable and self-sufficient man. Angus and I stayed at the crusher camp until nearly the middle of July when we were needed at home to help with the haying and summer work around the ranch.

That summer, in our spare time, we built an icehouse, because we had had no way to keep our milk, cream, butter, fresh meat and fish during the hot months. As usual we used logs, and sited it right next to the blacksmith shop. One end of the building was the milk house where the separating was done and the icehouse occupied the other end. We didn't have sawdust to pack the ice in to keep it from melting, so we used hay, having noticed that wherever ice or snow was covered with hay; it melted very, very slowly. We had plenty of ice on the lake in the wintertime, which we cut into good big chunks about eighteen by eighteen by thirty inches, using an ordinary six-foot crosscut saw. We laid the ice in twelve-foot squares on a layer of hay and built it up, layer upon layer, until we had a stack about eight feet high. Then we banked about two feet of hay around and over the stack and tramped on it to pack it down. In this way we were able to keep ice from one winter right through to the next.

When the icehouse was finished, I had my own idea what we should build next but I kept it to myself until the right opportunity came along. Then one morning while I was washing up the breakfast dishes, the others sat outside in the September sunshine discussing what other work should be done while the weather held. This is my moment, I thought.

I stood in the doorway and announced in a determined voice, "I'll tell you what we're going to do! We're going to dig a well. I'm sick and tired of packing two big buckets of water up that hill from the lake three or four times a day. Especially in winter when it's cold as hell and the wind's blowing a gale. I darn near freeze to death! And I'm not going on hauling water year after year!"

They were so surprised that at first none of them said a word. Little Ervin, the kid brother, getting up on his high horse and telling them what to do! He wasn't running true to form. Ervin was supposed to take orders not give them. When they recovered from the shock there was an uproar.

"That's a tremendous job!" said one.

"Where would we dig it?" asked another.

"Don't worry," I said, "I know exactly the place for it!" And I marched out and showed them where I wanted my well just ten feet from the east side of the house. They still had objections but I was determined.

"I'm through packing water from the lake," I said. "If I don't get a well, somebody else can carry the water from now on! I'm finished."

So they gave in and we started digging. We made the hole round and about five feet across to give us plenty of room to work and also so we could crib it with rock. There was a lot of flat rock a quarter mile from the house which would be just right for the job. At only twenty-four feet we got water, and since the soil was heavy clay, we hadn't even needed cribbing while we dug. Father hired our neighbour Frank Hansen to do the rock work, then we built a little roof over the well and rigged up a windlass to hoist the buckets of water. We now had a fine year-round well of clear, ice-cold water, one that we should have had years earlier as far as I was concerned.

At the end of September, father decided it was time to round up the cattle to see what we had left to ship to market. But we were in for more trouble. Most of the cattle from Henry Atwood that we had been able to pull through the winter, about 125 head, had drifted back onto their old range around the Big and Little Green lakes and the South Bonaparte River, an area about eighty miles square of timber, brush, mountains, lakes and potholes, and by now they would be mixed up with another thousand head of wild range cattle.

We had to round them up, but what a job it was going to be! We took six saddle horses—two apiece for myself, Angus and father—because chasing wild cattle through such rough range-land is a horse-killing job requiring a change of horses at least twice a day. It was impossible to take a chuck wagon over that wild country so we packed our camp supplies on two pack horses.

We set up our first camp at the forks of the North and South Bonaparte rivers. While father and Angus took a short ride around to see if they could locate any cattle, I picketed our spare horses, pitched the tent and prepared supper. It was just my luck to draw the disagreeable jobs every time.

We had three days of hard riding in that district to satisfty ourselves that we had got all the cattle bearing our reversible J brand: ſ J. It was the same brand we had used for all our stock at

Bear Creek Ranch and in Alberta, and we still used our original branding iron. However, several other ranchers in our part of the Cariboo used brands that were similar, so it took a keen eye to pick out our own animals among a herd. Whenever we found some, we drove them to a holding corral we had built on the Seven Mile Flats near Green Lake, where there was plenty of feed and water and a good strong fence to keep them in. Now we transferred our camp here.

There were a lot more cattle in this area, and a much larger range to cover. This territory was dotted with small lakes, pot-holes, sloughs, wild meadows, jack pine flats and fir ridges. All the animals were as wild as buffalo because they had been on the range since early spring, hardly ever seeing a human but often spooked by cougar, bear and other wild animals. As soon as a man appeared on horseback they took off on the dead run for the thickest patch of brush or jack pine they could find.

We had to run the bunch to a standstill before we could force them out into an open flat or meadow to check their brands, then cut out and drive any with our brand. It was a tough job, especially on days when we ran into duck and geese hunters. Whenever those wild cattle saw a man on foot, particularly one who was blazing away with a big twelve-gauge shotgun, they took off again. They never got so tired that they didn't have a little more run left in them.

We were about a week at that camp. Then we moved the whole herd to a fenced-in pasture on the North Bonaparte River, closer to the north end of Big Green Lake where we were going to be rounding up more cattle. We set up camp on a bench above Little Green Lake. As we had an even bigger expanse of rangeland to cover here, father rode off to see Roy and Stan Eden whose ranch was about three miles away on Watch Lake. They were first-rate cowboys and very familiar with the range we were working. Father persuaded Roy to come and give us a hand and he proved to be a real asset.

But when it came to rounding up cattle and driving them to the corrals, father was the best among us, and indeed one of the best and most active cowboys in the country. What was really amazing was that he never seemed to tire on the long drives, and he was always ready to lend a hand to anyone who needed help.

He was always "one of the boys": around the campfires in the evenings, he would tell stories about his prospecting days, and frequently he would sing his Gaelic songs. They were a novelty for the cowboys, especially for those who had never heard the Gaelic language. He was quite an entertainer.

The young cowboys were full of heck and always out for a lark. Once in a while one of them would challenge father to a wrestling match or a round of sparring, and when the challenger came out second best, he would scheme to get some newcomer to try. And that's exactly what happened to a young chap we called "Slim" when he and a bunch of young fellows stayed overnight with us a few months earlier at the ranch. John "Slim" Hansen was well nicknamed, for he was over six feet tall, lean and strong as an ox. He loved to box and very few fellows could beat him, but this was more because of his long reach and strength than his skill. He had become pretty conceited about his boxing ability, however, and some of the others were hoping to see him taken down a peg or two, so they started working on him to get him to challenge my father to a sparring match.

After a little persuasion, Slim succumbed and the next morning before breakfast approached father as soon as he came downstairs. As usual, father said good morning to everyone in turn, and to Slim he said, "And how are you feeling this fine morning, Slim?"

"Oh, I'm just fine, sir," he said, "and I would like to spar a few rounds with you."

The expression on father's face never changed. He just looked at Slim in his calm, friendly way, so Slim put his big fists up and started to dance around him. Now, ever since father had been hurt way back in 1884, he had been a little stiff on his feet first thing in the morning. "Take it easy, Slim," he said, "there's no need to get excited. Just wait till I get limbered up a bit." He shuffled around for a minute or two, keeping just out of his reach and putting up his hands to ward off his hard blows. All the time he kept talking to him, telling him that someone was going to get hurt, but Slim kept jabbing fiercely; they were awkward blows but would have hurt father had any landed. Finally, seeing that Slim had no intention of giving up, father began to watch for an opening and when it came, he let drive with his left, then followed it up with a terrific right that knocked poor Slim clear across the room. Father helped him to his feet.

"I'm real sorry, Slim," he said. "I didn't want to fight you but you kept on insisting!"

Slim was shaking his head to clear it but he managed to nod in agreement. He had already developed a brand new respect for father; he developed a beauty of a black eye shortly afterwards.

It was noon of 12 October when we rounded up the last of Henry Atwood's cattle. We planned to move them the next morning down to the pasture on the North Bonaparte where we were holding the rest of the stock. The weather had remained good with bright sunny days and frosty nights; at this camp above Little Green Lake we never even bothered to put up our tent, believing it warmer to sleep in the wide open spaces beside a big log fire. Consequently we were thoroughly surprised to wake up the last morning to find six inches of snow on our beds. With all that snow on top of the tarpaulin over us, we were as warm as bugs in a rug, but when we crawled out, the freezing air hit us. After a hot breakfast, we quickly saddled up for the cold, miserable cattle drive to the North Bonaparte pasture.

When father and I rode ahead to the pasture to start the animals on the trail, they began to run as soon as they were out of the gate. Fortunately, they were headed in the right direction, for the two of us couldn't hope to stop them. Meanwhile, Angus was having trouble with his horse, a fine big four-year-old Arab and Morgan cross that he called Nigger. He had only been ridden a few times but Angus thought this would be an opportunity to give him more training in neck-reining, a necessary skill for a good cow horse. But the colt, still half-wild and cold as well, was fighting the bit this morning and bucking and crow-hopping all over the place. Suddenly, his feet shot from under him on the snow-covered hillside and he went down hard on his side, all one thousand pounds of him, catching Angus's leg under his body.

Father turned just then to see what was keeping Angus and Roy and saw Nigger fall but there was no time to turn back. "Roy, look after Angus!" he shouted. That herd of cold, wild cattle were on the run with only two of us to handle them and keep them out of the brush. After all our hard, dangerous work rounding them up, we couldn't take the chance of losing them again.

241

Although father was seventy-four years old, there were not many cowboys in the country who could handle cattle better than he did. He knew exactly what to do with those animals — though we both knew our work was cut out for us. We had two things in our favour: there was a trail to follow and the terrain was pretty open allowing us to see if any of the cows slipped off into the bush. It was about two o'clock in the afternoon on Friday, 13 October 1913 when we got them safely into the big corral, then wheeled around and started back as fast as we could.

When we got to the camp we could see that something was terribly wrong. Tracks in the snow showed that somebody with a team and wagon had been there. Roy's saddle horses and Nigger were picketed with the other horses, yet there was no sign of the two men. On the ground we found some pieces of white cloth with bloodstains on them, but there was no note of explanation for us.

"Ervin, saddle a fresh horse for me," said father. "I'm going to follow those wagon tracks. You stay in camp till I get back!" He had already put in a hard, cold day of riding with nothing to eat or drink since six in the morning, but I don't think that man ever backed down from trouble or hardship in his entire life.

There was something familiar about the situation I found myself in. I was alone again in the middle of the wilderness with a snowed-in camp to shovel out and eight horses to feed and water. When the chores were done, I lit a fire and prepared some supper. Like father I had not eaten since six that morning and it was now nine at night. Poor father. I kept thinking about him pushing his horse along the trail, cold and hungry. Houses were few and far between in that country and God alone knew when he would take time to eat and rest a little. All I could do was care for the horses and myself and wait.

Father had little trouble following the wagon tracks in the fresh snow, and when he reached the west side of Big Green Lake he could see that the wagon had turned south toward the 70. He took a short cut and arrived at the 70 about one o'clock in the morning. He soon located Angus and Roy, who told him that after father and I had left following the cattle, he had dragged Angus the two hundred yards back to camp. He had tied his lasso rope to one end of a canvas pack cover and took a turn around his saddle horn, pulling this improvised sled along easily on the snow-covered ground. In camp, he had cut off Angus's boot, made him as comfortable as possible, and covered him up well. As a rule, we carried a quart of 35 overproof Hudson's Bay rum with us for emergencies, so Roy mixed a big hot drink for his patient and one for himself as well.

After much discussion, the two of them concluded that Angus had to be taken to a doctor, and Roy rode over to his ranch to bring back a wagon. He had to leave Angus by himself but could see no alternative, and took the two-mile short cut over a fir ridge behind the camp. His brother Stan came back with him, but they took more than three hours since they had to go by road with the team and wagon; it was close to eleven o'clock when they reached Angus. They had been very worried about him, but except for the dreadful pain he was in, he was all right.

The two men carefully lifted him onto a mattress on the floor of the wagon box and wrapped him up warmly in blankets. Around one o'clock they set off for the 70, travelling at a walk so as not to shake Angus up any more than could be helped, which meant they took nearly eight hours to get there. However, the nearest doctor, Dr. Sanson, was at Ashcroft. When he was con-tacted by phone, he promised to start out as soon as he could get transportation for the fifty-mile trip. In the meantime, Jack Boyd took over as nurse. Unfortunately, his cure-all for most ailments was hot rums, and more hot rums until all worry and pain disap-peared.

Besides their big, heavy four-horse coaches for long hauls, the BX Company had lighter ones for overloads and special trips, one of which Dr. Sanson was able to hire that night for his journey to the 70 Mile House. It was morning before he arrived to find that Angus had a compound fracture just above the ankle. But Angus was so full of Jack's special remedy that he would not respond to the doctor's injections of painkilling drugs and it was impossible to work on his leg. All he could do was bind it for the time being and arrange to get him to the hospital in Ashcroft where his leg could be set properly. Quite near the 70 lived a man who owned a small truck and agreed, for good pay, to take Angus into Ashcroft right away.

Angus was again laid on a thick mattress and covered with

blankets on the floor of the truck. But on this trip there was a new concern. The snow that had led to Angus getting injured had been general all over the southern Cariboo, and the roads were terribly slippery, especially for automobiles and trucks. The big question was how to keep the truck from sliding off the road. There were no such things as tire chains, so they came up with the bright idea of wrapping logging chains around the back wheels. It made for a darned rough ride but it was better than chancing an accident.

Just before they set off, good old pal Jack slipped Angus another bottle of rum to ease his pain. Consequently, Angus was moaning with pain one minute and the next minute he was singing like a bird all the way to Ashcroft. Even after he was admitted to the hospital, the doctor had to wait a few hours for the patient to sober up before attempting to do anything with his leg.

At the holding pasture, father, Roy and I cut out the range cattle and drove them to our ranch. This was a two-day trip. Then we rounded up all the mature beef cattle at the ranch. While I stayed behind, father, Roy and Dan drove them over to the holding pasture on the North Bonaparte, collected the animals that had been left there and started driving the 170 or so head toward Ashcroft. The six-day drive went off without a hitch.

In Ashcroft, father and Dan went to the hospital to see Angus, two weeks after father had seen him at the 70. They found him with his leg in a cast, kept immobile with pulleys and weights. But he was having the time of his life for it was the first occasion since the orphanage that he had had time for a good rest, and he had jolly young nurses for company to boot. He had only one complaint: he missed the stinky old pipe that he cherished so much. When he returned home he had to learn how to smoke all over again!

With Angus laid up, I had to work our trapline myself that winter. One day, about the middle of Feburary 1914, I set off up Willow Creek on my snowshoes, stopping here and there to look at a trap or a lynx snare. The blazed trail followed the north side of the creek which wound its way down a deep, narrow draw, through thick mats of willows, alders and the occasional cluster of balsam and spruce. I was having a hard time because of the narrowness of the trail between the thick jungle and a steep ridge. But at one little dip in the trail a big spruce tree had been uprooted and now a small cluster of young spruce had grown up there, making a nice sheltered nook. Angus and I had cut a log and placed it in front of this grove, because the spot got the full force of the noonday sun. Many times we had sat on this log to take a breather or eat our lunch.

Well, on this pleasant sunshiny day I stopped there as usual for a short while. I didn't bother to take my snowshoes off, but just slipped my packsack off to give my back a rest. I leaned back against the little spruce trees, enjoying the sunshine while I ate my lunch. Afterwards I dozed off for a moment or two, but awoke abruptly on hearing a slight noise close by. And there right in front of me was a great big cow moose. She was so close I could have reached out and touched her nose. I knew that I was in a very dangerous position, and though my brain was racing, I sat perfectly still. Cautiously, she pushed her big ugly head toward me and stuck her wet nose into my face and started sniffing. Slowly she sniffed me from my head to my feet while I sat frozen stiff. Every second I expected her to pick up one of her huge splayed front hoofs and split me in two, for I knew a moose could easily kill a man that way. I held my breath and waited.

After what seemed to be at least a month, but was probably only a minute or two, she slowly turned and wandered off down the creek. For several minutes I sat there unable to understand that I was still in one piece, then I grabbed my pack and headed up the creek with my knees shaking uncontrollably. I am still convinced that if I had lost my nerve and moved, it would have been the end of me. Instead, I have the distinction of being one of the few people who has ever been "kissed" by a moose and lived to tell about it.

It was later the same month that I found Billy Lame camped on the shore of a small lake about four miles east of our ranch. The lake was on my trapline and since there were a couple of beaver houses there, every year we trapped four or five beaver as well as a few muskrats and mink. Billy Lame had gone there to fish for freshwater ling cod through the ice at the outlet of the lake. The weather had been cold, at least fifty degrees below zero, and old Billy had had the misfortune to slip into the water and get his feet frozen. When I found him, he had used up all the

245

firewood in reach and was in danger of freezing to death.

We had known old Billy for some three or four years and had often marvelled at his ability to get around. When he was young he had been attacked by a grizzly bear, leaving his legs mauled and broken in so many places that it was a miracle he could walk at all. Most of the time he rode a little roan mare, but in winter when the snow was deep he dragged himself around on snowshoes, though we could never understand how he did it. As far as we could figure out, Billy didn't understand or speak English, and whenever we tried to talk to him he would only bleat like a sheep, baa-aa.

The toboggan he used to haul his camp equipment along the ice was lying nearby so I loaded him on board and started for home. When I reached the ranch, I left him on the lake to run up to the house for help. We got the poor old fellow into the house and, with father's guidance, doctored up his feet, soaking them in kerosene for an hour or so, then wrapping them in clean bandages. The cold kerosene took the frost out and disinfected them at the same time, leaving a sort of numbness in the frozen part and reducing the pain. Rubbing the old man's feet was out of the question because it would have taken all the skin off, and putting anything warm on his feet would have been terrifically painful.

We put a cot near the big heating stove and a pile of wood within reach, so that Billy could stoke up the fire when none of us was around. Then we fed him a big bowl of hot soup. After that, we soaked his feet in salt water and rebandaged them twice every day. It was weeks before he could put his weight on them, but by the middle of March he was out of bed most of the time. Though he still couldn't walk, he was able to crawl around the room.

One day, father was in his room writing letters when he suddenly heard Billy laugh out loud. He was obviously having the time of his life all by himself there by the heater, so father became curious and went in to see what was amusing the old boy. What he saw was Billy Lame with a pair of grey-backs — lice — on a big piece of split wood. The old fellow was poking the lice with a long sliver to make them run. It was a lice race!

Father snatched the piece of wood and threw it into the stove as fast as he could, and Billy's two little playmates perished in the flames.

When Angus and I came in for supper that night father greeted us with, "Boys, put a cot in the storehouse and get this lousy old Indian out of here!"

Angus and I were stunned, and then from the cot near the heater, we heard Billy say quite clearly, "Billy Lame no lousy. MacDonald lousy!"

We were floored. In all the time we had known him and in all the weeks he had been with us, he had never said more than "baa-aaa." We went to work at once putting up a heater in the store-house and moving our sly, lousy old invalid out of the house. After that, we took his meals to him every day and kept him well supplied with wood, but we never let him in the house again. He could race all the lice he wanted to out there in the storehouse.

Spring came and one morning when I took his breakfast to the storehouse, Billy Lame wasn't there. We had no idea where he had gone and actually we weren't sorry to be rid of him and his lice, but we thought he could have at least come to our door to say that he was leaving. We thought we had seen the last of old Billy, but one day in mid-May he showed up again on his little mare. We watched him go down to a spruce thicket by the lake and set up camp, then turn his horse into the calf pasture. We didn't say anything to him, but we wondered what he was up to. The next day, father happened to ride by the hay field and there he found Billy down on his knees at the edge of the field: he was grubbing out the stumps and willows that got in the way during haying.

"What are you doing, Billy?" asked father.

Billy looked up. "Me got no *chikamin* [money] to give you for keeping old Billy from going *mimaloos* [dying], so I chopum brush."

"You don't owe me anything, Billy," said father. "If I froze my feet you would help me, wouldn't you?"

But Billy refused to accept the logic. Finally, father decided that if the old Indian wanted to work, he would have to accept a dollar a day for clearing land, the going wage for labourers at that time and really good pay for slow Billy.

Every day after that for nearly a month, Billy grubbed at those roots. It was pitiful to watch since most of the time he was crawling on his hands and knees. Then one day when father saw a young man and a squaw working with Billy, he rode over to make it clear to them that we didn't need any more land cleared and that he certainly wasn't going to hire anyone but Billy.

"Oh," said the young Indian, "you no pay me. Billy pay me."

Father was thoroughly puzzled. "Why are you working for Billy?"

To this he replied, "Big potlatch at Canim Lake. Billy say he no come till he finish job. Me and my squaw come to help him. Faster she done, sooner he come."

Men like that crippled old Indian don't come along very often.

This was not the only time we had evidence of the Indians' generosity and unselfish ways. Many times when we had hired two or three of them to work for us, a couple of extra families would come to live off them. Frequently the ones we hired would ask to be paid in groceries instead of money so they could share with their friends; when the friends' turn came to get a job, the favours were returned. Their way of life was as socialistic as one would find anywhere.

On one particular occasion, we had hired three young fellows for the haying season. When there were only about three more days of stacking left, father had to go on a business trip, leaving us money to pay the men when the haying was finished. At noon the next day, the men came to the house just as we were ready to go back out to work, asking for their money right then.

"Our friends have come over the trail from Chu Chua. They want us to go with them to hiyu big potlatch at Canim Lake. So we want our money to go do some celebrating."

"You were hired to stay until the hay was all put up," said Angus. "You don't get any money till the job is done."

We couldn't let them go or we would be left with a lot of hay still out in the field, for chances were they wouldn't come back once they got paid. Angus and I could see that the men were angry and we watched them stalk off to have a powwow with their friends at their camp near the lake. We headed back to the field and started to haul in the hay, but before we finished pitching the first load onto the wagon, we saw all the Indians, both men and women, marching out onto the field. The women were on horseback and the men walked beside them. Many of them carried poles about ten feet long and three inches thick, sharpened at one end; rope was tied through a notch around the other end. Angus and I stared open-mouthed and then suddenly light dawned on us. They had come to help with the haying! Each woman rode up beside a big stook of hay, the men pushed the sharp pole under the stook, then tied the rope over top in a half hitch. The women took a turn of the rope around her saddle horn and headed for the stack at a dead run, dragging the stook behind her. Four other men waited to pitch the hay onto the stack.

Well, with eight Indian women on fast horses hauling the hay, a couple of men helping Angus haul with the wagon, and two more Indians and me on the stack, that hay field was cleaned up in about five hours. We never saw faster work or a more thorough job of moving hay than we saw that afternoon. Before nightfall we had paid them off and they were headed for Canim Lake. It was a distance of about forty miles so they probably rode all night but they were determined not to miss any of that celebration.

I was often amazed at the remarkable stamina and endurance of Indian people. I believe it was May one year that a group of Indians rode past our place about six o'clock in the morning, stopping only long enough to say "Klahowya, tilicum" because they were hurrying to get to a party at Canim Lake. About half an hour later I started off to our north range to check on some cattle that we had turned out a couple of weeks earlier, and much to my surprise, only half a mile or so out I found the Indians gathered around a campfire. Their horses were grazing nearby. I spotted Pierre, one of their lesser chiefs.

"Why are you camping here, Pierre?" I asked. "I thought you were in a big rush to get to the potlatch."

"We no camp," he said. "One squaw going to catchum papoose so we stop."

With the mystery cleared up I went on my way to the range, put out salt for the cattle and made a count to see if they were all there. Several calves had been born since I had last checked but everything was all right with them so I rode home. When I

reached the spot where the Indians were stopped I was aston-
ished to see them getting ready to go on their way again.

"What's the matter, Pierre?" I asked. "Why are you leaving so
soon?"

"Squaw catchum papoose so we go on to Canim now," he said
matter-of-factly.

The new mother had already ridden ten miles that morning
and was now preparing to ride another thirty or more miles
before being able to rest. The long ride by itself would be too
much for many able-bodied men, but the Indian women took it all
in their stride.

Father's efforts to get the land surveyed had paid off; the population grew quickly in those years just before the First World
War. There were the Higginses, the Prinzhouses, the Larsens, the
Hollands and the Calvin Smiths. The Ed Smiths had small children and were not able to afford a cow so father lent them a
couple of ours for their first summer. It was good to have neighbours and to have a little social life, too. People began organizing
sleighing parties. Dances became popular, held in the fall and
winter months, of course, when there was less work to do on the
ranches. Couples who had babies and small children brought
them all, and when the little ones got sleepy, they were bedded
down on beds or benches until the dance was over in the morning. The women brought enough food for a midnight supper and
for breakfast. Music was provided by the guests themselves;
often Dan played his violin and, though he had never had a
lesson, he did very well. The people who didn't care to dance just
sat around and gossipped.

Father refused to go to the dances, but he thoroughly
enjoyed the sports days and picnics that were held in the sum-
mertime. Folks came from miles around to join in the fun. The
older ones swapped "tall tales" and "fish stories" while the young
ones ran races. These activities always called for ice cream and
cold drinks, and since we were the only family who had an
icehouse we always supplied the ice. We would pack several big
chunks of it in a wagon well lined with hay; at the appointed
place of entertainment, the men took over the job of freezing the
ice cream in hand-operated ice cream freezers while the ladies

supervised. Only real thick fresh cream, eggs and flavouring were used, none of the artificial stuff they put in it today.

It was a bit of a nuisance hauling ice around this way, but one summer Dan and I solved the problem. We kept a rowboat on Bridge Lake where we liked to troll for big rainbow and lake trout, and one day after we had been trolling around the islands at the south end of the lake, we took a notion to hike over to the Roe Lake settlement to visit with friends. It was an easy walk except for a quarter mile of rocky ridges and cliffs: as we scrambled over this part, we suddenly felt a cold draft. Naturally we were puzzled because it was such a warm day, and we had never had this experience on any of our previous trips through the area, so we started to investigate. Eventually we found a crevice in the ground where the cold air was wafting out, and when we climbed down and around to the face of the cliff, we found the mouth of a cave. Inside was a huge ledge of ice. There must have been several tons of it. We figured that the water from the melting snow seeped through the rock crevices and into the cave where it refroze, and because the sun and wind could not penetrate this chamber, the ice stayed all year round.

Our discovery was quite near the settlement at Roe Lake, and we asked some of the younger men to come back with us to see it. After that, we never had to haul ice from our place for the summer picnics. Anyone wanting it knew where to find it.

When spring came in 1914, Angus and I went out to the Cariboo Road to work again, for we were still short of ready cash to pay the ever-present tax burden. We were not alone in this predicament; most of the new settlers had the same problem. We could grow a good part of our living, but cash for taxes and other necessities was hard to come by. Some families gave up and left, while others looked for work off the farm. Yet jobs were scarce. Angus managed to get one driving a tote wagon for the surveyors who were working the right of way for the Pacific Great Eastern Railway from the 100 Mile House north to Lac La Hache; I worked at Jimmy Boyd's sawmill near the 115 Mile House on Lac La Hache. I was just leaving the mill to go home to help with the haying when I heard that World War I had broken out. Angus quit his job at the same time and we got a ride with a freighter as far as the 70 Mile House, where there was a great deal of talk about the war; but it was generally agreed that it wouldn't last long.

In the first week of November 1914, Angus and I decided to have a look at some country fifteen or twenty miles north of our trapline, for we knew we must expand if we were going to make our trapping pay. The previous winter when Angus was laid up, I had made a quick trip on snowshoes to have a look. The snow had been deep and hard-crusted and the travelling easy, but though I liked the look of the country, I couldn't do anything about establishing a new line by myself. I had told the others about the high plateau I had found: it seemed to be about 4,000 or even 5,000 feet above sea level; it had a lot of beaver ponds and a few small lakes, and I had seen signs of marten, fisher and lynx.

Angus and I realized we would have to build a good cabin up there if we were going to establish a trapline, so we set off the following November with the necessary tools and materials. We packed a camp stove and some pots and dishes onto two pack horses and headed northeast from the ranch. Since we would be cutting trail, there was no use taking saddle horses. On the third evening we made camp at the edge of the new district in a small wild meadow with a little stream running through it. The next morning, as soon as we located a place to build our cabin, we unloaded our supplies and Angus started back with the pack animals. He would be able to make better time now following the trail we had blazed. Meanwhile I got busy cutting logs for the cabin. This one would be larger and better than our other cabins since we would be using it as our headquarters for the district, so I had to find longer, more uniform logs. By the time Angus returned, I had them all cut and had made a fair start on the walls. I had also been able to shoot a three-point mule deer which would stretch our grub supply. With Angus's help the cabin was soon complete, and we christened it "The Granite Creek Hotel" as we had already named the nearby creek Granite Creek. After cutting a good supply of firewood for winter, we set out some traps for marten, fisher and lynx, and prepared to move on.

On the morning of the twenty-seventh of November, we set off south to blaze a new trapline up and over a high mountain and through the plateau country, to connect up with a line we had already established a few years earlier. Our destination was "Big Stick Cabin." It was a cold, dull morning. A foot of snow had fallen overnight but it was too loose and soft for snowshoes so we just had to wade through it. Every now and then we stumbled over the rocks and sticks hidden under the snow cover. Considering the conditions, we were making good time and we figured on reaching the cabin before dark. The 1909 forest fire, about five years before, had burned through that country and all the big timber was gone: there wasn't much brush to cut, just clumps of balsam trees and a few willows here and there. We set a few traps in likely looking places, but we were in a hurry for we had a long way to go. After a while the cold seemed to be getting more intense with every step we took. Just above the treetops, a heavy blanket of cloud or fog had formed. Stubbornly we trudged on, until we reached the top of the mountain and came out onto the long plateau. Ahead we could see the small lakes and beaver ponds that I had seen last February. Angus agreed that it had the makings of a good trapline but neither of us wanted to stop and explore its possibilities right then because we suffered so much from the cold when we weren't moving.

Around noon we stopped to make a big campfire for boiling up a pot of good strong tea and thawing out a kettle of beans and salt pork. With our appetites appeased and our bodies warmed through, we went on again. By now we were beginning to really worry about the weather and wondered whether we could reach Big Stick Cabin before it got too dark to travel. We decided to climb the high peak to our right to see how far we still had to go.

But by the time we had climbed to the top it was already getting dark. In the distance we could see our destination but it was still too far away and to continue that night was too dangerous. All around us were big boulders and fallen timbers. It was terribly cold and the wind knifed through our clothing. We knew that we had to get a fire going fast so we slipped down into a little draw just below the peak — the only shelter we could find before darkness set in. Luckily we were still packing the sharp double-bitted axe that we had used to build the cabin. We chopped up some balsam logs and set a fire between two more logs. We built a windbreak out of balsam boughs between two big boulders, hoping this would also act as a heat reflector, but

253

there was such a draft of subzero air coming down the draw that it was impossible to get a really hot fire going. It was almost as though the frost in the air smothered the flame.

We kept cutting the available wood into kindling to feed the fire, but we couldn't get warm. In one of our packs we carried a four-point Hudson's Bay blanket which we cut up to make Mexican-style ponchos, and we wrapped smaller pieces around our feet to prevent them from freezing. All night long we took turns cutting kindling to keep that fire going. We knew how easy it would be to become discouraged and give up and perish in that awful cold.

There was no possibility of sleep for we were far too cold, and it was even dangerous to relax. We would have soon frozen stiff. To help us survive we melted snow and made strong tea in a five-pound lard pail, setting it close to the fire to steep, and though it simmered on the side next to the heat, slivers of ice formed on the other side where the draft of cold air was drawn into the flame. The cold beat at us all night until we were stiff and stupid and our every move was slow and awkward. It would have been so easy to give up but that stubborn MacDonald streak would not let us quit.

Oh, how thankful we were to see the grey light of dawn filtering into the draw. As soon as we could safely travel, we set off for the dark line of forest on the far side of the lake. We didn't bother to blaze a trail, putting all our energy into reaching that cabin. It was noon before we arrived, and at first we were too cold to even start a fire in the stove. We had to rub our hands and fingers for a while before attempting to light a match. When we had a good fire going we prepared a hot meal, and afterwards we hit our bunks for a delicious long rest. We were absolutely played out.

We stayed over the next day to put the cabin in shape and lay in a fresh supply of wood before the deep snows came. With the weather warming a little, we left the following morning for our cabin near the foot of Long Island Lake about ten miles distant. We stayed another day there cutting wood and setting out traps, then set off for home. Father told us that the temperature the night of the twenty-seventh had been fifty-seven degrees below zero at the ranch. We figured it must have hit nearly seventy below where we were because that mountain peak was almost

6,000 feet above sea level. I'm sure if I live to be a hundred years old, I'll never forget that dreadful experience, for I am certain that the wings of death touched my brother and me many times that terrible night.

In the years that we trapped in that high plateau country, we often marvelled at how clear and cold the air was. Some mornings the temperature went down to sixty degrees below zero. The air would be clear, deathly cold, and full of particles of frost sparkling in the bright sunlight. We couldn't even cook our breakfast until we thawed out the food, and that was indoors, not outdoors. Sometimes we could hear our nearest neighbour, four or five miles away, chopping wood or hear his dog barking.

At times when we were out on our traplines in the mountains high above the headwaters of Four Mile Creek, which drained the high plateau and flowed into the North Thompson River at Little Fort, we were able to look down into the valley below, where the Canadian National Railway had been built. And when the weather conditions were right we could hear the faint but unmistakeable sound of the train whistle, twenty miles away. It was a comforting sound, somehow, telling us that down there in the valley there were people living and travelling in the plush modern railway coaches. We were not alone in our silent world.

Sometimes the noises that a person hears in the mountains are not so comforting, but weird and frightening if he doesn't know what is causing them. The disastrous fire of 1909 had swept up a mountain approximately 1,500 feet straight up from Green Pine Lake. Hundreds of snags had been left, burned quite thin, with holes right through them here and there. Since there was no cover on the mountain but bare rocks and these burned husks, the wind vibrated the thin shells of the snags and whistled through the holes. They moaned and shrieked and howled. It sounded as if all the lost souls from hell were drifting around that peak! The first time Angus and I heard them was one night when we had just started building Big Stick Cabin on the shores of Green Pine Lake. The sound was terrifying, especially since it was night and we were so many miles into the wilderness. The next morning when we found the cause, we named the mountain Spook Mountain.

In the same district one January, Angus and I set out to locate two men who were overdue from a trapping trip. It was one of the few times we had a compass with us, because we only used it in unfamiliar country. On our second day away from home we ran into a blinding snowstorm. We knew we had to travel due north so we got out the compass to guide us Our snowshoes sank into the dry, powdery snow, making travel slow and tough.

For several hours we plodded along breaking trail and taking a look at our compass now and again. Then suddenly we came to snowshoe tracks. They were snowed under to be sure but there could be no mistaking that somebody had been there within the last few hours. Angus and I felt sure it could only be the missing men so we started to follow the tracks.

Suddenly, I stopped. "Wait a minute. These are our own tracks! Look at the shape of them!"

Angus agreed. "And look at that tree over there. We've passed that tree before! What's going on here?"

We had been travelling in a big circle, even with a compass! The mountain we were crossing had so much iron in its ore that it attracted the needle. In fact, it had so much iron that it tinted the snow red. And that is why we named that mountain Iron Cap Mountain.

When we finally realized what had happened, we switched to our old style of travel, taking a landmark and heading for it. A person can keep a fairly straight course this way, and it brought us to the creek we were looking for on the third day. We followed it to a big lake called Taweel, which we had recommended to the men as a possible location for a cabin, so we expected that this was where we would find them. It was a simple matter to spot their cabin by travelling along the shore ice, until we came to the hole they had cut to get water. The men were both in the cabin, very sick with the flu.

Angus and I prepared hot tea from balsam needles and hot moosemeat broth. We kept the two of them in bed until we were sure they were well on the way to recovery, then set off for home.

As a rule, January was a poor month to trap because fur-bearing animals don't move about much in the severe cold and the deep snow. Our patients now decided to take it easy out there in the peaceful wilds, until they had regained their strength, having been assisted so unexpectedly by our house call. They were very grateful for our help.

11

New Enterprise

IN THE TRAPPING season we got little news of the outside
world, but in the spring of 1915 when Angus and I learned that
the war was still going on, we set off for Kamloops a few days
later to enlist. We were told that raising beef cattle was a very
necessary part of the war effort, and that it would be better for us
to carry on for the time being. Besides, said the recruiting officer,
there were more men enlisting than they could outfit and train.
He took our names and addresses, including Dan's, and said we
would be notified when we were needed. Nevertheless, some of
the young men who had pre-emptions in the district were
accepted, and several of the Englishmen who had settled near us
went back home to enlist. That year, with so many men leaving
for the armed forces and others taking war jobs, we had a hard
time getting help to put up the hay.

In the spring of 1916, we received a letter saying that two of us
boys were to report for military service; the third was to remain
on the ranch since our father was too old to operate the place
alone. How were we to decide which one of us would stay home?
We agreed to push it from our minds until the hay was in; then
we would toss a coin to see who would be left behind.

The big day came and we asked father to flip the coin. We
were a pretty solemn foursome. Dan lost the toss; he would stay

with father. Angus and I packed our bags and left for Vancouver to enlist in the army.

We were sent to Victoria for training, where our company consisted mostly of loggers, trappers, cowboys and ranchers who had lived in isolated places for years. When these fellows hit civilization they came down with one childhood disease after another, even though they were perfectly strong and healthy. Angus and I had been through those illnesses when we were very young, in the orphanage at Spokane, but we were kept in quarantine along with the rest of the men. Four or five times our outfit even managed to get packed up to go overseas before we found ourselves quarantined again. We were all pretty disgusted, impatient to be on our way to Europe where things were happening.

Then in March 1918 the most serious illness of all broke out: spinal meningitis. I was the only man in our tent to get it and was rushed to hospital. Angus managed to avoid getting sick even though he slept in the same tent; nevertheless, he and the other ten men were isolated.

Many of the men in our outfit were struck down with meningitis. Some died within a few hours of the first symptoms. Most of them went into convulsions and became delirious, and nothing could be done for the poor fellows. However, a doctor in Victoria had just developed a new antitoxin, which had not yet been tested. Since I was the only patient who was not delirious I was chosen as the guinea pig; they needed someone who could be reasoned with. I would have to remain conscious and perfectly still throughout this painful procedure. Several men held me down to prevent me from moving. A hypodermic needle was inserted at the base of my spine to begin removing the pale-yellow syrupy fluid, then three more, and each one felt like a crowbar being stuck into me. The pain was indescribable. Then another hypodermic needle was used to insert the antitoxin. At last it was over. The cure was terrible but it was effective, and very slowly I began to recover.

I was placed in a private ward and given the best possible care. Of course, Angus was not allowed in to visit me, but since my room was on the ground floor he frequently came to my window to talk. One day he came to say good-bye: our outfit was finally going overseas, but I would not be going with all my buddies. I felt that fate had dealt me a very dirty blow. I spent nine months in hospital, and made a sad-looking spectacle when I was discharged from the army late in the fall as physically unfit for further service. I went home, but I was no longer the strong hunter, trapper and woodsman I had been. It was a long time before I was much use around the ranch.

After the Armistice in November 1918, Angus was sent to Belgium with the Seaforth Highlanders and did not get home to the Cariboo until August 1919. On the way he contracted jaundice, and had only recovered from that when he developed rheumatic fever. For nearly two years he suffered from its effects.

That fall our sister Lavena and her husband Jim came with their two sons, Eddie and Richard (or Buster as he was called), to pre-empt land on the north shore of Crooked Lake, fulfilling a long-held plan. Dan and I helped Jim build a good log house, happy to have them close by at last.

By November, I was able to begin trapping again, but not alone. Because Angus was too ill and Dan was needed at the meadow to look after the cattle, I got Slim Hansen's eighteen-year-old brother Lee to help me. He was a big strong fellow and a very good hunter, sure to have the makings of a first-rate trapper. I showed him how to set traps, how to distinguish one animal's signs from another—many of the things that old Cashmere and Ike Simmons had shown me long ago. He learned fast and we had a profitable season.

Our family had often wished we had a portable sawmill, which would be a tremendous help in building hay sheds and so on. There was a lot of good timber on our ranch. Consequently, in the spring of 1920 I took my winter's catch of furs to Vancouver to buy a sawmill and Titon tractor with the profits. I was the only one of us boys who had any experience around a sawmill. When I found exactly what I wanted in a mill and tractor and arranged to have them shipped to Ashcroft, most of the money I had made from my furs was gone, but I consoled myself that the mill would pay off in the long run. In Ashcroft we loaded the sawmill onto our steel-wheeled hay wagon along with some timbers to be used for a track for the mill carriage. It was a heavy load but the wagon was well built and strong enough to carry it, and the tractor would pull it. We headed for the Cariboo Road, and it wasn't long before the fun began. The road was just gravel, but had been packed down like cement by years and years of big freight wagons. With the jar of our heavy load on the steel wheels, something had to give, and it was the steel spokes, which started to break away from the rims. Everything had to come to a halt while we switched loads, putting the sawmill on a wagon with wooden wheels. It seems like we always had to learn the hard way.

At the ranch, we had the problem of setting up the mill and learning how to run it. A man living on Montana Hill claimed to be a millwright, so we hired him at an exorbitant price to help us, but quickly discovered that he didn't know as much as I knew myself. We managed after a while to get the mill running by ourselves, and had a nice pile of lumber cut before haying time.

That fall, when father got his annual urge to go prospecting, Dan went with him. He was past eighty now and though he was still able to ride horseback and got around well enough on foot with the help of his cane, we felt better that someone was going with him. Angus and I had gone once or twice in the past, but Dan had far more patience than either of us and by this time he got along with father better than we did. We knew that father would go anyway; nothing would stop him from striking out into the hills with his pick and shovel. He still had the notion that he would someday find his pot of gold. This time they were gone two weeks but they came back as usual empty-handed.

Ever since we came to the Cariboo we had tried to get the government interested in building a road from our ranch to Little Fort. It seemed too bad that people had to travel all the way to Ashcroft to reach the railway when the tracks ran past only thirty miles away. The most logical road, it appeared to us, would run through Three Mile Canyon, which was just south of our trapline, but when we talked to some of our Indian friends they were skeptical and a few even said it was impossible to build it through the canyon.

I had always wanted to have a look for myself, and in January 1921 when I was out alone on my trapline travelling along Long Island Lake, I took a notion to go down and investigate. The weather was cold, about twenty degrees below zero, but I was used to that. The small bushes, logs and rocks were all covered with deep snow, so that snowshoeing was quite easy. Breaking trail all the way was tiring, but like father, I was happiest exploring new country. Finally I came to the canyon wall at a point where it dropped about two thousand feet to the creek below. I started down. I knew I was taking a chance by venturing into strange territory without anyone knowing where I was going but I was determined to explore that canyon.

Most of the way the drop was too steep for me to use snowshoes, but wading through the snow prevented me from sliding down the wall too fast. When I began to wonder how I would ever climb back up if the canyon floor proved too difficult to travel, I had already gone too far to turn back. It was dark when I reached the bottom of the wall and found myself on a long, fairly open bench beside a big creek a few feet below. Some jack pine and fir trees grew on the bench and along the creek. I could see that beaver had cut a number of poplar and cottonwood trees, a good sign that there would be marten around as well. If the going was not too rough up and down the creek, I thought, this place had possibilities for a good trapline.

Because I was dreadfully tired after my trek down that treacherous wall, I then did something awfully foolish, something I ordinarily would not have done. Nearby was a big fir snag leaning toward the creek, partly rotten but containing a lot of pitch. It was about three feet thick at the stump and perhaps eighty feet high. I thought, why cut wood when that big snag is waiting there to be burned? A person needs a lot of wood to keep a fire going all night, or freeze to death in that temperature. So I set fire to the snag and it was soon burning from bottom to top in a tremendous tower of flame. Never before or since have I seen anything like that great torch. I had to stay thirty feet away because the heat was so intense. I cut myself a lot of spruce boughs and stretched out on them well away from the fire with my packsack as a pillow.

I had little hope of sleeping because the night was terribly cold, but I rested a little and the burning snag kept me warm. Sparks and pieces of burning bark fell occasionally but not on my bed which was at the opposite side of the leaning snag. As the night wore on I must have dozed off for a few minutes, because all of a sudden I was aware of sparks showering down on me and then I felt a hard blow across my legs, just above my knees. When

I regained my senses I found a huge chunk of burning timber lying right across my legs. I struggled out from under it but the damage was already done. Both my legs were very badly bruised, and the pain was excruciating. I had been saved from worse injury only by the springiness of my spruce bed and the cushioning snow.

I was thankful to be alive but I was sure in a mess, more than twenty-five miles from the ranch at the bottom of an unfamiliar canyon. I hadn't the faintest clue what kind of territory I would have to travel through to get home, and nobody knew I was down there. I simply had to get out on my own before my legs got too sore and stiff for walking. I gathered up my equipment, put on my snowshoes and headed up the creek in the direction of home. It was about two in the morning and the sky was clear and moonlit. I had to break trail all the way but I travelled slowly and steadily, in spite of the pain in my legs which was growing worse with every step.

The creek bottom was fairly open though the deep snow probably covered a lot of fallen timber and stumps. I was amazed to find that the canyon was easier to get out of than we had always been led to believe by the Indians: there was only a quarter mile of cliffs with boulders and large rocks, which I got around without much difficulty. Around three o'clock in the afternoon I reached Beaver Lake and I knew that I was past the worst part. There were only twelve more miles to go. Although I was feeling the pangs of hunger, I was afraid to stop to eat for my legs would get stiffer, and made do with a package of raisins and some jerky in my pocket.

I reached the ranch at one in the morning after walking twenty-five miles in about twenty-three hours. The house was dark when I let myself in, but father and Angus leaped out of bed to find out what I was doing there at that hour; my usual trip around the trapline would have kept me from home for another three or four days. When they lit a lantern they saw how tired I was, and that my legs were not working right. While they got my clothes off and put me to bed, I explained what had happened. Lying down I got my first good look at my legs; they had swelled to an enormous size and were all black and blue. Father and Angus were simply astounded that I had managed to walk so far in such condition, but I explained that it had been a case of walk or freeze to death—and that the old MacDonald stubbornness had won out. They made me as comfortable as they could and brought me food. For days father doctored up my legs with hot compresses until most of the swelling was gone, but it was nearly two weeks before I could walk again.

As soon as I was fit, Angus and I headed back to the canyon with the idea of establishing a new trapline and looking for a possible road route. We found quite a number of beaver houses and ponds along the creek and signs of mink, marten and fisher. About fifteen miles east of Beaver Lake, we built a lean-to shelter above the creek bed.

We found good possibility of a water grade for a road through the canyon, so in the spring of 1921 when father went out to Clinton for supplies, he urged Mr. Soues, the government agent, to send an engineer to have a look. Early in June, an engineer named Jones arrived at the ranch and Angus took him through to Little Fort on our proposed route along Three Mile Creek. It took them four days to make the round trip on horseback, but Jones agreed that since it was a natural water grade, a good trail and eventually a road could be put through quite easily. He told us to hire men to cut the trail and the government would reimburse us. Angus got three men at Little Fort to work with him toward Lac des Roches, while I hired another three men near home to start at the lower end of the lake and work east to meet Angus's crew. It took us ten days to complete the trail, including some grading along the sidehills, but most of the route lay across jack pine flats where we just cut a few trees and logs out of the way. The new trail was certainly a big improvement over that old Indian trail over which we had ridden with our pack animals in search of our rainbow in 1907.

By the summer of 1921 we were somewhat short-handed because Dan was away from the ranch most of the time now. One of his jobs was in California, working in the oil fields. When winter came, father and Angus took turns feeding the cattle at the meadow while I tended the trapline. And that was how we carried on until the spring of 1925 when Dan returned, the same spring we heard about a herd of dairy cows for sale at Forest Grove near Canim Lake. We had been in the cream business twenty years earlier in Colville and decided it would be ideal extra income for the ranch. We got only one cheque a year for selling our beef cattle, which we had to drive over a hundred miles to a shipping centre. We couldn't depend on furs for an income; some years, in fact, the prices were so low they did not begin to compensate for all the danger, hardships and labour that a season's trapping entailed.

It took Dan and me a day and a half to ride to the Forest Grove farm that Fred Slater was giving up. His herd consisted of fourteen head of fine Jersey cows, a registered Jersey bull, and a few one- and two-year-old heifers. Slater told us that the cream he shipped was graded number one sour when it was received at Spencer's Store in Vancouver, and he averaged about forty dollars a week. He invited us to stay overnight to see for ourselves the large quantity of milk the cows gave at the evening and morning milkings and how rich it was. We were well satisfied and bought the herd, paying forty-five dollars a head for the cows and the bull and twenty-five dollars apiece for the heifers. The dairy business would require us to work much harder than we had with our beef cattle, but it would bring in the ready cash we needed.

We already had a cream separator but bought Slater's cans to ship the cream. It took us three days to drive the herd home, giving milk away wherever we stopped for the night. We were soon up to our ears in the cream business, but the cheques came in regularly and we were very pleased with our new venture. However, with all the extra milk on our hands we needed more pigs to use it up. Lavena and Jim also had a few cows and they, too, wanted a couple more pigs.

One summer day, therefore, their son Eddie, who was now eighteen years old, went with me to Clinton in his parents' Dodge to buy some young ones. We bought six eight-week-old pigs at the Pollard ranch—four for us and two for the Cases. We crated them and loaded them into the car and drove home: the round trip, which used to take us six days with a team and wagon, was done in a single day. Time and mechanization were changing everything.

When we unloaded the Cases' pigs into their pen, one managed to find a hole in the fence almost immediately and he was

264

out like lightning. We set off after that darn little thing but, having been badly scared by the car and in a strange place, he wouldn't let us get close. When he came to the narrow outlet of Crooked Lake, he swam right across and got into the swampy, bushy piece of ground along the north shore. We headed in after him but it was like trying to catch the wind. He could dodge through the tall grass and thick willows like a scared rabbit. Next, he crossed the road heading for the shore of Bridge Lake; Jim, Eddie and I were in hot pursuit. We hoped to corner him along the lake but he jumped into the water and swam off. We were stumped. The nearest rowboat was about a mile along the shore and it would be dark before we could start after our runaway. Besides, we would have little chance of finding him among the high waves. We watched him swim at least two miles out into the lake and then lost sight of him, convinced he would drown before long. We turned back in frustration, and concentrated on getting our four pigs safely into a pen.

A couple of days later a neighbour spotted a forlorn little pig on the shore of Bridge Lake. He was quite near the place where he had plunged into the water, only about two hundred yards from the Cases' farm. Eddie and Jim started putting food out for him hoping he would find it and stay close by. Sure enough, the little fellow was attracted and eventually caught. We never could fathom how he had managed to swim so far and then turn around and swim right back to the spot he had started from.

That fall, Angus and I built a large addition to the old house at the main ranch. Dan was busy at the meadow working with the beef cattle, but father, though he had given up actively helping when we built anything, gave us valuable advice. The new wing was at right angles to the old house. The walls were log but since we now had a sawmill, we cut boards for finishing the inside, making a big improvement over the old building.

We had made up our minds that the addition was going to have a large room for parties and neighbourly gatherings, but also a kitchen, dining and living room, and two bedrooms. The best way was to partition the two bedrooms from the kitchen with removable panelling. We sawed out about a thousand board feet of spruce lumber half an inch thick and made up panels four feet wide and eight feet high, fastened to each other with bolts.

Whenever we needed a larger room we simply removed the bolts and took the panels out to the verandah where we had arranged a storage rack. We pushed all the furniture back against the walls and—presto!—we had a room large enough for square-dancing. At times we had twenty-five or thirty people dancing up a storm. There were plenty of musicians around now: violin, mandolin, guitar and even mouth organ players.

Father loved these affairs because he loved to have people in his home. He would even step-dance when he took the fancy, though as a rule he sat and watched. Until he was about seventy years old he would do the sword dance to entertain us, and he did it well, too; but we never got him on his feet for a waltz or two-step, popular dances in those days.

People came from all over the area for these get-togethers. Sometimes they were planned but more often they were spontaneous gatherings: people would just suddenly appear, carrying all the food needed for a party. Our house was a favourite place to congregate because it was the only one with a space big enough for dancing. Usually the parties were in wintertime when farm work was not so pressing, and sometimes instead of dancing we went skiing, or sleigh-riding with four-horse teams hitched to big bobsleighs, always homemade and designed by Angus.

12

Father

BY 1926 WE had a good general store at Bridge Lake, as well as a weekly mail service, a school and a community hall. The point of land that father had recommended for a park had been reserved, and in the fall of 1921 the people of the immediate district had received permission from the provincial department of education to move the first school, which was an old log building on land that had reverted to the government, to a new site on this parkland. Local men donated their time, and once reassembled it was used as a community centre and a schoolhouse both. There were only eight pupils at first but the little building gradually filled up. Eventually, it was torn down and a modern building was constructed elsewhere. Some years later a forestry camp was located on the point, which also became a popular camping spot.

Father was very pleased to think he had helped to get the community started, and that his foresight in getting the district surveyed had opened the country up. And he liked to look over our own spread of ranchland with pride; over the years he and his three boys had bought and pre-empted land until we now owned 2,240 acres.

One day in February 1926, father hitched a driving team to the cutter and drove from the home ranch to the Bridge Lake store and post office. It was a cold day and very windy, with the snow drifting badly. About a mile and a half from home, loaded down with the mail and groceries, he came to a huge drift across the road at the west end of Lac des Roches. The horses were travelling fast and they plunged into the drift before he was able to stop them. The cutter upset, the tongue broke and father was thrown out into the snow. The team took fright and tried to run. Father managed to get to his feet, but he had hurt his side painfully. He had lost one rein in the spill, but hung on to the other one with all his strength, determined to keep the horses from getting away. He hadn't the strength to prevent them from running, but he could keep them going in a circle. He had to stand clear of the cutter because they were still hooked to the singletree. As they pulled the sleigh around and around in circles, plunging through the drift, father stood in the centre and hung on to that single rein until at last they were played out and he was able to calm them down. Then he unhooked them from the doubletrees, got the reins fastened up onto the hames and prodded them toward home. He began to follow on foot, but his side was so sore that he barely crept along.

Angus was at the home ranch when the horses came up to the barn without father or the cutter. He rushed out to hook them up to the big sleigh and headed back down the road, finding father only two hundred yards from the wrecked cutter.

When we got him into bed we found that he had a large bruise on his left side where the edge of the cutter seat had landed on him. Though it was giving him a lot of pain, in a few days he was up and around again. Father was a hard man to keep down.

He gave up driving a team after that accident, yet he continued to ride horseback around the ranch to check on the cattle. He still insisted on doing his share of the chores, but that summer he was unable to run the mowing machine in haying time as he had every summer before.

Angus and Dan were both away most of the winter of 1926–27, and so father, who was now eighty-seven, stayed alone at the meadow feeding the big herd of beef cattle all winter. I was at the home ranch with the horses and the dairy cattle to look after. I trapped a little around the ranch but the price of furs was so low that it was hardly worth my while to set a trap at all.

Once a week I rode over to see how father was making out and to cut him a supply of firewood. Every day he had to harness up a team to a sleigh and haul out two big loads of hay for the stock. He had to keep the water holes free from ice, shovel snow, keep the fires going in the cabin and do his own cooking. It was a full-time job that would have kept a much younger man on the jump. To make things worse, the weather that winter was the coldest we had experienced in all our twenty years in the country, and the snow was very deep. How father managed to carry on and do all the necessary work was a puzzle to me.

He still looked after all the paperwork for the ranch and kept up with his correspondence; he read a lot, too, the only other activity for which he needed glasses. He was always exceptionally neat and clean, and he brushed his teeth three times a day without fail. There wasn't a single cavity in that third set of teeth of his.

In the wintertime, he liked to sit by the fire in the rocking chair that Angus had designed and built for him years earlier. Over his knees he would place a llama rug, sent to him by a man from South America who had once stayed at the ranch. It kept his legs warm on the coldest days when he was bothered by arthritis. How he treasured that rug! He even used it as a bed throw.

Every summer he would take a trip to Kamloops, often to attend to business. He would dress in his Sunday-go-to-meeting clothes and have someone drive him to Lone Butte to get the PGE train to Clinton. From there he would take the stage to Ashcroft and finish the trip on the CPR. He would stay in Kamloops with his special friends Jim and Katie Lapin, whom he had met shortly after we came to the Cariboo.

Whenever he went to the city he took the fancy blackthorn cane that Dr. Burns had given him in Spokane in 1884. The handle still carried the silver plate inscribed with his name. Another item he never forgot to take with him was his extraordinary toothpick, because without it a man was not considered a well-dressed mountaineer. It was actually gristly bone taken from the front ankle of a deer's foot, very carefully cleaned and dried so that it was tough and almost impossible to break.

Father lived to know his young grandchildren. He took a great interest in them and liked to take them with him in the evening when he went down to the big gate to drive the cows home for milking. He had to use a cane more often now, one that Angus had made for him from a small spruce tree with a natural handhold.

Father lost his eyesight in his ninetieth year. He knew now that his search for his rainbow was over, but it was not until he packed up his prospector's pick, his gold pan and a small grubstake for one more trip that this proud, brave, adventurous spirit left on his last journey to that prospector's paradise where there is a gold nugget in every pan.

He died on the first day of January 1929 at the home of his first-born, Lavena, after about a month's illness. We buried him in Kamloops near the hills he loved so well.

Epilogue

AFTER FATHER'S death, all our property was sold, for our circumstances had changed, and we entered a completely new phase in our lives. In the last years of father's life each of us thirtyish bachelors were married—Dan to a local Bridge Lake girl, Maude Smith, and Angus to a girl from Birmingham, Margaret Garner, whom he had first met in a tobacconist's shop while he was posted in London at the end of the war; they were finally reunited seven years later. I married the first school teacher to come to the Bridge Lake log schoolhouse—Ann Botterill, the daughter of Matt Botterill who had won the pulling contest so ably with our stallion Walter years before. We had become friends while she boarded at Lavena and Jim's place. Our ranch now could not support three young families, who needed more cash income and amenities than had we MacDonald men alone. The ranch had no running water or electricity, and with the Depression on, we could not hope to get them; the nearest school was ten miles away, and medical facilities were no closer than Ashcroft. Dan and I were fortunate to find steady employment at the Cominco smelter in Trail, while Angus ended up farming for several years at Blackpool on the North Thompson River, getting the land through the veterans affairs department.

Our Cariboo land was sold for a fraction of its real worth, the market for isolated ranches being very poor during those years, and when our mounting ranch expenses were finally paid off, we ended up with very little to show for all our years of hard work. Gardner Boultbee, a real estate man, bought our Lac des Roches property and raised fine thoroughbred Hereford cattle, bringing in breeding stock from as far away as England. For us MacDonalds, however, the rainbow we had sought in ranching faded with the Depression.

Father did not live to see one of his pet projects fulfilled: the road to Little Fort. It was 1946 before the government highways department started to work on it, and it was September 1949 before it was finished and officially opened to the public. Hundreds of cars, campers and trucks travel its length every day now. Father would be pleased, I know.

I often wondered what had happened to the ranch at Bear Creek near Colville where we were all born. Who was living there now? How much had it changed? In the summer of 1963 I finally had an opportunity to go back. The narrow, winding road leading to it was just the same, but there was more timber and much more underbrush on the hills. The neighbouring farms looked more prosperous than they had been when I was a child.

A new barn and new fences had been built on our little ranch, but the house was just as I remembered it. It had been well kept up though no one seemed to be there. I walked around the yard, thinking of the good times and the sad times we had had. I stood on the verandah and remembered my mother pointing out the "pretty rainbow" so long ago.

Only then did I notice a sign posted nearby: it announced a government wild bird and game sanctuary. I felt very happy, partly because father would have been so pleased, for he loved the outdoors and believed especially in the preservation of wildlife.

My father left a marvellous legacy to his family and all who knew him throughout his long life — a memory of his outstanding and eventful life, his courage in adversity, his unfailing love of God's creatures, the great outdoors and his fellow man.

Although he never found his "pot of gold," truly he touched the rainbow.

The author would like to thank Betty Keller, who saw in the MacDonald family's story those experiences that might speak to the reader, and whose sensitive editing of the manuscript brought welcome new direction without sacrificing any of its spirit.